PARENTHOOD AND RACE CULTURE

PARENTHOOD AND RACE CULTURE

An Outline of Eugenics

By

CALEB WILLIAMS SALEEBY

M.D., CH.B., F.Z.R.EDIN.
FELLOW OF THE OBSTETRICAL SOCIETY OF EDINBURGH, MEMBER OF COUNCIL OF THE EUGENICS EDUCATION SOCIETY, THE SOCIOLOGICAL SOCIETY, THE NATIONAL LEAGUE FOR PHYSICAL EDUCATION AND IMPROVEMENT, MEMBER OF THE ROYAL INSTITUTION, THE SOCIETY FOR THE STUDY OF INEBRIETY, ETC,

GYAN

Published by

Gyan Publishing House
5, Ansari Road
Daryaganj, New Delhi-110002
Phone: 011-47034999, 9811692060
E-mail: books@gyanbooks.com

Distribution Network
gyanbooks.com
India, USA, Canada, UK, Australia, France

ISBN : 978-81-212-6256-9 (PB)
First Published, 1909

2nd Impression 2022

Printed at: Gyan Press, Delhi.

PARENTHOOD AND RACE CULTURE
Author: CALEB WILLIAMS SALEEBY

PARENTHOOD
AND
RACE CULTURE

An Outline of Eugenics

BY

CALEB WILLIAMS SALEEBY

M.D., CH.B., F.Z.R.EDIN.

FELLOW OF THE OBSTETRICAL SOCIETY OF EDINBURGH,
MEMBER OF COUNCIL OF THE EUGENICS EDUCATION SOCIETY,
THE SOCIOLOGICAL SOCIETY,
THE NATIONAL LEAGUE FOR PHYSICAL EDUCATION AND IMPROVEMENT,
MEMBER OF THE ROYAL INSTITUTION,
THE SOCIETY FOR THE STUDY OF INEBRIETY, ETC.

1909

THIS BOOK IS

Dedicated

TO

FRANCIS GALTON

THE

AUGUST MASTER OF ALL EUGENISTS

CONTENTS

PART I

THE THEORY OF EUGENICS

PART II

THE PRACTICE OF EUGENICS

PREFACE

THIS book, a first attempt to survey and define the whole field of eugenics, appears in the year which finds us celebrating the centenary of the birth of Charles Darwin and the jubilee of the publication of *The Origin of Species.* It is a humble tribute to that immortal name, for it is based upon the idea of *selection for parenthood* as determining the nature, fate and worth of living races, which is Darwin's chief contribution to thought, and which finds in eugenics its supreme application. The book is also a tribute to the august pioneer who initiated the modern study of eugenics in the light of his cousin's principle. A few years ago I all but persuaded Mr. Galton himself to write a general introduction to eugenics, but he felt bound to withdraw from that undertaking, and has given us instead his Memories, which we could ill have spared.

The present volume seeks to supply what is undoubtedly a real need at the present day — a general introduction to eugenics which is at least considered and responsible. I am indebted to more than one pair of searching and illustrious eyes, which I may not name, for reading the proofs of this volume. My best hopes for its utility are based upon this fact. If there be any other reason for hope it is that during the last six years I have not only written incessantly on eugenics, but have spoken upon various aspects of it some hundreds of times to audiences as various as one can well imagine — a mainly clerical assembly at Lambeth Palace with the Primate in the Chair, drawing-rooms of title, working-class audiences from the Clyde to the Thames. It has been my rule to invite questions whenever it was possible. Such a discipline is invaluable. It gives new ideas and points of views, discovers the existing forms of prejudice, sharply corrects the tendency to partial statement. It is my hope that these many hours of cross-examination will be profitable to the present reader.

It has been sought to define the scope of eugenics, and my consistent aim has been, if possible, to preserve its natural unity without falling into the error, which I seem to see almost everywhere, of excluding what is strictly eugenic. Our primary idea, beyond dispute, is selection for parenthood based upon the facts of heredity. This, however, is not an end, but a means. Some eugenists seem to forget the distinction. Our end is a better race. If then, beyond selecting for parenthood, it be desirable to take care of those selected — as, for instance, to protect the expectant mother from alcohol, lead or syphilis — that is strict eugenics on any definition worth a moment's notice. It then appears, of course, that our demands come into contact with those prejudices which political parties call their principles. A given eugenic proposal or argument, for instance, may be stamped as "Socialist" or as "Individualist," and people who have labelled their eyes with these catchwords, which eugenics will ere long make obsolete, proceed to judge eugenics by them. But the question is not whether a given proposal is socialistic, individualistic or anything else, but is it eugenic. If it is eugenic, that is final. To this all parties will come, and by this all parties will be judged. The question is not whether eugenics is, for instance, socialist, but whether socialism is eugenic. I claim for eugenics that it is the final and only judge of all proposals and principles, however labelled, new or old, orthodox or heterodox. Some years ago I ventured to coin the word eugenist, which is now the accepted term. With that label I believe any man or woman may well be content. If this be granted, the old catchwords and the bias they create forgotten, we may be prepared to consider what the scope of eugenics really is.

Eugenics is not, for instance, a sub-section of applied mathematics. It is at once a science, and a religion, based upon the laws of life, and recognising in them the foundation of society. We shall some day have a eugenic sociology, to which the first part of this volume seeks to contribute: and the sociology and politics which have not yet discovered that man is mortal will go to their own place.

Only when we begin to think and work continuously at eugenics is its range revealed. The present volume is a mere introduction to the principles of the subject: the full elucidation of its practice is a problem for generations to come. Nor is it easy to set logical limits to our inquiry. We may say that eugenics deals with conceptions: and that the care of the expectant mother is outside its scope: but of what use is it to have a eugenic conception if its product is thereafter to be ruined by, for instance, the introduction of lead into the mother's organism? Again, the care of the individual is, in part, a eugenic concern: for if we desire his offspring we desire that he shall not contract transmissible disease nor vitiate his tissues with such a racial poison as alcohol. Plainly, everything that affects every possible parent is a matter of eugenic concern: and not only those factors which affect the choice for parenthood.

It follows that the second portion of this volume, which deals with the practice of eugenics, cannot be more than merely indicative. In the available space it has been attempted to define certain constituents of practical eugenics, but in any case the entire ground has not been surveyed. The concept of the *racial poisons* may be commended to special consideration. Whether a poison be so-called "chemical," as lead, or no less chemical, as the poison of syphilis, is of great practical importance, because of the infection involved in the second case: but, in principle, both cases belong to the same category. Sooner or later, eugenists must face the transmissible infections, and repudiate as hideous and devilish the so-called morality which discountenances any attempt to save unborn innocence from a nameless fate. He or she who would rather leave this matter is placing "religion" or "morality" or "politics" above the welfare of the life to come, and therein continuing the daily prostitution of those great names.

Again, the practice of eugenics may be commended and accepted as the business of the patriot: and two chapters have been devoted to the question as seen from the national point of view. I am of nothing more certain than that the choice for Great Britain to-day is between national eugenics and the fate of all her Imperial predecessors from Babylon to Spain. The whole book might have been written from this standpoint, but such a book would have been beneath the true eugenic plane, which is not national but human. I believe in the patriotism of William Watson, who desires the continuance of his country because, as he addresses her,

> "O England, should'st thou one day fall,
> . . . .
> Justice were thenceforth weaker throughout all
> The world, and truth less passionately free,
> And God the poorer for thine overthrow."

This is a patriotism as splendid and vital as the patriotism of the music-halls and the political and journalistic makers of wars is foul and fatal: and it is only in terms of such patriotism that the appeal to love of country is permissible in the advocacy of eugenics, which is a concern for all mankind.

The prophet of that kind of Imperialism which has destroyed so many Empires, has lately approved the emigration of our best to the Colonies, on the ground that "it is good to give the second eleven a chance." But as students of history know, it is at the heart that Empires rot. The case of Ireland is at present an insoluble one because the emigration of the worthiest has had full sway. So with the agricultural intellect: the "first eleven" having gone to the towns. Rome sent her "first eleven" to her Colonies: If you were not good enough to be a Roman soldier you could at least remain and be a Roman father: and the children of such fathers perished in the downfall of the Empire which they could no longer sustain. I can imagine no more foolish or disastrous advice than this of Mr. Kipling's, in commending that transportation of the worthiest which, thoroughly enough persisted in, must inevitably mean our ruin.

The national aspect of eugenics suggests its international aspect, and its inter-racial aspect. Not having spent six weeks rushing through the United States, I am unfortunately dubious as to the worth of any opinions I may possess regarding the most urgent form of this question to-day. I mistrust not merely the brilliant students who, unhampered by biological knowledge, pierce to the bottom of this question in the course of such a tour, but also the humanitarian bias of those who, like M. Finot, or the distinguished American sociologist, Mr. Graham Brooks, would almost have us believe that the negro is mentally and morally the equal of the Caucasian. Least of all does one trust the vulgar opinions of the man in the street. Wisdom on this matter waits for the advent of real knowledge. Similarly in the matter of Caucasian — Mongolian unions. I question whether any living man knows enough to warrant the expression of any decided opinion on this subject. Merely I here recognize miscegenation in general as a problem in eugenics, to which increasing attention must yearly be devoted. But it would have been ridiculous to attempt to deal with that great subject here. As for the marriage of cousins, to take the opposite case, I always reply to the question, "Should cousins marry?" that it depends upon the cousins. The good qualities of a good stock, the bad qualities of a bad stock, are naturally accentuated by such unions: I doubt whether there is much more to be said about them.

In the following general study of a subject to which no human affair is wholly alien, it has been impossible to deal adequately with the great question of eugenic education — that is to say, education *as for parenthood.* If only to emphasize its overwhelming importance, one must here insist upon the argument. There is, I believe, no greater need for society to-day than to recognize that education must include, *must culminate in,* preparation for the supreme duty of parenthood. This involves instruction regarding those bodily functions which exist not for the body nor for the present at all, but for the future life of mankind. The exercise of these functions depends upon an instinct which I have for some time been in the habit of terming the *racial instinct* — a name which at once suggests to us that we are to represent this instinct, to the boy or girl at puberty, not as something the satisfaction of which is an end in itself — that is the false and degrading assertion which will be made by the teachers whom youth will certainly find, if we fail in our duty — but as existing for what is immeasurably higher than any selfish end. Youth must be taught that it is for man the self-conscious, "made with such large discourse, looking before and after," as Hamlet says, to deal with his instincts in terms of their purpose, as no creature but man can do. The boy and girl must learn that the racial instinct exists for the highest of ends — the continuance and ultimate elevation of the life of mankind. It is a sacred trust for the life of this world to come. We must teach our boys what it is to be really "manly"— the fine word used by the tempter of youth when he means "beast-ly." To be manly is to be master of this instinct. And the "higher education" of our girls, as we must teach ourselves, will be lower, not higher, if it does not serve and conserve the future mother, both by teaching her how to care for and guard her body, which is the temple of life to come, and how afterwards to be a right educator of her children. The leading idea upon which one would insist is that the key to any of the right and useful methods of eugenic education is to be found in the conception of the racial instinct as existing for parenthood and to be guarded, reverenced, educated for that supreme end. It is for the reader who may be responsible for youth of either sex with this key to solve the problem on the lines best suited to his or her particular case.

By the application of mathematical methods to statistics we can ascertain their real meaning, if they have any. If, as frequently happens, they have none, mathematical analysis is worse than useless. Mr. Galton is the pioneer of this study, which Professor Karl Pearson has named biometrics. Biometrics is not Eugenics, as some have supposed, but is a branch of scientific inquiry which, like Genetics, Obstetrics and many more, contributes to the foundations of Eugenics. In Appendix A reference is made to various publications, mostly inexpensive, which deal with biometrics. In the text I have availed myself of biometric, genetic and other results impartially. Differences of opinion between this school and that of scientific workers are to be regretted by the eugenist; but it is for him to accept and use knowledge of eugenic significance no matter by what method it has been obtained. Directly he fails to do so he ceases to be a Eugenist and becomes the ordinary partisan. No reference is made in the following pages, for instance, to the *law of ancestral inheritance,* formulated by the Master to whom the volume is dedicated and of whom all eugenists are the followers. I believe that law, despite its beauty, to be without basis in fact and incompatible with demonstrated Mendelian phenomena: and though the book is dedicated to Mr. Galton, it is more deeply dedicated to the Future. This, indeed, is the *Credo* of the Eugenist: *Expecto resurrectionem mortuorum, et vitam venturi saeculi.*

Woman is Nature's supreme instrument of the future. The Eugenist is therefore deeply concerned with her education, her psychology, the conditions which permit her to exercise her great natural function of choosing the fathers of the future, the age at which she should marry, and the compatibility between the discharge of her incomparable function of motherhood and the lesser functions which some women now assume. Obstetrics, and the modern physiology and psychology of sex must thus be harnessed to the service of Eugenics, and I hope to employ them for the elucidation, in a future volume, of the problems of woman and womanhood, thus conceived.

PART 1

THE THEORY OF EUGENICS

PARENTHOOD AND RACE CULTURE

CHAPTER I

INTRODUCTORY

"A Little Child Shall Lead Them"

THIS book will be mere foolishness to those who repeat the inhuman and animal cry that we have to take the world as we find it — the motto of the impotent, the forgotten, the cowardly and selfish, or the merely vegetable, in all ages. The capital fact of man, as distinguished from the lower animals and from plants is that he does not have to take the world as he finds it, that he does not merely adapt himself to his environment, but that he himself is a creator of his world. If our ancestors had taken and left the world as they found it, we should be little more than erected monkeys to-day. For none who accept the hopeless dogma is this book written. They are welcome to take and leave the world as they find it; they are of no consequence to the world; and their existence is of interest only in so far as it is another instance of that amazing wastefulness of Nature in her generations, with which this book will be so largely concerned.

Beginning, perhaps, some six million years ago, the fact which we call human life has persisted hitherto, and shows no signs of exhaustion, much less impending extinction, being indeed more abundant numerically and more dominant over other forms of life and over the inanimate world to-day than ever before. It is a continuous phenomenon. The life of every blood corpuscle or skin cell of every human being now alive is absolutely continuous with that of the living cells of the first human being — if not, indeed, as most biologists appear to believe, the first life upon the earth. Yet this continuous life has been and apparently always must be lived in a tissue of amazing discontinuity — amazing, at least, to those who can see the wonderful in the commonplace. For though the world-phenomenon which we call Man has been so long continuous, and is at this moment perhaps as much modified by the total past as if it were really a single undying individual, yet only a few decades ago, a mere second in the history of the earth, no human being now alive was in existence. "As for man, his days are as grass: as a flower of the field, so he flourisheth. For the wind passeth over it, and it is gone; and the place thereof shall know it no more." Indeed, not merely are we individually as grass, but in a few years the hand that writes these words, and the tissues of eye and brain whereby they are perceived, will actually *be* grass. Here, then, is the colossal paradox: absolute and literal continuity of life, every cell from a preceding cell throughout the ages — *omnis cellula e cel-*

lula; yet three times in every century the living and only wealth of nations is reduced to dust, and is raised up again from helpless infancy. Where else is such catastrophic continuity?

Each individual enters the world in a fashion the dramatic and sensational character of which can be realized by none who have not witnessed it; and in a few years the individual dies, scarcely less dramatically as a rule, and sometimes more so. This continuous and apparently invincible thing, human life, which began so humbly and to the sound of no trumpets, in Southern Asia or the neighborhood of the Caspian Sea, but which has never looked back since its birth, and is now the dominant fact of what might well be an astonished earth, depends in every age and from moment to moment upon here a baby, there a baby and there yet another; these curious little objects being of all living things, animal or vegetable, young or old, large or small, the most utterly helpless and incompetent, incapable even of finding for themselves the breasts that were made for them. If but one of all the "hungry generations" that have preceded us had failed to secure the care and love of its predecessor, the curtain would have come down and a not unpromising though hitherto sufficiently grotesque drama would have been ended for ever.

This discontinuity it is which persuades many of us to conceive human life to be not so much a mighty maze without a plan, as a mere stringing of beads on an endless cord of which one end arose in Mother Earth, whilst the other may come at any time — but goes nowhere. The beads, which we call generations, vary in size and color, no doubt, but on no system; each one makes a fresh start; the average difference between them is merely one of position; and the result is merely to make the string longer. Or the generations might be conceived as the links of an indeterminate chain, necessarily held to each other; but suggesting not at all the idea of a living process such that its every step is fraught with eternal consequence. In a word, we incline to think that History merely goes on repeating itself, and we have to learn that History never repeats itself. Every generation is epoch-making.

It is thus to the conception of parenthood as the vital and organic link of life that we are forced: and the whole of this book is really concerned with parenthood. We shall see, in due course, that no generation, whether of men or animals or plants, determines or provides, as a whole, the future of the race. Only a percentage, as a rule a very small percentage indeed, of any species reach maturity, and fewer still become parents. Amongst ourselves, one-tenth of any generation gives birth to one-half the next. These it is who, in the long run, make History: a Kant or a Spencer, dying childless, may leave what we call immortal works; but unless the parents of each new generation are rightly chosen or "selected"— to use the technical word — a new generation may at any time arise to whom the greatest achievements of the past are nothing. The newcomers will be as swine to these pearls, the immortality of which is always conditional upon the capacity of those who come after to appreciate them. There is here expressed the distinction between two kinds of progress: the traditional progress which is dependent upon transmitted achievement, but in its turn is dependent upon racial progress — this last being the kind of progress of which the history of pre-human life upon the planet is so largely the record and of which mankind is the finest fruit hitherto.

It is possible that a concrete case, common enough, and thus the more significant, may appeal to the reader, and help us to realize afresh the conditions under which human life actually persists.

Forced inside a motor-omnibus one evening, for lack of room outside, I found myself opposite a woman, poorly-clothed, with a wedding ring upon her finger and a baby in her arms. The child was covered with a black shawl and its face could not be seen. It was evidently asleep. It should have been in its cot at that hour. The mother's face roused feelings which a sonnet of Wordsworth's might have expressed, or a painting by some artist with a soul, a Rembrandt or a Watts, such as we may look for in vain amongst the be-lettered to-day. Here was the spectacle of mother and child, which all the great historic religions, from Buddhism to Christianity, have rightly worshiped; the spectacle which more nearly symbolizes the sublime than any other upon which the eye of a man, himself once such a child can rest; the spectacle which alone epitomizes the life of mankind and the unalterable conditions of all human life and all human societies, reminding us at once of our individual mortality, and the immortality of our race —

> "While we, the brave, the mighty and the wise,
> We Men, who in our morn of youth defied

> The Elements, must vanish;—be it so.
>   Enough, if something from our hands have power
> To live, and act, and serve the future hour:"

— the spectacle which alone, if any can, many reconcile us to death; the spectacle of that which alone can sanctify the love of the sexes; the spectacle of motherhood in being, the supreme duty and supreme privilege of womanhood —" a mother is a mother still, the holiest thing alive."

This woman, utterly unconscious of the dignity of her attitude and of the contrast between herself and the imitation of a woman, elegantly clothed, who sat next her, giving her not a thought nor a glance, nor yet room for the elbow bent in its divine office, was probably some thirty-two or three years old, as time is measured by the revolutions of the earth around the sun. Measured by some more relevant gauge, she was evidently aged, her face gray and drawn, desperately tired, yet placid — not with due exultation but with the calm of one who has no hope. She was too weary to draw the child to her bosom, and her arms lay upon her knees; but instead she bent her body downwards to her baby. She looked straight out in front of her, not at me nor at the passing phantasms beyond, but at nothing. The eyes were open but they were too tired to see. The face had no beauty of feature nor of color nor of intelligence, but it was wholly beautiful, made so by motherhood; and I think she must have held some faith. The tint of her skin and of her eyeballs spoke of the impoverishment of her blood, her need of sleep and rest and ease of mind. She will probably be killed by consumption within five years and will certainly never hold a grand-child in her arms. The pathologist may lay this crime at the door of the tubercle bacillus; but a prophet would lay it at the reader's door and mine.

While we read and write, play at politics or ping-pong, this woman and myriads like her are doing the essential work of the world. *The worm waits for us as well as for her and them: and in a few years her children and theirs will be Mankind.* We need a prophet to cry aloud and spare not; to tell us that if this is the fate of mothers in the ranks which supply the overwhelming proportion of our children, our nation may number Shakespeare and Newton amongst the glories of its past, and the lands of ancient empires amongst its present possessions, but it can have no future; that if, worshiping what it is pleased to call success, it has no tears nor even eyes for such failures as these, it may walk in the ways of its insensible heart and in the sight of its blind eyes; yet it is walking not in its sleep but in its death, is already doomed and damned almost past recall; and that, if it is to be saved, there will avail not "broadening the basis of taxation," nor teaching in churches the worship of the Holy Mother and Holy Child, whilst motherhood is blasphemed at their very doors, but this and this only — the establishment, not in statutes but in the consciences of men and women, of a true religion based upon these perdurable and evident dogmas — that all human life is holy, all mothers and all children, that history is made in the nursery, that the individual dies, that therefore children determine the destinies of all civilizations, that the race or society which succeeds with its mammoth ships and its manufactures but fails to produce men and women, is on the brink of irretrievable doom; that the body of man is an animal, endowed with the necessary animal instincts necessary for self-preservation and the perpetuation of the race, but that, if the possession of this body by a conscious spirit, "looking before and after," is anything more than a "sport" of the evolutionary forces, it demands that, the blind animal instincts notwithstanding, the desecration of motherhood, the perennial slaughter and injury of children, the casual unconsidered birth of children for whom there is no room or light or air or food, and of children whose inheritance condemns them to misery, insanity or crime, must cease; and that the recurrent drama of human love and struggle reaches its happy ending not when the protagonists are married, but when they join hands over a little child that promises to be a worthy heir of all the ages. This religion must teach that the spectacle of a prematurely aged and weary and hopeless mother, which he who runs or rides may see, produced by our rude foreshadowings of civilization, is an affront to all honest and thoughtful eyes: that where there are no mothers, such as mothers should be, the people will assuredly perish, though everything they touch should turn to gold, though science and art and philosophy should flourish as never before. I believe that history, rightly read, teaches these tremendous lessons.

* *

In our own day the bounds of imagination are undoubtedly widening. Means of communication, the press, the camera, the decadence of obsolete dogmas, making room for the simple daily truths of morality which have "the dignity of dateless age" and are too hard for the teeth of time — these account in large measure for the fact that the happier half of the world is at last beginning to realize how the other half lives. There is perhaps more divine discontent with things as they are than ever heretofore; this being due, as has been suggested, perhaps as much to the modern aids of imagination as to any inherent increase of sympathy. Science, too, in the form of sociology and economics, adds warrant to the demand for some radical reform of the conditions of life. It teaches that all forms of life are interdependent; that society is thus an organism in more than merely loose analogy; that the classes pay abundantly for the state of the masses, whilst medicine teaches that the tuberculosis, for instance, which slays so many members of the middle and upper classes, is bred by and in the overcrowding of the lower classes, this and many other diseases promising to resist all measures less radical than the abolition of half our current social practice.

Hence it is that we hear so much of social reform; and the promises of representatives of many political-isms jostle one another at the gates of our ears. The Anarchist at one extreme, and the Collectivist at the other, with the Individualist and the Socialist somewhere beween, offer their panaceas. To me, I confess, they seem little better than the scholastic metaphysicians of old days, like them, mistaking words for things, incapable of understanding each other, evading precise definition and using terms which never mean the same thing twice as missiles and weapons of abuse: and, above all, mistaking means for ends.

But the leading error common to them all, as I seem to see it, is their conception of society as a stable thing — a piece of machinery which must be properly "assembled," as the engineers say; forgetful of the extraordinary discontinuity which inheres in the swift-approaching death of all its parts, and their replacement by helpless immaturity. The first fact of society really is that all its individuals are mortal. This we all know, but I question whether even Herbert Spencer fully reckoned with it; and certainly the common run of social speculators have not begun to realize what it means. Human life is made up of generations, and the key to all progress lies in the nature of the relation between one generation and another. Spencer records the case of an Oxford graduate, desirous to be his secretary, who did not know that the population of Great Britain is increasing. Here is a capital present fact of the — merely quantitative — relation between successive generations. So far as any influence on their theory or practice is concerned, it is still unknown to nearly all our advisers. Yet this fact of the ceaseless multiplication of man, which has distinguished him from the first, and is absolutely peculiar to him of all living species, animal or vegetable, as Sir E. Ray Lankester has lately pointed out is the source of the major facts of history and the besetting condition of every social problem that can be named at this hour.

The professional and dedicated teachers of morality seem to be in little better case. They believe in babies, perhaps, as the prime and only really valid source of the weal and wealth and strength of nations, and as the great moralizers and humanizers of the generation that gives them birth. They are beginning to join in that public outcry against infant mortality which will yet abolish this abominable stain upon our time. But they are lamentably uninformed. They do not know, for instance, that a high infant mortality habitually goes with a high birth-rate not only in human society but in all living species; and they have yet to appreciate the proposition which I have so often advanced and which, to me at any rate, seems absolutely self-evident, that until we have learned how to keep alive all the healthy babies now born — that is to say not less than ninety per cent. of all, the babies in the slums included — it is monstrous to cry for more, *to be similarly slain.* These bewailings about our mercifully falling birth-rate, uncoupled with any attention to the slaughter of the children actually born, are pitiable in their blindness and would be lamentable if they had any effect — of which there is fortunately no sign whatever, but indeed the contrary.

Humanitarian sentiment, also, is terribly misguided. "Why always the benefit of the future, has the present no claim upon us?" I have been asked. Assuredly all sentient life, and therefore pre-eminently all human life, in which sentiency is so incommensurably intensified by self-consciousness, the power of "looking before and after," has a claim upon us: but the question could have been asked by no one whose imagination had been worthily employed. Our posterity will in due course be as actual and present as we, their deeds and sufferings and hopes as actual and present as ours. They outnumber us as the ocean outweighs a raindrop;

to avert evil from one of them is as much as to relieve evil in one of us,—how much more to prevent the misery of five in the next generation, fifty in the next and outnumbered hosts beyond? To serve the future of the race is not to benefit a fiction: the men and women of a hundred and a thousand years hence will be as real as we. And to serve the future is to put out our talent at compound interest a thousand-fold compounded. The weak imagination would rather build a sanatorium for consumptives and see it filled with grateful patients. This is a palpable, sensible good, for which the meanest visual faculty suffices: but the strong imagination would rather open the closed windows of nurseries or work at the mechanical problems of ventilation, aye, or even at the structure of bacteriological microscope — finding the spectacle, in the mind's eye, of healthy men and women fifty years hence as grateful and as real a reward as the sight of a sanatorium in the present. The pace of progress will be incalculably hastened when men, whether workers or bequeathers or administrators, enlarge their imaginations so as to perceive that the future will be, and therefore indeed is, as real as the present.[1] I appeal to the reason of the kind-hearted reader. Would you rather make one man or child happy now, or two or a thousand a century hence?

It is, in a word, the idea of continuous causation or evolution that explains the remarkable contrast between our outlook on the future and our fathers'. In

[1] A tribute is due to the anonymous pioneer of sane and provident philanthropy who lately gave £20,000 to the London Hospital for research. Such a thing is a commonplace in New York, it is unprecedented in London.

older — that is to say, younger — days, men's interest in posterity was most naïvely and quaintly selfish. If they raised a monument or did any piece of work which obviously would endure beyond the span of their own lives, their chief motive seems to have been that we should think well of them, nor forget how well they thought of themselves. They were not concerned with us but with our opinion of them. They were anxious about the verdict of posterity; and the verdict is that they little realized their responsibility for us, or betrayed it if they did. There is also the frank attitude of Sir Boyle Roche's famous bull, "What has posterity done for us?" This is a quite familiar and conspicuous sentiment — as familiar as any other form of selfishness: but it is as if a father should say, "What have my children done for me?" and is open to the same condemnation. We are assuredly responsible for posterity as any parent for any child. Before the nineteenth century this fact could be realized by very few. To-day, when the truth of organic evolution is a commonplace, and when the plasticity of the forces of evolution is slowly becoming realized, we must face our tremendous responsibility and privilege in a spirit worthy of those to whom such mighty truths have been revealed.

Parenthood and birth — in these the whole is summed. At the mercy of these are all past discovery, all past achievement in art or science, in action or in thought. The human species, secure though it be, is only a race after all; only a sequence of runners who *quasi cursores, vitai lampada tradunt* — like runners, hand on the lamp of life, as Lucretius said. This it is which, to the thoughtful observer, makes each birth such an overwhelming event. It is a great event for the mother and the father, but how much greater if its consequences be only half realized. Education in its full sense, "the provision of an environment," as I would define it, is a mighty and necessary force, for nothing but potentiality is given at birth: but no education, no influence of traditional progress, can avail, unless the potentialities which these must unfold are worthy. The baby comes tumbling headlong into the world. The fate of all the to-morrows depends upon it. Hitherto its happenings has depended upon factors animal and casual enough, utterly improvident, concerned but rarely with this tremendous consequence. Fate may be mistress, but she works only too often by Chance, as Goethe remarked. Fate and Chance hitherto have never failed to keep up the supply which the death of the individual makes imperative: and forces have been at work determining for progress, to some extent, but most imperfectly, the parentage of these headlong babies. Yet the human intelligence cannot remain satisfied with their working — and much less so when it realizes how they can be controlled, how effectively, and to what high ends. The physician may and must concern himself, on these occasions, with the immediate needs of the mother and the child, and when these are satisfied he may feel that his duty has been done; but, as he journeys homewards, he must surely reflect — that this astonishing thing, then, has happened again, as indeed it has happened many times this very day; that whilst this baby is to become an individual man or woman, an end in himself or herself, in its young loins and in those of its like are the hosts of all the unborn who are yet to be. If, then, these babies differ widely from each other, as they do; if these differences are, on the whole, capable of prediction in terms of heredity; if the future state of mankind is involved in these differences, which will in their turn be transmitted to the children of such as themselves become parents; and if this business of parenthood will be confined to only a *small* proportion of these babies, *of whom one-third will be dead within five years;* if these things be so, as they are, cannot these babies be chosen in anticipation, there being thus effected an enormous vital economy, Nature being commanded to the highest ends by the only method, which is to obey her as Bacon said; and the human intelligence thus making its supreme achievement — the ethical direction and vast acceleration of racial progress? What man can do for animals and plants, can he not do for himself? Give imagination its fleetest and strongest wing, it can never conceive a task so worth the doing.

This, and this alone, is what requires to be brought home to the general reader and the reformer alike. Says Mr. H. G. Wells: "It seemed to me then that to prevent the multiplication of people below a certain standard, and to encourage the multiplication of exceptionally superior people, was the only real and permanent way of mending the ills of the world. I think that still." And then, in a few sketchy pages, Mr. Wells discredits, as with one glance of great eyes, the very proposal which he thinks to be the only real and permanent way of mending the ills of the world. Not one man in thousands has got sd far as to hold this opinion; and it is the more lamentable that Mr. Wells, having reached it, should hold it in the loose, formal, and inoperative fashion in which the man in the street or the woman in the pew holds the dogmas of orthodox theology. We need to educate public opinion — that "chaos of prejudices"— up to Mr. Wells' standard, and then we need to accomplish the much harder task of converting a mere intellectual speculation into a living belief.

But so surely as this belief is the crowning and practical conclusion to which all the teachings of modern biology converge, comes to life in men's minds, so surely the difficulties will be met, not only on paper but also in practice. "Where there's a will there's a way." Meanwhile men are content to work at the impermanent, if not indeed at measures which directly war against the selection of the best for parenthood: they do not realize the stern necessity of obeying Nature in this respect — for it is Her selection of parents that alone has raised us from the beast and the worm — and since necessity alone, whether inner or outer, whether of character or circumstance, is the mother of invention, they fail to find the methods by which our ideal can be carried out. There is nothing, either in the character of the individual man and woman, or in the structure of society, that makes the ideal of race-culture impossible to-day: nor must action wait for further knowledge of heredity. Little though we know so far, we have abundance of assured knowledge for immediate action in many directions — knowledge which is agreed upon by Lamarckians and neo-

Lamarckians, Darwinians and Weismannians, Mendelians and biometricians alike. All of these agree, for instance, as to the fact that the insane tendency is transmissible and is transmitted by heredity. We need only public opinion to say, "Then most surely those who have such a tendency must forgo parenthood."

For it is public opinion that governs the world. If it were, as it will be one day — which may these pages hasten — an elementary and radical truth, as familiar and as cogent to all, man in the House or man in the public-house, as the fact of the earth's gravitation — that racial maintenance, much more racial progress, depends absolutely upon the selection of parents; if the establishment of this selective progress in the best and wisest manner were the admitted goal of all legislation and all social and political speculation — who can question that the thing would be practicable and indeed easy? Without the formation of public opinion this is as hopelessly Utopian and inaccessible an ideal as words ever framed; public opinion once formed, nothing could be more palpably feasible. Hence Mr. Galton's wisdom in demanding that before we dictate courses of procedure, and even before we can expect profit from scientific investigation, whether by the biometric method of which he is the founder, or by any other, *public opinion must be formed;* that the idea of eugenics or good-breeding must be instilled into the conscience of civilization like a new religion — a religion of the most lofty and austere, because the most unselfish, morality, a religion which sets before it a sublime ideal, terrestrial indeed in its chosen theater, but celestial in its theme, human in its means, but literally superhuman in its goal. If the intrinsic ennoblement of mankind does not answer to this eulogy, where is the ideal that does?

CHAPTER II

THE EXCHEQUER OF LIFE

"This last lustrum has enabled us to make an astounding discovery, of which neither Adam Smith nor Cobden nor Malthus dreamed — that a nation is composed not of property nor of provinces, but of men."— TILLE (1904) quoted by FOREL.

THE main thesis which the last chapter was intended to introduce is, in the words of Ruskin, simply this: "There is no wealth but life." The assumption throughout this book is that Ruskin is the real founder of political economy, he first of moderns having seen this supreme truth.

We speak of a nation's possessions, but possessions imply a possessor or possessors. Wealth, as Ruskin teaches us, is "the possession of the valuable by the valiant." If our national possessions were made over to a race of monkeys, "they being inherently and eternally incapable of wealth," what would they be worth? Furthermore, to possess and be possessed by, are totally diverse things. Says Ruskin, "Lately in a wreck of a Californian ship, one of the passengers fastened a belt about him with two hundred pounds of gold in it, with which he was found afterwards at the bottom. Now, as he was sinking — had he the gold or had the gold him?"

VITAL ECONOMICS.—We have already alluded to the unique property of mankind in virtue of which the radical character of the essential wealth, which is life, has only too commonly been forgotten. In the case of any animal or vegetable species we should have no difficulty, if asked regarding its "success" and "prospects," in directing our inquiry to essentials. We should examine the individuals of that species, young and old, its death-rate and its birth-rate, and these would supply us with the answer. In the case of man there is the almost incalculable complication involved in the fact that he is capable of making external acquirements,—material possessions and spiritual possessions which, so long as he remains capable of possessing them, are of real value and, on account of what they mean for life, are a true though secondary wealth. Amongst civilized mankind, therefore, the essential question as to the breed of men and women is obscured by the secondary question as to their traditional or transmitted possessions or external acquirements. But if we remember the case of the drowning man and his gold we shall realize that fundamentally, the case is the same for the human as for any other species. No one can openly question this, but not one publicist or politician in a thousand believes it in any living sense. The true function of government, said Ruskin, is the production and recognition of human worth. This has only to be said to be admitted; it is one of the thoughts that shine, as Joubert says. No one denies it and no one acts upon it.

In this sense such a phrase as the National Exchequer begins to take on a new meaning, and the Chancellor of the Exchequer loses every whit of his importance, except in so far as his proceedings tend towards, or away from, the production and recognition of human worth. He plays with money, whereas the Chancellor of the real Exchequer would work for life.

THE FACTS OF CHILDHOOD TO-DAY.—But since human life is discontinuous, since three times in a century the essential wealth of nations is reduced to dust, and raised again from helpless infancy, our urgent business is with the children of the nation. What, then, in general, are the facts of the National Exchequer thus conceived?

We find that, so far as ordinary physical health is concerned, the majority of human babies — including, for instance, so-called Anglo-Saxon babies — are physically healthy, at birth. On the other hand, a certain proportion are as definitely and obviously unhealthy at the very start as the more fortunate majority are healthy. If certain influences, such as alcohol and *some few* diseases, have been in operation, the babies may be already doomed —not national wealth, but national *illth*. In the absence of these pernicious factors, there is, on the whole, *physical* fitness. The ratios are perhaps as ninety to ten per cent.

Here then, is, on the whole, a ceaseless supply of essential wealth; physically, at any rate, of good enough quality. As every one knows, or should know, the greater part of it we immediately proceed to deface and destroy. Our mouths are full of argument concerning the principles of what we are pleased to conceive as political economy. The principles of vital economy we do not inquire into but outrage and defy at every turn. So horribly and wastefully are we misguided that in point of fact we actually destroy altogether the greater number, not of all the children merely, but even of the fit and healthy children; and it may forcibly be argued that, before any one proceeds to attempt any choice amongst the children, as to which shall in their turn become parents and which shall not, it would be well, apart from any question of discrimination to revise radically the methods which at present permit this wholesale destruction. Whilst we kill outright by hundreds of thousands every year, we damage for life far more, including a very large proportion of those who, as things at present are, will in their turn become the parents who alone are the makers of the real wealth of nations. If this destructive process had the effect which common notions of heredity would lead us to expect, then most certainly not merely would Britain, for instance, be doomed, but the very name would long ago have become "one with Nineveh and Tyre." But though this destructive process (which it is best to describe as resulting in deterioration rather than degeneration) has been long continued, and though, in consequence of the great economic changes of last century and the rush into the cities with their overcrowding, it is perhaps more disastrous now than ever before: *yet* it remains true that most of the babies born in the slums are splendid little specimens of humanity—so far as physique is concerned—bearing no marks of degeneration to correspond with the deterioration of their parents. In a word, heredity works—the racial poisons apart, as we shall see—so that each generation gets a fresh start. *If there be no process of selection,* each new generation begins where its predecessor began and is as a whole neither worse nor better, whether physically or psychically.

EUGENICS AND INFANT MORTALITY.— In the face of the foregoing, which merely outlines the appalling indictment that ought to be framed against civilization for its treatment of its children, it is evidently incumbent upon us to answer the objector who should say that the whole purpose and argument of our present inquiry is premature, and that surely our first business should be not to propose any novel and revolutionary doctrine as to the choice of parents and of children, but rather to stop this child slaughter and child damage — in other words, that we should devote ourselves rather, not to providing children with a good heredity, but to providing them with a good environment, it being only too demonstrable that the environment we at present provide for the great majority of them is deadly and abominable in the extreme. This argument is all the stronger because most of the children are admittedly fit physically at birth. It would seem as if there were little to complain of in their heredity, whilst there is certainly almost everything to complain of in their environment.

If this objection is to be met at all, we must be most careful and serious in our going. Whatever conclusions we come to we must at any rate be sure that we do not impugn or deny the instant, immediate and constant law of love which declares that there can be no adequate ideal short of doing our best for all children, once they are born — nay, more, from the very moment, months before, at which their individual history starts. Whoso suggests that, as a present and immediate policy, it is not right to care for all children, healthy or diseased, welcome or unwelcome, nursed in Park Lane or in the slums, may have plausible and even apparently eugenic arguments on his side, but his proposal is essentially immoral and therefore essentially false. For all children actually in being — whether they await or have passed the particular moment of birth — it is our duty, ideal and real, to do our utmost. The believer in the principle of race-culture or eugenics — whom I shall hereafter, as for some years past, call the eugenist — may believe that it would have been better had some of these children never been born; he may believe that, in the present unorganized state of society, in the present dethroned state of motherhood, it were vastly better had many even of the healthy majority never been born. He may be convinced that, since so many of them will certainly die, failing our feeble efforts to save childhood, their birth is a misfortune: but on no terms and for no objects whatever does, or can, the eugenist propose that any of these children, even though from the moment of birth they be riddled with disease, should be allowed to die. Though some will say that the keeping alive of diseased children, or even of many children at first healthy, is a disaster, I maintain that no such question of choice, selection or discrimination can find any warrant in any form of morality — eugenic or other — from the moment at which the child in question began its individual existence. Those of us who advocate the eugenic idea must be perpetually on our guard against the insidious alliance of any who, agreeing with our premises, declare that it is a mistake, for instance, to prosecute a campaign against infant mortality. I myself have had a share — by a continuous propaganda started in 1902 — in making this last a publicly recognized question, whilst, on the other hand, I have done my best to popularize the idea of eugenics. Let me repeat here what I have already said elsewhere: that I strenuously repudiate any suggestion that the eugenic end is legitimately or effectively to be served by permitting the infant mortality to continue. The distinguished Egyptologist, Professor Flinders Petrie, in his recent book *Janus in Modern Life,* describes as follows the results of the present crusade against infant mortality, as he conceives them: — "We must agree that it would be of the lower or lowest type of careless, thriftless, dirty, and incapable families that the increase [of surviving children] would be obtained. Is it worth while to dilute our increase of population by ten per cent. more of the most inferior kind? Will England be stronger for having one-thirtieth more, and that of the worst stock, added to the population every year? This movement is doing away with one of the few remains of natural weeding out of the unfit that our civilization has left to us. And it will certainly cause more misery than happiness in the course of a century."

Here, plainly, is a serious argument. We are bound to sympathize with its underlying assumption, viz., that not all babies are such as we can desire to carry on the race. Still more must we sympathize with any author whatever who has the imagination and foresight enough to write anywhere, on any subject, wrongly or rightly, such a sentence as "and it will certainly cause more misery than happiness in the course of a century." We need more such authors. But without going into the whole argument here — as, for instance, regarding the singular use of the word "natural" — I do most entirely deny the right of the eugenic idea to any voice or place as to the fate of children *once they have come into being*. Another writer, arguing on the same lines, says *à propos* of the abolition of infant mortality: "This last change which, as the Huddersfield experiment shows, is easy of accomplishment, is likely to be completely affected in the next few years, and we shall then have abolished the one factor which in any important degree at present tends to redress the balance between the rates of reproduction of the superior and the inferior classes." These are the words of Dr. W. McDougall, the distinguished psychologist. Dr. McDougall has subsequently shown that he repudiates the apparent deduction from them, and entirely approves of the present campaign of mercy to childhood. Nevertheless, these arguments, plainly derived from the principle of natural selection, do express a most important truth — viz., that indiscriminate survival must lead to racial dacadence, whether in man, microbe or moss. I submit that the difficulty can be solved only by the eugenic principle.

The fittest must become parents, and the unfit [1] must not; then kill the unfit, says Nature. And this indeed, in all living species other than man, is what Nature

[1] The word is used in the ordinary loose sense, to which there is no objection provided that there be no misunderstanding of its exact scientific meaning, as in Spencer's phrase "survival of the fittest"—i.e., not the best, but the most adapted.

does But "thou shalt not kill," says the moral law — not even the unfit. As the foregoing will have shown, some thinkers to-day propose to avail themselves in this dilemma of the "New Decalogue": —

> "Thou shalt not kill but need'st not strive
> Officiously to keep alive."

This is no solution of the problem. There is only one solution, and that is the eugenic solution. Nature can preserve a race only by destroying the unfit. We who are intelligent must preserve and elevate the race by preventing the unfit from ever coming into existence at all. We must replace Nature's relative death-rate by a relative birth-rate. This is merciful and supremely moral; it means vast economy in life and money and time and suffering; it is natural at bottom, but it is Nature raised to her highest power in that almost supra-natural fact — the moral intelligence of man.

THE DILEMMA DEFINED.— The moral law, and our natural human sympathy, insist that we should seek to preserve all the children that come into the world, to amplify the health of the healthy, and to neutralize, as far as possible, the unfitness of the unfit. A mother brings her malformed baby to the surgeon, and he does his best to patch up the gaps left by the imperfect processes of development. Otherwise the baby will die. Who dares look that mother in the face and say "Ah, but it is better for the race that your child should die!" Such a doctrine, I submit, blasphemes our humanity; it is intolerable to any decent person who will pause to think what it means: and yet, in so saying, we seem to defy Nature with her imperative law of the survival of the fittest only. Recent writers on evolution state the case in all its hardness. Dr. Archdall Reid says that "If we wish to improve the individual, we must attend to his acquirements by providing proper shelter, food, and training." Well, we do wish to improve the individual, and to preserve the individual! We do not wish the super-man on the terms of Nietzsche — the super-man obtained at the cost of love would turn out to be inferior to any brute-beast, an intellectual fiend. But, Dr. Reid goes on to say, "such means will not effect an improvement of the race. . . . On the contrary, they will cause deterioration [1] by an increased survival of the unfit." The provision of "proper shelter, food and training" will cause racial decadence! Is it not evident, then, that such provisions must rather be styled improper, and that we must refrain from doing anything for the defects and needs of the individual, lest a worse thing befall the race? This is an outrageous proposition, yet it is offered us as a necessary inference from the principle of natural selection or the survival of the fittest — which no one now dares to dispute.

Herbert Spencer, to whom we owe the phrase "the survival of the fittest," expresses this critical difficulty as follows: "The law that each creature shall take the benefits and the evils of its own nature has been the law under which life has evolved thus far. Any arrangements which, in a considerable degree, prevent superiority from profiting by the rewards of superiority, or shield inferiority from the evils it entails — any

[1] "Degeneration," I think, is the best word for the racial, "deterioration" for the individual, change.

arrangements which tend to make it as well to be inferior as to be superior, are arrangements diametrically opposed to the progress of organization, and the reaching of a higher life." This is permanently and necessarily true, and in our care for childhood we have to reckon with it. Yet Spencer did not or would not pursue this supremely important inquiry to what I shall in a moment submit to be its logical and almost incredibly hopeful conclusion.

Huxley, writing his well-known Romanes Lecture, "Evolution and Ethics," at a time when, unfortunately, he had somewhat parted company with Spencer, and was too ready to accept any argument that made against Spencer's political views, cuts the Gordian knot in an astonishingly unsatisfactory fashion. He declares that "the ethical progress of society depends, not on imitating the cosmic process [that is, the selection of the fittest] still less running away from it, but in combating it." This is shallow thinking and very poor philosophy. One wonders how Huxley can have forgotten the great dictum of Bacon that Nature can be commanded only by obeying her. He declares that moral evolution is the direct contradiction and antithesis of the processes of organic evolution hitherto. He says, "Social progress means a checking of the cosmic process at every step and the substitution for it of another, which may be called the ethical process;" and he declares it to be a fallacy to suppose "that because on the whole animals and plants have advanced in perfection of organization, by means of the struggle for existence and the consequent survival of the fittest; therefore men in society, men as ethical beings, must look to the same process to help them towards perfection."

With all this Huxley offers us no real solution whatever, no hint that he has realized in any degree what must be the consequences of indiscriminate survival. It is astonishing how personal bias, so alien to the whole character of the man as a rule, blinded him to a solution which, as it seems to me, stared him in the face. Assuredly we can transmute and elevate and raise to its highest power what he calls the cosmic process, and can reconcile cosmic with ethical evolution, *by extending to the unfit all our sympathy but forbidding them parenthood.* I deny that the provision of a proper environment for the individual entails racial deterioration. Cosmic and moral evolution are compatible if, whilst caring for each individual, whether maim, halt, blind, or insane, and whilst admitting the categorical imperative of the law of love which demands our care for him, we continue to obey the indication of Nature, which forbids such an individual to perpetuate his infirmity. Nature has no choice; if she is to avert the coming of the unfit race she must summarily extinguish its potential ancestor, but we can prohibit the reproduction of his infirmity whilst doing all we can for the success of his individual life. This is the ideal course indicated and approved by biology and morality alike.

THE EUGENIC RECONCILIATION.— I submit, then, that there is no inconsistency in fighting simultaneously for the preservation and care of all babies and all children without discrimination of any kind — and, on the other hand, in declaring that, if the degeneration of the race is to be averted, still more if racial, which is the only sure, progress, to be attained, we must have the worthy and only the worthy to be the parents of the future. I submit further that only the eugenist can maintain his position in this matter at the present day.

On this one hand is the improvident humanitarian with his feeling heart, he who, seeing misery and disease and death, whether in babyhood, childhood, or at any other time of life, seeks to improve the environment and so relieve these evils. Close beside this wholly indiscriminate humanitarianism is that which declares that with childhood is the future and therefore devotes its energies especially to the young, is grateful for every baby born, whatever its state, and when adult years are reached, assumes that all will be well for the future, though the principle of natural selection is thus made of none effect.

On the other side of the eugenists stand those whom we may for short call Nietzscheans. They see one-half of the truth of natural selection; they see that through struggle and internecine war, species have hitherto maintained themselves or ascended. They declare that all improvement of the environment, or at any rate all humanitarian effort, tends to abrogate the struggle for existence, and even, as is only too often true, to select unworth and let worth go to the wall. This school then declares that infant mortality is a blessing and charity an unmitigated curse. In short, that we must go back as quickly as possible to the order of the beast.

Between these two, surely, the eugenist stands, declaring that each has a great truth, but that his teaching, and his alone, involves their co-ordination and reconciliation. He agrees with the humanitarian that no child should cry or starve or work or die — or at any rate this particular eugenist does — and he agrees with the Nietzschean that to abrogate, and still more, to reverse, the principle of natural selection, is to set our faces for the goal of racial death. But further, the eugenist declares that the indiscriminate humanitarian, blind to the truth which the Nietzscheans sees, would heap up, if permitted, disaster upon disaster; whilst he repudiates as horrible and ghastly the Nietzschean doctrine that morality must go by the board if the race is to be raised: — that we must be damned to be saved.

Our age is now awakening, at last, to the cry of the children. The tendency of legislation and opinion in every civilized country is one and the same. For this humanitarianism let only him who thinks of any child as a brat refuse to give thanks. But it is the business of all who, whilst loving children and still in love with love, are yet acquainted with the principles of organic evolution — in short, the business of all humane men of science, men of science who have not ceased to be human — whilst aiding, abetting and directing this humanitarian effort by every means in their power, to teach and preach, in season and out of season, that unless meanwhile we make terms with the principle of selection, the choice of worth for parents, and the rejection of the unworthy, *not as individuals but as parents,* we shall assuredly breed for posterity, whose lives and happiness and moral welfare are in our hands, evils that can adequately neither be named nor numbered. Already, together with much blessed good, this indiscriminate humanitarianism has done much evil. Many of our most instant and, for this generation, insoluble problems are the lamentable fruit of this inherently good thing. The eugenist declares that this fruit is not necessary, that if it were necessary he could see no way out of our morass and would echo the half-wish of Huxley for some kindly comet that should put a term to human history altogether; and, in short, that only by the eugenic means can the humanitarian end be attained.

During the last year or two of the campaign against infant mortality many things have become clear, and none clearer than the fundamental compatibility between this campaign and the principles of eugenics. As these two efforts will be predominant in the real politics of many years to come, a few more words must here be devoted to the relation between them.

Granted that the highest of all objects is the making of worthy human beings, it is quite evident that we must attend equally to the two factors which determine all human life — heredity and environment. Eugenics stands for the principle of heredity — the principle that the right children shall be born. The campaign against infant mortality stands for a good environment [1]— so that children, when born, may survive and thrive. Obviously eugenics would be of no use if the children could not survive, and no human infant can survive unless it be born into a moral environment:

[1] That is in the ordinary sense of the words, not in the more exact sense — as I think — in which a good environment would be defined as that which selects the good for parenthood.

no motherhood, no man. The two campaigns, then, are strictly complementary. We must endeavor to rid ourselves of the popular notion that the whole result of the campaign against infant mortality can be measured by the number of babies whose death is prevented. The infant mortality is merely an index of a widespread social disease — an index and an extreme symptom. But for every baby killed many are damaged; and to remove the causes of infant mortality is to remove the causes which at present effect the deterioration of millions of human beings. The eugenic campaign, then, without the other would be almost futile.

THE TIME FOR EUGENICS.— On our principles the eugenic question can be decently raised only *before conception.* The unyoked germ-cells of any individual, though alive, are not entitled to claim protection from the principle that life is sacred. It is permitted to allow them to die; but from the moment of conception a new individual has been formed — a new living human individual, even though it only consists of a single cell, product of the union of the parental germ-cells: and we shall not be safe unless we regard this being as sacred and its destruction — except in order to save the life of the mother — as murder, even at this as at any later stage. If the eugenist should raise his voice, and say that this individual should not be born, he must be regarded exactly as if he were to recommend infanticide or the lethal chamber for unfit individuals. In such a case he would have entirely mistaken the whole principle of (negative) eugenics, which is *not* to elevate the race by the destruction of the unfit, at any stage, ante-natal or post-natal, but to do so by prohibiting the conception of the unfit. Directly the new human individual is formed the eugenic question is too late in that case. It is now the eugenist's duty, because it is every one's duty, to regard the new individual, whether born or yet unborn, as an end in himself or herself. But when the question arises whether that individual is to become a parent, then the eugenic question can and must be raised.

Circumstances might arise in which "case-law" might be applicable. It might be thought better to destroy the syphilitic child rather than allow it to come into the world. But we cannot make these distinctions. The question is simply one of expediency, and the only expedient thing is that there shall be no paltering with the principle that when a new human life is conceived our duty is to preserve it, whether it were conceived only twenty-four hours ago or whether it be a decrepit and helpless centenarian. The instant we let this principle go we are proposing to revert to nature's method of keeping up the level of a race by murder. It is improper, then, for any one on eugenic grounds to protest against proposals for the arrest of infant mortality. He should have spoken sooner; at this stage he must hold his peace.

THE TWO CAMPAIGNS COMPLEMENTARY.— Yet further: not only is it evident that the campaign against infant mortality (which is, in a word, the campaign for the provision of a proper environment for the young) is obviously necessary for the fulfillment of the eugenic ideal — since what would be the good of choosing the right parents if their children are then to be slain? — but it can be shown conversely that the object of those who are working against infant mortality can never be fully attained except by means of eugenics. Eugenics apart, we can and shall reduce the infant mortality to a mere fraction of what it is at present, by preventing the destruction of that great majority of babies who are born healthy. Even, however, when we have provided an ideal environment for every baby that comes into the world, we shall not have abolished infant mortality, since there will always remain a proportion, say ten per cent., whom not even an ideal environment can save. They should never have been conceived. At the Infantile Mortality Conference held in London in 1908, this was clearly recognized by more than one speaker. We who are working against infant mortality must have the eugenist to help us if our ideal is to be attained.

Not only is the ideal of the two campaigns one and the same; not only is each necessary for the other, but their methods are the same. It is true that at first this was not evident, since when we began to fight against infant mortality many temporary expedients of no eugenic relevance were adoped, such as the *crèche* and the infant milk *depôt*. But in the interval between the Conferences of 1906 and 1908 many things became clear: so that, whereas the papers at the first Conference were only accidentally connected, the programme of the second proceeded upon a principle — the principle of the supremacy of motherhood. We see now that the one fundamental method by which infantile mortality may be checked is by the elevation of motherhood. In the words of our President, Mr. John

Burns, "you must glorify, dignify, and purify motherhood by every means in your power." Thus the first two papers read at the first morning's meeting of the Conference — a brief paper by the present writer on "The Human Mother," and an admirable paper by Miss Alice Ravenhill on "Education for Motherhood" — might equally well have been read at a Eugenics Conference. The opponent of infant mortality and the eugenist appeal to the same principle and avow the same creed: that parenthood is sacred, that it must not be casually undertaken, that it demands the most assiduous preparation of body and intellect and emotions. When, at last, these principles are believed and acted upon, infant mortality will be a thing of the past and national eugenics a thing of the present.

It is essential in this first general study of the subject to state the true nature of the relation between these two campaigns, to which every succeeding year of the present century will find more and more attention devoted. Between them they succeed in beginning at the beginning, and it would be a disaster, indeed, if they were incompatible. On the contrary, they are complementary and mutually indispensable. As the years go on they will engage between them the sympathy and the assistance of all serious people. In the year 1907 infant mortality was first named in a speech by a Prime Minister, and in the same year it was first mentioned in the Christmas-Day sermon at St. Paul's Cathedral; in that year also Parliament passed the Early Notification of Births Act, the first substantial legislative provision which sets our foot on the road towards the goal of a true national estimate of the value of parenthood. We are about to discover that the true politics is domestics, since there is no wealth but life and life begins at home. We are going to have the right kind of life born, and we are going to take care of it when it is born. We shall raise a generation which looks upon the ordinary money-changing politician as an impudent public nuisance, and the brutal brazen-mouthed Imperialist, shouting about the Empire which his very existence is sufficient to condemn, whilst he pockets the profits of the sale of alcoholic poison to babies and the mothers of future babies, as the kind of thing for which some effective sewer must be contrived. We propose to rebuild the living foundations of empire. To this end we shall preach a New Imperialism, warning England to beware lest her veins become choked with yellow dirt, and demanding that over all her legislative chambers there be carved the more than golden words, "There is no Wealth but Life."

CHAPTER III

NATURAL SELECTION AND THE LAW OF LOVE

Truth justifies herself; and as she dwells
With hope, who would not follow where she leads?
WORDSWORTH.

La plus haute tâche de l'action morale est le travail pour le bien des générations futures.— FOREL.

BEFORE looking more closely than we are commonly apt to do at the meaning of the phrases "natural selection" and "survival of the fittest," let us exercise the right of man the moral being, as distinguished from man the scientist or observer of Nature, to pass ethical judgments upon the facts which it is the business of all the sciences, except ethics itself, merely to record and interpret in and for themselves. We are beginning at last, half a century after the publication of the *Origin of Species* in 1859, to realize the power of the law of selection; what is the moral judgment which is to be passed upon it? In a passage from the last page of Herbert Spencer's Autobiography, we find words which may be quoted on both sides: "When we think of the myriads of years of the Earth's past, during which have arisen and passed away low forms of creatures, small and great, which, ***murdering and being murdered, have gradually evolved,***[1] how shall we answer the question — To what end?

[1] The Italics are mine.

"Murdering and being murdered" suggests the adverse, and "have gradually evolved," the favorable, ethical judgment.

Many thinkers, finding Nature "so careless of the single life," finding the murderous struggle for existence the dominant fact of the history of the living world, return an adverse verdict. Amongst them are to be found not merely those who are inclined, by temperament or imperfect education, to rebellion against any conclusions of science, but also, as we saw in the second chapter, such a great biologist as Huxley. In another part of the lecture already cited he says that the Stoics failed to see

". . . that cosmic nature is no school of virtue, but the headquarters of the enemy of ethical nature. The logic of facts was necessary to convince them that the cosmos works through the lower nature of man, not for righteousness, but against it. . . . The practice of that which is ethically best — what we call goodness or virtue — involves a course of conduct which, in all respects, is opposed to that which leads to success in the cosmic struggle for existence."

In other words, honesty is the *worst* policy: and to worship natural selection is to deify the devil.

The reader will realize that, if we are to succeed in establishing the claim of natural selection to be the natural model upon which those who desire the progress of society are to base their policy, it is necessary to controvert the doctrine that natural selection is an anti-moral process. But let us hear the other side.

The directly contrary view, then, is taken that though, truly enough, there has been and is much "murdering and being murdered," yet organisms "have gradually evolved" towards fitness for their surroundings or the *milieu environnant* of Lamarck, which we translate environment; and that since fitness or adaptation obviously makes for happiness, and since the moral being man has himself been thus evolved, the process of natural selection, "murdering and being murdered" notwithstanding, is essentially beneficent.

The controversy is embittered and complicated by the fact that ultimate questions of religion and philosophy are involved. Is the Universe moral, as Emerson asserted it was, or is it immoral? A recent opponent of the orthodox creed of a benevolent Deity teaches that "The Lesson of Evolution" is to disprove the idea of benevolence behind or in Nature: "The story of life has been a story of pain and cruelty of the most ghastly description." The agelong fact of "murdering and being murdered" is the weapon with which he attacks the theist, who, *per contra,* points to the beneficent result, the exquisite adaptaion of all species to the circumstances of their life, and the evolution of love itself.

We may remind ourselves of those great lines of Mr. George Meredith.

". . . sure reward
We have whom knowledge crowns;
Who see in mould the rose unfold,
The soul through blood and tears."

The one camp points to the "blood and tears" and asks for a verdict accordingly. The other points to "the soul" as their product, and asks for a verdict accordingly. But surely we need only to have the case fairly stated, in order to realize that the "blood and tears" are true but only half the truth, "the soul" true but only half the truth. Natural Selection is a colossal paradox — the doing evil that good may come. The evil is undoubtedly done, and the good undoubtedly comes. Is not this the only verdict that is in consonance with all the facts? Is it not less than philosophic to look at the process alone, or to look at the result alone? Is any real end to be served by the incessant cry that we should keep our eyes fixed on the "blood and tears" alone, or on "the soul" alone? Is not the poet right when he says that the sure reward of knowledge is not to see either half of the truth as if it were the whole, but to see unfold "the soul through blood and tears?"

Any attempt to cast up accounts between the evil of the process and the good of the result — especially any attempt based on the assumption that the process has yet achieved its final result — would be not only premature in the eyes of those who can look forwards, but would be irrelevant to our present inquiry. I certainly am with those who repudiate as misleading Mill's description of Nature as a "vast slaughter-house" and will declare that, apart from self-conscious and supremely sensitive man, it is easy to exaggerate the misery and to minimize the joy of the sub-human world. But our business here is with the process and its results in man himself, in whom alone are possible the heights of ecstasy and the depths of agony: and the thesis — the sublime thesis, we may avouch — of the present discussion is that, whatever the balance between the evil of the process of Natural Selection and the good of its results in the natural state, yet when it is transmuted, as it may be, by the moral intelligence of man, according to the principles of race-culture or eugenics, the good of the result can be attained, more abundantly and incomparably more rapidly, than ever heretofore, *whilst the evil of the process can be abolished altogether.* True or false, is this not a sublime thesis?

NATURE MUST BE CRUEL TO BE KIND.—If organic fitness or adaptation to the circumstances of life is to be secured, Nature must choose for future parents, out of every new generation, only those whose inborn characters make for this adaptation, and who, in virtue of the fact we call heredity, will tend to transmit this fitness to their offspring. Now it is often convenient to personify Nature, but we must not be misled. The process is really an automatic, not an intelligently directed one. In order that it shall be possible, certain conditions must obtain. The choice or selection depends not merely upon the provision of a variety from which to choose — this being afforded by what is called variation, which is the correlative of heredity, both being obvious facts in any well-filled nursery — but also upon the production of *more* young creatures than there is or will be room for. (If there be room for all, so that all survive, there can be no selection, and instead of survival of the fittest there will be indiscriminate survival.) The choice is effected amongst this superfluity by an internecine "struggle for existence": hence the "murdering and being murdered," hence the "blood and tears." The motor force of the whole process may be symbolized as the "will to life," ever seeking to realize itself in more abundance and with more success — with more and more approximation to perfect adaptation. The will to death is no ingredient of the will to life. Nature is, so to say, by no means desirous of the process of "murdering and being murdered": very much on the contrary. It is life, more life, and fitter life, that is her desire: the "murdering and being murdered," the "blood and tears" are no part of her aim. But they are inevitable, though lamentable, if her aim is to be realized. She *must* be cruel to be kind.[1]— a little cruel to be very kind.

It is *imaginable,* though no more, that natural selection, in certain circumstances, might have worked otherwise: the penalty for less as against greater fitness might *imaginably* have been not death but merely sterility — the denial of future parenthood. This is the ideal of race-culture. Had this been possible, Nature could have effected her end, which is fitter and fuller life, without having incidentally to mete out premature death to such an overwhelming majority of all her creatures. But, actually, this was not possible: and, unless the end was to be sacrificed, Nature was compelled — to keep up the figure — summarily to kill

[1] We have seen that Huxley's assertion of the fundamental opposition between moral and cosmic evolution is unwarrantable. We do recognize, however, that in our present practice this opposition exists. Our ancestors were cruel to the insane, but at least they prevented them from multiplying. We are blindly kind to them, and therefore in the long run cruel. But the dilemma, kind to be cruel, or cruel to be kind, is not necessary. It is quite possible, as we have asserted, to be at once kind to the individual and protective of the future. On the other hand, it is also possible to be cruel to both. The London County Council offers us, at the time of writing, a demonstration of this. Sending wretched inebriates on the round of police-court, prison and street, with intermittent gestations, rather than expend a shilling a day, per individual, in decently detaining them, it serves at least the philosophic purpose of demonstrating that it is possible to combine the maxim of brutality to the individual and the present with the maximum of injury to the race and the future.

right and left. Permitted to reach maturity, the unfit as well as the fit would multiply; and since, in general, the lower the form of life the greater its fertility, the species could not possibly advance, or even maintain itself at the level already gained.

To drop the figure, the process is a mechanical and automatic one, and its appalling wastefulness and indisputable cruelty are inevitably involved, whilst it so remains.

INTELLIGENCE MAY BE KIND TO BE KINDER.—But, — and here is the great event — this mechanical, automatic, non-intelligent process has latterly given birth to intelligence, the moral intelligence of man: and the question now to be answered is, what modification can intelligence effect in the moral-immoral process that has created it? Must intelligence abrogate that process altogether, as Huxley declares, on the grounds of its murderous methods? Must intelligence simply look on, recognize, but not reconstruct? Must intelligence reverse the process — as indeed it is now doing in many cases — so that in the new environment of which itself is a factor, that which formerly was unfitness shall become fitness, and *vice versâ? Or* is it conceivable that intelligence can transmute the process, so that, whilst hitherto mechanical, automatic, and therefore inevitably murderous, it shall become *intelligent,* pressing towards the sublime end, and reforming the murderous means?

Hear Mr. Galton himself (*Sociological Papers,* 1905, p. 52): —

"Purely passive, or what may be styled mechanical evolution, displays the awe-inspiring spectacle of a vast eddy of organic turmoil . . . it is moulded by blind and wasteful processes, namely, by an extravagant production of raw material and the ruthless rejection of all that is superfluous, through the blundering steps of trial and error. . . . Evolution is in any case a grand phantasmagoria, but it assumes an infinitely more interesting aspect under the knowledge that the intelligent action of the human will is, in some small measure, capable of directing its course. Man has the power of doing this largely so far as the evolution of humanity is concerned; he has already affected the quality and distribution of organic life so widely that the changes on the surface of the earth, merely through his disforestings and agriculture, would be recognizable from a distance as great as that of the moon."

Hear also Sir E. Ray Lankester, in the Romanes Lecture[1] for 1905: "Man is . . . a product of the definite and orderly evolution which is universal, a being resulting from and driven by the one great nexus of mechanism which we call Nature. He stands alone, face to face with that relentless mechanism. It is his destiny to understand and to control it."

"Nature's Insurgent Son," Professor Lankester calls man in this lecture; and yet again there recurs that mighty aphorism of Bacon, which might well be printed on every page of these chapters, "Nature is to be commanded only by obeying her." The struggle for existence is the terrible fact of Nature, but is only a means to an end. It is our destiny to command the end whilst *humanizing* the means.

THE STRUGGLE FOR EXISTENCE.—The ideal eugenics or race-culture is to abolish the brutal elements of the struggle for existence whilst gaining its great end. The nature of this struggle is commonly misapprehended and, as I cannot improve upon the words of

[1] Reprinted in *The Kingdom of Man*, London.

Professor Lankester, I shall freely use them in the attempt to show what it really is. He says: —

"The world, the earth's surface, is practically full, that is to say, fully occupied. Only one pair of young can grow up to take the place of the pair — male and female — which have launched a dozen, or it may be as many as a hundred thousand, young individuals on the world. . . . The 'struggle for existence' of Darwin is the struggle amongst all the superabundant young of a given species, in a given area, to gain the necessary food, to escape voracious enemies, and gain protection from excesses of heat, cold, moisture, and dryness. One pair in the new generation — only one pair — survive for every parental pair. Animal population does not increase: 'Increase and multiply' has never been said by Nature to her lower creatures. Locally, and from time to time, owing to exceptional changes, a species may multiply here and decrease there; but it is important to realize that the 'struggle for existence' in Nature — that is to say, among the animals and plants of this earth untouched by man — is a desperate one, however tranquil and peaceful the battlefield may appear to us. The struggle for existence takes place, not as a clever French writer glibly informs his readers, between different species, but between individuals of the same species, brothers and sisters and cousins. . . . In Nature's struggle for existence, death, immediate obliteration, is the fate of the vanquished, whilst the only reward to the victors — few, very few, but rare and beautiful in the fitness which has carried them to victory — is the permission to reproduce their kind — to carry on by heredity to another generation the specific qualities by which they triumphed.

"It is not generally realized how severe is the pressure and competition in Nature — not between different species, but between the immature population of one and the same species, precisely because they are of the same species and have exactly the same needs. . . . A distinctive quality in the beauty of natural productions (in which man delights) is due to the unobtrusive yet tremendous slaughter of the unfit which is incessantly going on, and the absolute restriction of the privilege of parentage to the happy few who attain to the standard described as 'the fittest.'"

THE SURVIVAL OF THE FITTEST.— Now let us look closely at this most famous of all Spencer's phrases, "the survival of the fittest," and try to understand its full and exact meaning. There is no phrase in any language so frequently misinterpreted. Even a writer who should know better makes this mistake. Mr. H. G. Wells speaks [1] of "that same lack of a fine appreciation of facts that enabled Herbert Spencer to coin those two most unfortunate terms *Evolution* and the *Survival of the Fittest.* The implication is that the *best* reproduces and survives. Now really it is the *better* that survives and not the *best.*" What the correction is supposed to signify I do not know, but the whole passage is nonsense. The implication is neither that the *best* nor the *better* survive, but the fittest — or if Mr. Wells prefers, for it matters not one whit — the fitter. This lack of fine appreciation of words is not, unfortunately, peculiar to Mr. Wells. There is no word in the language that more exactly expresses the fact than the word fittest: as Darwin recognized when he promptly incorporated Spencer's phrase in the second edition of the *Origin of Species* as the best interpretation of his own phrase "Natural Selection" [2] Fitness is the capacity to fit: a thing that is fit is a thing that *fits.* A living creature survives in proportion as it fits its environment — the physical environment in the case of vegetables and the lower animals, the physical, social, intellectual and moral environment in the

[1] *Sociological Papers,* 1905, p. 59.

[2] Whilst allowing due weight to Mr. Wells' opinion, we may also note that Charles Darwin, who, referring to his own phrase, 'natural selection,' says, "But the expression often used by Mr. Herbert Spencer of the Survival of the Fittest is more accurate." (Origin of Species, Popular Edition, page 76.)

case of man. The kind of glove that most perfectly fits the hand is the fittest glove and will survive in the struggle for existence between gloves. If, instead of a glove, we take a living creature, say a microbe, the kind of microbe that best fits into the environment provided by, say, human blood, is the fittest and will survive and be the cause of our commonest disease. Thus the tubercle bacillus is at once the *fittest* microbe and, not the best, but the worst. Among ourselves, the newspaper devoted to yesterday's murder is the fittest and survives, ousting the newspaper which reckons with the crucifixion or the murder of Socrates or Bruno. In a society of blackguardism, the biggest blackguard is the fittest man and will survive: he is also the worst. In another society the best man is the fittest and survives. The capacity to fit into an environment is the capacity that determines survival: it has no moral connection whatever. If Herbert Spencer had written the survival of the better, as Mr. Wells desires, he would have written palpable nonsense: as it was he used the fittest word — in this case also the best, because the truest. Referring to the queen-bee, who destroys her own daughters, Darwin says: "Undoubtedly this is for the good of the community; the maternal love or maternal hatred, though the latter fortunately is most rare, is all the same to the inexorable principle of natural selection."

If natural selection were the survival of the better, as Mr. Wells would have us believe, there would be nothing for eugenics or race-culture to do: and heaven would long ago have come to earth. If in all ages the better men and women had survived and become parents earth would long ago have become a demi-paradise indeed, there would have been no arrests, no reversals in the history of human progress, and life would be already what, some day, it will be, when there is achieved the eugenic ideal — which is precisely that the best or better members of our race shall be the selected for the supreme profession of parenthood. In other words, the eugenic ideal, the ideal of race-culture, is *to ensure that the fittest shall be the best.* Always, everywhere, without a solitary exception, human, animal or vegetable, the fittest have ultimately survived and must survive. Once realize what is the meaning of the word fit — best seen in the verb "to fit" — and we shall see that, as Herbert Spencer pointed out in his overwhelming reply to the late Lord Salisbury's attack on evolution, the idea of the survival of the fittest is a necessity of thought.[1]

But, alas, the idea of the survival of the best or the better is not a necessity of thought! The fittest microbes are the worst from our point of view, because they are most inimical to the highest forms of life; the fittest newspaper may be the worst, because it panders to the worst but most widespread and irresponsible elements in human nature; everything and every one that succeeds, succeeds because it or he fits the conditions: but to succeed is not necessarily to be good. Indeed everything that exists at all, living or lifeless, an atom or an animal, a molecule or a moon, exists because it can exist, because it fits the conditions of existence: there is no moral question involved, but

[1] *Collected Essays,* vol. i. p. 493. A valuable controversy but poor sport. Thinker *versus* politician is scarcely a match.

only a mechanical one. The business of eugenics or race-culture is to make an environment, conditions of law and public opinion, *such that the fittest shall be the best and the best the fittest therein.*

If memory may be trusted, the primary meaning of the word *fit* has not hitherto been called in by any one to elucidate the meaning of Spencer's phrase: perhaps it may be hoped that we shall at last begin to understand it, if we remember that a thing is fit because it fits. It is best not to be too sanguine, however, and therefore we may attempt to illustrate the case from another aspect.

SURVIVAL-VALUE.— Every living thing and really every character or feature of a living thing that survives, survives because it has value or capacity for life — which may be called, in Professor Lloyd Morgan's phrase, *survival-value.* The character that gives an organism survival-value or value for life, the character that enables it to fit its environment, may be of any order. The atom, as I have said elsewhere, is an organism writ small. The kinds of atoms that have survived in the agelong struggle for existence between atoms are those that have survival-value on account of their internal stability: as Empedocles argued ages ago. In the case of living things, which individually die, it is evident that capacity to reproduce themselves is one of supreme survival-value. If mankind lost this capacity, all its other characters of survival-value, such as intelligence, would obviously avail it nought. Certain valuable members of society may fall short in this cardinal respect, and therefore become extinct. Indeed, other forms of survival-value, as we shall see, seem to be in large measure inimical to fertility: and this is perhaps the chief obstacle to eugenics.[1]

Fertility apart, the character having survival-value may take a thousand forms. In the case of the parasitic microbe it is an evil character, the power to produce toxins or poisons. In the case of the tiger it is the possession of large and powerful bones and claws and muscles and teeth. In the case of the ox it is a complicated and efficient digestive apparatus, enabling it to fit into a food-environment which is too innutritious to sustain the life of creatures not so endowed. Nature seeks only the fittest; not the best but the best-adapted; she asks no moral questions. A Keats, a Spinoza or a Schubert must go under if his factors of survival-value do not enable him to resist those of the tubercle bacillus, its toxins or poisons. She welcomes the parasitic tapeworm, all hooks and mouth or stomach, because these give it survival-value; and so on.

The business of eugenics or race-culture, then, is to create an environment such that those characters which we desire as moral and intelligent beings, shall be endowed with the highest possible survival-value, as against those which ally so many men with the microbe and the tapeworm. There are those who live in society to-day, and reproduce their like, in virtue of the poisons they produce, in virtue of their tenacious hooks and voracious stomachs. If society be organized so

[1] This is discussed at length in the writer's papers, "The Obstacles to Eugenics," read before the Sociological Society, March 8, 1909.

that these are factors of more survival-value than the disinterested search for truth, or mother-love, or the power to create great poetry or music — then, according to the inevitable and universal law of the survival of the fittest, our parasites will oust our poets and our poisoners our philosophers. These things have happened and may happen again at any time. It does not matter that the good thing, in virtue of survival-value then superior, has been evolved. Nature never gives a final verdict in favor of good or bad but only and always in favor of the fit. Let the conditions change, so that rapacity fits them better than righteousness, or — as in a completely "collectivist" state — vegetableness rather than virility, and the thing we call high will go under before the thing we call low. Nature recognizes neither high nor low but only fitness or value for life in the conditions that actually obtain. These laws enthroned and dethroned the civilizations of the past: they have enthroned and may dethrone us. But this end is not inevitable, since man — and this is his great character — not merely reacts to his environment, as all creatures must, but can create and recreate it. The business of eugenics or race-culture is to create an environment such that the human characters of which the human spirit approves shall in it outweigh those of which we disapprove. Make it fittest to be best and the best will win — not because it is the best, but because it is the fittest: had the worst been the fittest it would have won. In society to-day both forms of the process may be observed. The balance between them determines its destiny. It is the business of eugenics to throw the whole weight of human purpose into the scale of the good.

EVOLUTION NOT NECESSARILY PROGRESS.— No excessive space has been devoted to this distinction between the fittest and the best and to the real meaning of Spencer's famous phrase, if perchance it should avail in any degree to dispel one of the commonest of the many common delusions regarding the nature of organic evolution and its outcome. This delusion is that progress is an inevitable law of nature.[1] The great process of history, as revealed by biology, displays as its supreme fact the occurrence of progress. The principles of evolution teach that this progress — as, for instance, in the evolution of man — is a product of the survival of the fittest; whilst we are also reminded that the survival of the fittest is a necessary truth; but it does not follow that progress is inevitable.

In the first place, natural selection involves selection. Where all the young members of a new generation of any species survive, and parenthood becomes not a privilege but a common and universal function, plainly the process is in abeyance: and, in the second place, since the survival of the fittest is the survival of the best adapted, the process may at any time take the form of retrogression rather than that of progress. The assumption that, because progress has been affected through natural selection, we need do no more than fold our hands or unfold them merely to applaud, involves the denial of one of the most

[1] Spencer introduced the non-moral word evolution in 1857, *in order to* avoid the moral connotation of the word progress, which he had formerly employed.

familiar facts of natural history — the fact of racial degeneration. The parasitic microbes, the parasitic worms, the barnacles, innumerable living creatures both animal and vegetable individuals and races of mankind, to-day as in all ages —these prove only too clearly that the process of the survival of the fittest may make as definitely for retrogression in one case as for progress in another.

By all means let us infer from the facts of organic evolution the conclusion that further progress must surely be possible, so much progress having already been achieved as is represented by the difference between inorganic matter or the amœba or microbe on the one hand, and man on the other hand. But let us most earnestly beware of the false and disastrous optimism which should suppose that because the survival of the fittest has often, and indeed most often, meant the survival of the best, it means always that and nothing else. On the contrary, we must learn that, even in natural circumstances, apart from any interference by man, the survival of the fittest often means racial degeneration — a tapeworm kept in spirits should stand upon the study mantelpiece of all who think with Mr. Wells that the survival of the fittest means the survival of the better; and still more notably we must learn that the interference of man in the case of his own species, sometimes of evil intent, sometimes for the highest ends, with the process of natural selection, has repeatedly led, and is now in large part leading, to nothing other than process of racial degeneration of which the tapeworm and the barnacle should be our perpetual reminders. The case becomes serious enough when man interferes with the process of selection merely with the effect of suspending it, wholly or in part: but it becomes far more serious when his interference constitutes a reversal of the process. This most supremely disastrous of all conceivable consequences of man's intelligence and moral sense is known as reversed selection, and must be carefully studied hereafter. Meanwhile, we must devote some space to a most important consideration — namely, that though Nature is impartial in her choice, and will, for instance, allow the poisons of a microbe such as the tubercle bacillus to destroy the life of a Spinoza or a Keats or a Schubert, yet, on the whole, the survival-value of the mental, spiritual, or physical in all its forms, does persistently tend to outweigh that of the physical or material — of this great truth the evolution and dominance of man himself being the supreme example.

The very fact of progress, which I would define as the emergence and increasing dominance of mind, demonstrates — it being remembered that natural selection has no moral prejudices — that even in a world of claws and toxins the psychical must have possessed sufficient survival-value to survive. It is quite evident that even the lowliest psychical characters, such as sharpness of sensation, discrimination, and memory, must be of value in the struggle for life. More and more we might expect to find, and do actually find in the course of evolution, that creatures live by their wits, rather than by force of bone or muscle. The psychical was certainly given no unfair start — on the contrary. It has had to struggle for its emergence;

it has emerged only where there has been struggle and has done so because it could — because of its superior survival-value. It has the right which belongs to might — in the world of life there is no other.[1]

By no means less evident is the inherently superior survival-value of the psychical, if we turn from its aspects of sensation and intelligence to those which are all summed up under the word love. Notwithstanding Nietzsche's mad misconception of the Darwinian theory, no one who has studied the facts of reproduction and its conditions in the world of life can question the incalculable survival-value of love in animal history. The success of those most ancient of all societies, of which the ant-heap and the bee-hive are the types, depends absolutely upon the self-sacrifice of the individual. If we pass upwards from the insects to the lowest vertebrates, we find the survival-value of love proved by the comparison between various species of fish, and its increasing importance may be traced upwards through amphibia, reptiles, birds and mammals in succession, up to man. Natural selection thus actually selects morality. Without love no baby could live for twenty-four hours. Every human being that exists or ever has existed or ever will exist is a prod-

[1] In his recent work, "The Origin of Vertebrates," Dr. W. H. Gaskell, F.R.S., has adduced much evidence in support of this thesis. He says, "The law of progress is this: The race is not to the swift nor to the strong, but to the wise." And again; "As for the individual, so for the nation; as for the nation, so for the race; the law of evolution teaches that in all cases brain-power wins. Throughout, from the dawn of animal life up to the present day, the evidence given in this book suggests that the same law has always held. In all cases, upward progress is associated with the development of the central nervous system. The law for the whole animal kingdom is the same as for the individual. Success in this world depends upon brains."

uct of mother-love or foster-mother-love, and I am well entitled to say, as I have so often said, *no morals, no man.* The creature in whom organic morality is at its height has become the lord of the earth in virtue of that morality which natural selection has selected, not from any moral bias, but because of its superior survival-value.

CHAPTER IV

THE SELECTION OF MIND

"Many are the mighty things, but none is mightier than man. . . . He conquers by his devices the tenant of the fields."—SOPHOCLES.

"L'homme n'est gu'un yoseau, le plus faible de la Nature; mais c'est an yoscau pensant."—PASCAL.

"The soul of all improvement is the improvement of the soul." —BURCHELL.

WHEREAS, in its beginning, *mind,* or the psychical in all its aspects, was merely a useful property of *body,* all organic progress may be conceived in terms of a change in this original relation between them. In man, the mental or psychical has become the essential thing, and the body its servant. We are well prepared, then, to accept the proposition that in our own day and for our own species, the plane upon which natural selection works has largely been transferred, and, indeed, if any further progress is to be effected, *must* be transferred, from the bodily or physical to the mental or psychical. A certain most remarkable fact in the anatomy of man may be cited, as we shall see, in support of this proposition.

We need not venture upon the controversial ground of the relation or ultimate unity of mind and body; nor need we set up any suggestion of antagonism between them. All, however, are absolutely agreed that the psychical in all its forms, whatever it really be, has a consistent relation of the most intimate kind with that part of the body which we call the nervous system. For our present purposes the nature of this relation matters nothing at all, and in place of the phrase the "selection of mind," I should be quite content, if the reader so prefers, to speak of the selection of nerve or nervous selection. And if I may for a moment anticipate the conclusion, we may say that, in and for the future, the process of selection for life and parenthood, as it occurs in mankind, must be based, if the highest results are to be obtained, upon the principle that the selection of bodily qualities other than those of the nervous system is of value only in so far as these serve the nervous or psychical qualities. For practical and for theoretical purposes we must accept the dictum of Professor Forel that "the brain is the man"—or, to be more accurate and less epigrammatic, the nervous system is the man. If, then, we counsel or approve of any selection of bone or muscle or digestion, or any other bodily organ or function; if we select for physical health, physical energy, longevity, or immunity from disease—our estimate of these things, one and all, must be wholly determined by the services which they can perform for the nervous system, whether as its instruments, its guarantors of health and persistence, or otherwise. But we are not to regard any of these things as ends in themselves—notwithstanding the fact that this temptation will constantly beset us. So to do is implicitly to deny and renounce the supreme character of man—which is that, in him, mind or nervous system is the master and the rest of the body, with all its attributes, the servant.

THE BODY STILL NECESSARY.— Should any one suppose that the principles here laid down would speedily involve us, if executed, in a host of disasters, let him reconsider that conclusion. Utterly ignorant or jocose persons have hinted, more or less definitely, that if a race of mankind were to be bred for brains, the product would be a most misbegotten creature approaching as near as possible — and that imperfectly enough — to the ideal of disembodied thought, a creature monstrous as to head, impotent and puny as to limbs, and, in effect, the least effective of living creatures. This supposition may be commended as the last word in the way of nonsense. It depends upon an abysmal ignorance of the necessary and permanent relations which subsist between mind and body. It assumes that the healthy mind can be obtained without the healthy body; it is totally unaware that the nervous system cannot work properly unless the blood be well aerated by active lungs and distributed by a healthy heart; that unless certain glands, of which these people have never heard, are acting properly, the nervous system falls into decadence, and the man becomes an imbecile. To breed for brains is most assuredly to breed for body too: only that the end in view will guide us as to what points of body to breed for. For instance, it would prevent us from having any foolish ambitions as to increasing the stature of the race, or the average weight of its muscular apparatus. Stature may be a point to breed for in the race-culture of giraffes and muscle in the race-culture of the hippopotamus: but such bodily characters are of no moment for man, who is above all things a mind. Whilst we shall pay little attention to these, we or our descendants will be abundantly concerned with the preservation and culture of those many bodily characters upon which the health and vigor and sanity and durability of the nervous system depend. Further, notwithstanding all the nonsense that has been written concerning the man of the future, with bald and swollen head, begoggled eyes, toothless gums, and wicker-work skeleton, those who know the alphabet of physiology and psychology are warranted in believing that wisely to breed for brains will be to breed for beauty too — not of the skin-deep but of the mind-deep variety — and also for grace and energy and versatility of physique. Those who worship brawn as brawn may be commended to the ox; those who respect brawn as the instrument of brain, and value it not by its horse-power but by its capacity as the agent of purpose, will find nothing to complain of in the kinds of men and women whom a wise eugenics has for its ideal.

The erect attitude.— And now we must briefly consider that "most remarkable fact in the anatomy of man" to which allusion was made in the first paragraph. It is that, as the most philosophic anatomists are now coming to believe, the body of man actually represents the goal of physical evolution. Of course the common opinion is quite apart from science, that man is the highest of creatures, and that there is no more to be expected. But the doctrine of evolution regards man as the latest, not necessarily the last, term in an agelong process which is by no means completed, and from the evolutionary point of view it is thus a daring, and at first hearing, a preposterous thing to say that, so far as the physical aspects of organic evolution are concerned, the body of man apparently represents the logical and final conclusion of the agelong process which has produced it. Let us attempt very briefly to outline the argument.

We may say that a great step was taken when from the chaos of the invertebrate or backbone-less animals there emerged the first vertebrates. This unquestionably occurred in the sea, the first backbone being evolved in a fish-like creature which, in the course of time, developed two lateral fins. These became modified into two pairs of limbs, the sole function of which was locomotion. In the next group of vertebrates, the amphibia — such as the frog — we see these limbs terminating each in five digits. (The frog, so to say, decided that we should count in tens.) Now some creatures have specialized their limbs at the cost of certain fingers. The horse, for instance, walks on the nails (the hoofs) of its middle fingers and its middle toes. In the main line of ascent, however, none of these precious fingers (and toes) — how precious let the typist or the pianist say — have been sacrificed. There has been, however, in later ages a tendency towards the specialization of the front limbs. Used for locomotion at times, they are also used for grasping and tearing and holding, as in the case of the tiger, a member of the carnivora, a relatively late and high group of mammals. But the carnivore does not carry its food to its mouth, and the cat carries her kittens in her mouth and not with her paws. In the apes and monkeys, however, this specialization goes further, and things are actually carried by the hands to the mouth — a very great advance on the tiger, who fixes his food with his "hands," and then carries his mouth to it. Food to mouth instead of mouth to food is a much later stage in evolution, a fact which may be recalled when we watch the table manners of certain classes. Finally, in man the specialization reaches its natural limit by the *complete* liberation of the fore-limbs from the purpose of locomotion — though the crawling gait of a child recalls the base degrees by which we did ascend. This great change depends upon an alteration in the axis of the body. The first fishes, like present fishes, were horizontal animals, but gradually the axis has become altered, in the main line of progress, until the semi-erect apes yield to man the erect, or "man the erected," as Stevenson called him. The son of horizontal animals, he is himself vertical: the "pronograde" has become "orthograde." Thus the phrase, "the ascent of man," may be read in two senses. This capital fad has depended upon a shifting of the center of gravity of the body, which in adult man lies behind the hip-joints, whereas in his ancestors and in the small baby (still in the four-footed stage) it lies in front of the hip-joints. Thus, whilst other creatures tend naturally to fall forwards, so that they must use their fore-limbs for support and locomotion, the whole body of man above the hip-joints tends naturally to fall backwards, being prevented from doing so by two great ligaments which lie in front of the hip-joints and have a unique development in man. The complete erection of the spine means that the skull, instead of being suspended in front, is now poised upon the top of the spinal column. The field of vision is enormously enlarged, and it is possible to sweep a great extent of horizon at a moment's notice. But the complete discharge of the fore-limbs from the function of locomotion has far vaster consequences, especially as they now assume the function of educating their master, the brain, and enabling him to employ them for higher and higher purposes.

Thus, when we ask ourselves whether there is any further goal for physical evolution, the answer is that none can be seen. So far as physical evolution is concerned the goal has been attained with the erect attitude. Future changes in the anatomy of man will not be positive but negative. There doubtless will be a certain lightening of the ship, the casting overboard of inherited superfluities, but that is all: except that we may hope for certain modifications in the way of increasing the adaptation of the body to the erect attitude, which at present bears very hardly in many ways upon the body of man, and much more so upon the body of woman.

Thus race-culture will certainly not aim at the breeding of physical freaks of any kind, nor yet at such things as stature. It must begin by clearly recognizing what are the factors which in man possess supreme survival-value, and it must aim at their reinforcement rather than at the maintenance of those factors which, of dominant value in lower forms of life, have been superseded in him. A few words will suffice to show in what fashion man has already shed vital characters which, superfluous and burdensome for him, have in former times been of the utmost survival-value.

THE DENUDATION OF MAN.— As contrasted with the whole mass of his predecessors, man comes into the world denuded of defensive armor, destitute of offensive weapons, possessed alone of the potentialities of the physical. So far as defense is concerned, he has neither fur nor feathers nor scales, but is the most naked and thinnest skinned of animals. In his *Autobiography,* Spencer tells us how he and Huxley, sitting on the cliff at St. Andrews and watching some boys bathing, "marvelled over the fact, seeming especially strange when they are no longer disguised by clothes, that human beings should dominate over all other creatures and play the wonderul part they do on the earth." [1] But man is not only without armor against either living enemies or cold; he is also without weapons of attack. His teeth are practically worthless in this respect, not only on account of their small size but also because his chin, a unique possession, and the shape of his jaws, make them singularly unfit for catching or grasping. For claws he has merely nails, capable only of the feeblest scratching; he can discharge no poisons from his mouth; he cannot envelop himself in darkness in order to hide himself; his speediest and most enduring runner is a breathless laggard. And, lastly, he is at first almost bereft of in-

[1] We may recall the words of Lear:—

"Is man no more than this? Consider him well: Thou owest the worm no silk, the beast no hide, the sheep no wool, the cat no perfume: . . . Thou art the thing itself: unaccommodated man is no more but such a poor, bare, forked animal as thou art."

stinct, has to be burnt in order to dread the fire, and cannot find his own way to the breast. His sole instrument of dominance is his mind in all its attributes.

On the grounds thus indicated, we must be wholly opposed to all proposals for race education and race-culture, and to all social practices, which assume more or less consciously that, for all his boasting, man is after all only an animal: whilst we must applaud the selection and culture of the physical exactly in so far as, but no further than, it makes for health and strength of the physical — or, if the reader dislikes these expressions, the health and strength of that particular part of the physical which we call the nervous system.

It used to be generally asserted that whilst, in a civilized community, we do not expect to find the biggest or most muscular man King or Prime Minister, yet amongst savage tribes it *is* the physical, muscle and bone and brutality, that determines leadership. This, however, we now know to be untrue even for the earliest stages of society that anthropologists can recognize. The leader of the savage tribe is not the biggest man but the cleverest. The suggestion is therefore that, even in the earliest stages of human society, the plane of selection has already been largely transferred from brawn to brain or from physique to *psyche*. It has always been so, we may be well sure. The Drift men of Taubach, living in the inter-glacial period, could kill the full-grown elephant and rhinoceros. Says Professor Ranke: "It is the mind of man that shows itself superior to the most powerful brute force, even where we meet for the first time." This remains true whether the brute force be displayed in brutes or in other men.

The great fact of intelligence, as against material apparatus of any kind and even as against rigid instinct, is its limitless applicability. With this one instrument man achieves what without it could be achieved only by a creature who combined in his own person every kind of material apparatus, offensive and defensive, locomotor or what not, with animal life, and vegetable life too, have invented in the past — and not even by such a creature. Man is a poor pedestrian, but his mind makes locomotives which rival or surpass the fish of the sea, the antelope on land, if not yet the bird of the air; his teeth are of poor quality, but his mind supplies him with artificial ones and enables him to cook and otherwise to prepare his food. All the physical methods are self-limited, but the method of mind has no limits; it is even more than cumulative, and multiplies its capacities by geometrical progression.

THE CULT OF MUSCLE.— A word must really be said here, in accordance with all the foregoing argument, against the recent revival of what may be called the Cult of Muscle. This cult of muscle, or belief in physical culture, so called, as the true means of race-culture, undoubtedly requires to have its absurd pretensions censured. We now have many flourishing schools of physical culture which desire to persuade us to a belief in the monstrous anachronism that, even in man, muscle and bone are still pre-eminent. They want as many people as possible to believe that the only thing really worth aiming at is what they understand by physical culture. They pride themselves upon knowing the names and positions of all the muscles in the body, and on being able to provide us with instruments to develop all these muscles: they are there and they ought to be developed, and you are a mere parody of what a man ought to be unless they are developed — none of them must be neglected. Many people have been persuaded of these doctrines, and there is no doubt that the physical culture schools do thus develop a large number of muscles which have no present service for man and would otherwise have been allowed to rest in a decent obscurity.

In order to prove this point, let us instance a few muscles which it is utterly absurd to regard as still possessing any survival-value for man. In the sole of the foot there are four distinct layers of muscles, by means of which it is theoretically possible to turn each individual toe to the left or the right, independently of its neighbors, and to move the various parts of each toe upon themselves, just as in the case of the fingers. All this muscular apparatus is a mere survival, worth nothing at all for the special purpose of the human foot. In point of fact the human foot is now decadent, and probably not more than two or three specimens of feet in a hundred contain the complete normal equipment of muscles, bones and joints — as Sir William Turner showed many years ago. Thus many feet are possessed of muscles designed to act upon joints which have not been developed at all in the feet in question and which, if they were there, would not be of the smallest use. To take another instance, we do not now use our external ears for the purpose of catching sound, though we still possess muscles which, if thrown into action, would move the external ear in various directions. Again, there is a flat, thin stratum of muscle on the front of the neck, corresponding to a muscle which in the dog and the horse is quite important, but which is of no use to us. All would be agreed as to the absurdity of devoting continued conscious effort to the development of these particular muscles; but in point of fact we have a whole host of muscles which are in a similar case, and which are nevertheless objects of the most tender solicitude on the part of the physical culturist. In general, this modern craze, whilst highly profitable to those who foster it, is most misguided and reactionary. Modern knowledge of heredity teaches us that our descendants will not profit muscularly in the slightest degree because of our devotion to these relics: the blacksmith's baby has promise of no bigger biceps than any one else's. Further, the over-doing of muscular culture is responsible for the consumption of a large amount of energy. A muscle is a highly vital and active organ, requiring a large amount of nourishment, which its possessor has to obtain, consume, digest and distribute. The more time and energy spent in sustaining useless muscles, the less is available for immeasurably more important concerns. Man does not live by brawn alone: he *does* live by brain alone.

Strength versus skill.— So far as true race-culture is concerned, we should regard our muscles merely as servants or instruments of the will. Since we have learnt to employ external forces for our purposes, the mere bulk of a muscle is now a matter of little importance. Of the utmost importance, on the other hand, is the power to co-ordinate and graduate the activity of our muscles, so that they may become highly trained servants. This is a matter, however, not of muscle at all but of nervous education. Its foundation cannot be laid by mechanical things like dumb-bells and exercises, but by games, in which will and purpose and co-ordination are incessantly employed. In other words, the only physical culture worth talking about is nervous culture.

The principles here laid down are daily defied in very large measure in our nurseries, our schools, and our barrack yards. The play of a child, spontaneous and purposeful, is supremely human and characteristic. Although, when considered from the outside, it is simply a means of muscular development, properly considered it is really *the* means of nervous development. Here we see muscles used as human muscles should alone be used — as instruments of mind. In schools the same principles should be recognized. From the biological and psychological point of view the playing-field is immeasurably superior to the gymnasium. But it is in the barrack yard that the pitiable confusion between the survival-value of the mind and muscle respectively in man is most ludicrously and disastrously exemplified.

The glorious truth upon which we appear to act is that man is an animated machine; that the business of the soldier is not to think, not to be an individual, but to be an assemblage of muscles. We see the marks of this idea even in a fine poem: "Their's not to reason why, their's but to do or die"— which, of course, might just as well be said of a stud of horses or motor-cars. Further, our worship of the machine is, consistently enough, an unintelligent worship. We do not even recognize the best conditions for its action. Every year hundreds of young soldiers, originally healthy, have their hearts and lungs and other vital organs permanently injured by the imbecile attitude of chest — that of abnormal expansion — which they are required to adopt during hard work. Army doctors are now protesting against this, but it is in accordance with the fitness of things that the cult of muscle as against intelligenee should be unintelligent.

I repeat that whilst in the study of race-culture the physical cannot be ignored, since the psychical is so largely dependent upon it, yet the physical is of worth to us only in so far as it serves the psychical. The race the culture of which we propose to undertake has long ago determined to abandon the physical in itself as an instrument of success. We are not attempting the culture of the cretaceous reptiles, which staked their all upon muscle, and finally, having become as large as houses — and as agile — suffered extinction. We are attempting the culture of a species which, so far as the physical is concerned, has long ago crossed the Rubicon or burnt its boats. Even if Mr. Sandow and the drill-sergeant had their way to the utmost, and having finally eliminated all traces of mind, succeeded in producing the strongest and most perfect physical machine that could be made from the human body, the species so produced would go down in a generation before the beast and the microbe — before any living species that may be named. Man has staked his all upon mind. The only physical development that is really worth anything to such a race is that which educates intelligence and morality, on the one hand, and serves for their expression, on the other.

If there is any salient and irresistible tendency in our civilization to-day, it is the persistent decadence of muscle and of all of which muscle is the type, as an instrument of survival-value. The development of machinery, much deplored by the short-sighted, is in the direct line of progress, because it reduces the importance of muscle and throws all its weight into the scale of mind. Hewers of wood and drawers of water are becoming less and less necessary, not because mechanical force is not needed but because the human intelligence is learning how to supersede the human machine as its source. Every development of machinery makes the man who can merely offer his muscles of less value to the community. Long ago — not so very long ago in some cases — it was quite sufficient for a man to be able to say "I am a good machine:" he was worth his keep and had his chance of becoming a parent; but the man whom society wants now-a-days is not the man who is a good machine but the man who can make one. These elementary truths are hidden, however, from the political quacks who discourse to us upon unemployment.

Herbert Spencer's remark that it is necessary to be a good animal has an element of truth in it which was utterly ignored and needed proclamation at that time;

but it is necessary to be a good animal only in so far as that state makes for being a good man — and not an iota further.

The present interest in many most important aspects of physical education, such as may be summed up under the phrase "school hygiene," must not blind us to the great principle that physical education is a means and not an end. Our present educational system, which permits schooling to end just when it should begin, or rather sooner, and which, even through our Government Departments, permits boys to be used as little more than animated machines, such as telegraph boys — is very largely responsible for the great national evil of unemployment, which we treat with soup-kitchens. We shall revise a great proportion of our educational, political and social methods just so soon as — but not before — we get into our heads the idea that in human society, and pre-eminently in society to-day, the survival-value of mind and consequently the selection of mind must predominate over the survival-value and consequent selection of muscle. Further, whatever factors tend to enhance the survival-value of the physical are *ipso facto* making for retrogression and a return to the order of the beast. Whatever tend to enhance the survival-value of the psychical — by which I most assuredly include not only intelligence but, for instance, motherhood — are *ipso facto* forces of progress. The products of progress are not machinery but men and the well-drilled-machine idea of a man ought to be as obsolete as more than one recent war has proved it disastrous.

There is here to be read no pessimistic suggestion

that the psychical is in any permanent danger. No one can think so who knows its strength and the relative impotence of the physical, but it is certainly possible that the course of progress may be greatly delayed in any given nation or race by worship of the physical, or even, as Sparta shows, by worship of what may be called the physical virtues as against the moral and intellectual virtues. But those who are interested in the survival of any particular race or nation have to remember that arrest or retardation of progress therein, relatively to its wiser neighbors, must, before long, result in its utter downfall.

WHAT ARE WE TO CHOOSE? — The argument that the selection of mind has been dominant throughout human history is reinforced by such knowledge of that history as we possess. There is no record of any race that established itself in virtue of great stature or exceptional muscular strength. Even in cases of the most purely military dominance, it was not force as such, but discipline and method, that determined success; whilst some of the greatest soldiers in history have been physically the smallest. The statement of the anthropologists, already alluded to, regarding the selection of the leading men in primitive tribes, may safely be taken as always true: selection in human society has always been, in the main, selection of that which, for survival-value, is the dominant character of man, *mind* in its widest sense. We shall see, later, that *physical eugenics* can by no means be ignored: but our guiding principle must be that the physical is of worth only in so far as it serves the psychical, and is worse than worthless in so far as it does not. It would surely be well, for instance, that we should breed for "energy," to use Mr. Galton's term: but the energy we desire, and the energy he commends, is nervous, not muscular. The confusion between two radically different things, vitality and muscularity, is however, almost universal, though it will not stand a moment's examination. In a volume devoted to personal hygiene I have discussed this point, which is of real moment both for the individual and for the theory of eugenics.[1]

It is of interest to note, in passing from this question, that inherent facts of the human constitution would interdict us if we thought it a fit ideal to breed for stature or bulk. Giants are essentially morbid — not favorable but unfavorable variations. They are very frequently childless and almost constantly slow-witted. Their condition is really a mild form of a well-marked and highly characteristic disease known as acromegaly, and distinguished by great enlargement of the face and extremities. The malady depends upon peculiarities in the glandular activities of the body: *and the state of these which makes for great stature and bulk makes against intelligence.* It is suggested, then, that any considerable increase of human bulk and stature could only be obtained at the cost

[1] Says Darwin, "So little is this subject understood, that I have heard surprise repeatedly expressed at such great monsters as the Mastodon . . . having become extinct; as if mere bodily strength gave victory in the battle of life. Mere size, on the contrary, would in some cases determine . . . quicker extermination from the greater amount of requisite food." In the Russo-Japanese War, one of the effective factors was the disparity between the food requirements of the little victors and the big losers.

of intelligence. They would be very dear at the price.

When we come to the subject of selection for parenthood in man through the preferences exhibited by individuals for members of the opposite sex, we shall see that what Darwin called "sexual selection" is certainly a reality in the case of man, whether or not it be so in the case of the lower animals. We shall see that this most potent factor in human evolution acts even now very favorably and is capable of having its value enormously enhanced. In the selection of husbands, nervous or psychical factors are notably of high survival-value in civilized communities. In the selection of wives the survival-value of the physical is still very high: but it may be hoped and believed that the present tendency is to attach relatively less importance to them and more to the psychical elements of the chosen. This tendency must be furthered to the utmost point beyond which the physical requisites for motherhood would suffer weakening — but no further.

HOW ARE WE TO ESTIMATE CIVIC WORTH? — We have already observed that it is incorrect to use the word "fit" as if it were synonymous with "worthy." If we insist on using this term, which means only adapted to conditions, we must define those conditions. We must say that we desire to further the production of those who are fit for citizenship, and to disfavor the production of those who are unfit for citizenship. We shall thereby dispose at least of those vexatious objectors who tell us that many eminent criminals are individually superior to many eminent judges. The statement is doubtless untrue, but if it were true it would still be irrelevant. A criminal may be individually a remarkable personality, but in so far as he is a criminal, he is unfit for citizenship.

It is far better to use consistently Mr. Galton's phrase, "civic worth," or, for short, "worth." We may here note Mr. Galton's most recent remarks on what he meant by worth: —

> "By this I mean the civic worthiness, or the Value to the State, of a person, as it would probably be assessed by experts, say, by such of his fellow-workers as have earned the respect of the community in the midst of which they live. Thus the worth of soldiers would be such as it would be rated by respected soldiers, students by students, business men by business men, artists by artists, and so on. The State is a vastly complex organism, and the hope of obtaining a Proportional Representation of its best parts should be an avowed object of issuing invitations to these gatherings.
>
> "Speaking only for myself, if I had to classify persons according to Worth, I should consider each of them under the three heads of Physique, Ability, and Character, subject to the provision that inferiority in any one of the three should outweigh superiority in the other two. I rank Physique first, because it is not only very valuable in itself and allied to many other good qualities, but has the additional merit of being easily rated. Ability I should place second on similar grounds, and Character third, though in real importance it stands first of all."[1]

We shall certainly misunderstand this quotation unless we clearly realize that Mr. Galton is speaking of eugenic worth — that is to say, of worth in relation to parenthood and heredity. No one, of course, would assert for a moment that inferiority in the matter of

[1] Quoted from a Paper read by Mr. Galton before the Eugenics Education Society, October 14, 1908, and published in *Nature*, October 22, 1908.

physique outweighed superiority in ability and character, so far as our estimate of an individual as an individual is concerned, nor yet so far as our estimate of him as a citizen is concerned. But from the eugenic standpoint, as a parent of citizens to come, such a person, though he may have himself saved the State, is on the average rightly to be regarded as unworthy on the eugenic scale — it being assumed, of course, that the inferiority of physique in the person in question is either native and therefore transmissible, or else due to forms of disease, or poisoning, such as, according to our knowledge of ante-natal pathology, will probably involve degeneracy on the part of his children. I would add that love is as precious as ability, if not more so, and that we should aim at its increase by making parenthood the most responsible act in life, so that children are born only to those who love children, and who will transmit their high measure of the parental instinct and the tender emotion which is its correlate.[1]

[1] See the Author's paper, "The Psychology of Parenthood," *Eugenics Review*, April, 1909.

CHAPTER V

THE MULTIPLICATION OF MAN

"Increase and multiply"

THE ceaseless multiplication of man is one of the facts which distinguish him from all other living species, animals or vegetable.[1]

We must not be misled by such a case as that of the multiplication of rabbits in Australia. Apart from such circumstances as human interference, the earth is already crammed with life of a kind, not the highest life nor the most intense life, but at any rate fully extended life. Man alone multiplies, persistently, irresistibly, and has done so from the very first, so that, arising locally, he is now diffused over the whole surface of the earth. To quote from Professor Lankester again: "Man is Nature's rebel. Where Nature says Die! Man says I will live! According to the law previously in universal operation man should have been limited in geographical area, killed by extremes of cold or heat, subject to starvation if one kind of diet were unobtainable, and should have been unable to increase and multiply, just as are his animal relatives, without losing his specific structure. . . . But man's wits and his will have enabled

[1] An authoritative statement on this point has already been quoted from Sir E. Rav Lankester's Romanes Lecture of 1905,

him . . . to 'increase and multiply,' as no other animal, without change of form."

Not only has man made himself the only animal which constantly increases in numbers, but this increase, as Professor Lankester points out in another part of his lecture, already threatening certain difficulties, will be much more rapid than at present, assuming the birth-rate to remain where it is, when disease is controlled. It is within our power, as Pasteur declared long ago, to abolish all parasitic, infectious or epidemic disease. This must be and will be done — within a century, I have little doubt. The problem of the increase of human population will become more pressing than ever. Professor Lankester suggests that in one or five centuries the difficulty raised by our multiplication, "would, if let alone, force itself upon a desperate humanity, brutalized by over-crowding and the struggle for food. A return to Nature's terrible selection of the fittest may, it is conceivable, be in this way in store for us. But it is more probable that humanity will submit to a restriction by the community in respect of the right to multiply." The lecturer added that we must therefore perfect our knowledge of heredity in man, as to which "there is absolutely no provision in any civilized community, and no conception among the people or their leaders, that it is a matter which concerns any one but farmers."

THE SECRET OF MULTIPLICATION.— Professor Lankester, however, omits to point out the astonishing paradox involved in the fact that — as I pointed out at the Royal Institution in 1907 — man, the only ceaselessly multiplying animal, has the lowest birth-rate of any living creature.[1] From the purely arithmetical point of view, what does it mean? We may defer at present any deeper interpretation.

It means necessarily and obviously that the effective means of multiplication is not a high birth-rate but a low death-rate. It is a necessary inference from the paradox in question that the infant death-rate and the general death-rate in man are the lowest anywhere to be found. Producing fewer young he alone multiplies.[2] It follows that a smaller proportion of those young must die. Unless it is supposed by bishops and others, then, that a peculiar value attaches to the production of a baby shortly to be buried, the suggestion evidently is the same as that to which every humanitarian and social and patriotic impulse guides us, namely, the reduction of the death-rate and especially the infant mortality. This is the true way in which to insure the more rapid multiplication of man, if that be desired. I believe it is not to be desired, but in any case the reduction of the death-rate and especially of the infant mortality is a worthy and necessary end in itself, and need not inevitably lead to our undue multiplication provided that the birth-rate falls. Hence the eugenists and the Episcopal Bench may

[1] The exception of one or two large animals, like the elephant, is not important. In proportion to body weight man's birth-rate is lower than theirs. And it is to be noted that the "infant" mortality is very low in this case, where the birth-rate is so low. Says Darwin, of the young elephant, "None are destroyed by beasts of prey; for even the tiger in India most rarely dares to attack a young elephant protected by its dam." The dam has no factory to go to, and no beast of prey to sell her alcohols.

[2] "The Fulmar petrel lays but one egg, yet it is believed to be the most numerous bird in the world." (*Origin of Species*, popular edition, p. 81.)

join hands so far as the reduction of the death-rate is concerned, and the only persons with whom a practical quarrel remains are those who applaud the mother who boasts that she has buried twelve.

THE FACTS OF HUMAN MULTIPLICATION.— Human population continues to increase notwithstanding any changes in the birth-rate. This fact remains true, as shown by the latest obtainable figures. It should be one of the dogmas never absent from the foreground of the statesman's mind. Apparently nothing, however, will induce us to take this little forethought. When we build a bridge across the Thames, we ignore it; when we widen a bridge we ignore it likewise. When we make a new street we ignore it; when we build railways and railway stations we ignore it — excusably, perhaps, in this case; when we build hospitals we ignore it; four times out of five there is no room for the addition of a single ward in time to come. We have not yet even learnt, as they are learning in America and Germany, how to acquire the outlying lands of cities for the public possession, so that they may be properly employed as the city grows. The man who builds himself a villa on the outskirts of a city, ignores it, and is staggered by it in ten years. The lover of nature and the country ignores it: "Just look at this," he says, "this was in the country when first I knew it, look at these horrible rows of villas!" The only possible reply to such a person is simply, "Well, my dear sir, what do you propose? General infanticide?" Most important of all, this fact, that, to take the case of Great Britain, some half million babies are born every year in excess over the number of all who die at all ages, is forgotten by our statesman — or rather by our politicians. It could, of course, not be forgotten by a statesman. Quite apart from remoter consequences, especially in relation to the wheat supply, this persistent multiplication — which one has actually heard denied on the ground that the birth-rate is falling — is of urgent moment to all of us.

In 1907 the Census Bureau of Washington published some figures on the mortality statistics of nations, a summary of which may be quoted: "In all parts of the civilized world both the birth-rates and death-rates tend to decrease, and, as a rule, those countries having the lowest death-rates have also the lowest birth-rates. In Europe the lowest birth-rate is that of France, the highest those of Servia and Roumania. The lowest death-rates are in Sweden and Norway; the highest in Russia and Spain. The downward tendency of the birth and death-rates is best shown by diagrams prepared by the French Government, and it is probable that the downward tendency is actually steeper than the diagrams show because both births and deaths are more accurately registered than formerly."

But these statements are by no means necessarily incompatible with steady increase of population, which, of course, increases so long as the birth-rate exceeds the death-rate. I quote a few figures from the *Science Year Book* of 1908:

In 1890 the total population of the world was estimated at 1,487,900,000.

Aryan (Europe, Persia, India, etc.) ..	545,000,000
Mongolian (N. and E. Asia)	630,000,000
Semitic (N. Africa)	65,000,000
Negro (C. Africa)	150,000,000
Malay and Polynesian	35,000,000
American Indian	15,000,000

The total figure now must be something like sixteen hundred millions at least.

Density of population, in so far as it means what is commonly called over-crowding, is an important factor in the death-rate, and has a most inimical influence upon race-culture, in virtue of the opportunity afforded to the racial poisons—syphilis, alcohol, etc. Thus Sweden has the lowest death-rate in Europe, and has much the least density of population — only 29 per square mile as compared with our own 341. If now the fact of the increase of population, with all that it means and will mean, may be taken as dealt with and accepted, there will be no danger of leading the reader to false conclusions if we insist upon the fall of the birth-rate, which in Great Britain in 1908 was the lowest on record. The death-rate, however, persistently falls also. The reader who thinks that the birth-rate alone determines the increase of population, and those who believed in polygamy on the ground that it necessarily makes for the rapid multiplication and therefore strength of a nation, should compare the death-rate of London, which is under 16, with that of Bombay, which is just under 79. It is asserted that in many large Indian cities the infant mortality approaches one-half of all the children born. What it amounts to in such cities as Canton and Pekin we can only surmise with horror.

Notwithstanding the persistent fall in the birth-rate of London the rate of increase in population remains stupendous, according to the calculations of Mr. Cottrell, which may be quoted from the *Science Year Book* of 1908. He estimates the population of Greater London 1910 at about 7½ millions and in 1920 at well over 8½ millions — the falling birth-rate notwithstanding.

The increase of population of five great countries may be briefly noted here. In all, with the possible exception of Russia, the birth-rate is rapidly falling. In the course of the nineteenth century the population of

Russia (in Europe) ..	rose	from	38	to	105,000,000
France	"	"	26	"	38,000,000
Germany	"	"	23	"	55,000,000
Great Britain ..	"	"	15	"	40,000,000
United States ..	"	"	5	"	75,000,000

These are merely approximate figures but accurate enough to be of value. It need hardly be pointed out that immigration accounts for the disproportionate increase of population in the United States. But it may be added that the imminent arrest or control of this immigration will assuredly have the most serious and pressing consequences for Europe. Plainly it must hasten the coming of national eugenics.

THE CASE OF GERMANY.—Especial interest and importance attach for many reasons to the case of Germany in this connection, and, as might be expected, many precise facts are available. Here I shall avail myself freely of the paper contributed by Dr. Sombart to the *International* for December, 1907. In the first seven years of this century the population of Germany increased almost ten per cent. The figure in 1870 was 40.8 millions and in 1907, 61 millions. The population is increasing yearly at the rate of about 800,000, as compared with about half a million in the case of Great Britain. In France in 1907 the population actually declined by a few thousands. In regard to the growth of population Germany is now at the head of all civilized countries, excepting those cases in which immigration has augmented the number of inhabitants. Does this expansion of population depend upon an increasing birth-rate or a diminishing death-rate? The fact, in strict parallel with the biological generalization already made, is that "Germany's population is increasing so swiftly because the death-rate has been falling steadily. At the beginning of the period, 1870-1880, there were nearly 30 deaths per thousand inhabitants, while in recent years only about 20 deaths in every thousand inhabitants have taken place each year. . . . Notwithstanding, the birth-rate during the last ten years, during which the principal growth of population occurs, has not in anywise increased in Germany. Indeed, by careful investigation it becomes apparent that it has declined almost unintermittently for a generation." The average birth-rate for the ten years, 1871–1880 was 40.7 for 1891–1900 the average was 37.4 Since then it has fallen further, and in 1905 the figure was 34, the lowest on record. As Dr. Sombart observes, we shall only appreciate these figures if we regard them as an expression of a tendency which will continue, and that this is so he proves. He observes that "the more highly advanced the country, the lower its birth-rate. . . . From this we may already draw the conclusion that a diminution of births is a concomitant of our progress in civilization. Secondly, this is confirmed by the fact that the falling off in the birth-rate must be attributed largely to the big cities. . . . As a third statistical argument that the birth-rate declines with the advance of civilization, the fact may be cited that in the quarters of the well-to-do still fewer children are born than in those of the poor." (In London, as we have seen, the birth-rate is highest in Stepney and lowest in Hampstead.)

Dr. Sombart finally points out what must never be forgotten — that an increase in population, dependent upon a fall in the death-rate, whilst the birth-rate also falls, is necessarily self-limited. The decrease of the death-rate is limited by definite natural age-limits, and "this indicates that the increase of population in Germany is gradually entering upon a period of less activity, and will perhaps quite cease within a conceivable period unless other causes operate in the opposite direction."

THE YELLOW PERIL.— The facts regarding the yellow races are extremely difficult to ascertain. It appears, however, that the birth-rate in Japan has almost doubled in 27 years — rising from 17.1 to 31. (I doubt the accuracy of the earlier figure.) In China the population is largely controlled by infanticide, but there is little doubt that the main contention of Pearson was correct, and that the yellow races are multiplying much more rapidly than the white races. It does not necessarily follow, however, as we shall see, that this means yellow ascendancy, any more than a similar conparison would mean microbic ascendancy. It is not quantity but quality of life that gives survival-value and dominance. This disparity between white and yellow rates of increase is by far the most pregnant of contemporary phenomena. In the present introductory volume it can merely be named. But since we shall not survive in virtue of quantity, I, for one, am well assured that the choice for Western civilization will ere long be the final one between eugenics or extinction.

THE WHEAT PROBLEM.—Meanwhile, we must consider briefly the question evidently raised by this fact of human multiplication. As an expert has lately said, the rise in the price of wheat "is not the transitory result of market manipulation and 'corners,' forcing prices up to an unnatural level, but of perfectly natural and irresistible causes which, for all that, are the more anxious and disquieting. The truth is we are for the first time beginning to feel individually the effect of a great natural process — the race which started long ago between the population of the world and the growth of the world's wheat supply. In this race the growth of the world's population has been outstripping the growth of its wheat-food production, and the consequence has been a total growing shortage, in spite of the opening of vast new areas in Canada and the Argentina." In this connection one of the best papers in Great Britain — the *Westminster Gazette* — cheerfully remarked in a leading article that, after all, we need not be alarmed as to the difficulty in increasing the supply of wheat, since population would, in any case, adapt itself to the food-supply. This is true, indeed: there will never be more human beings than there is food to feed. But the question is, how will the population be kept down? In a word, is it to be by the awful and bloody processes of Nature or by the conscious, provident and humane methods of man?

We are reminded of the argument advanced by Sir William Crookes in his Presidential Address to the British Association in 1898. The distinguished author has himself written an invaluable book on the subject which has been carefully revised and supplemented, and must be read by the serious student.[1] We may note from the point of view of the student of dietetics that wheat is and remains, on physiological examination, what the proverb suggests. Bread is the staff of life, wheat being, in proportion to its price, by far the best and cheapest of all foods.

The argument of Sir William Crookes was advanced exactly a century after the publication of the great essay of Malthus which we must soon consider. In the whole intervening century no one, capable of being heard, had considered the question. The relation of Crookes to the earlier thinker remains, though it is curious that Malthus was not mentioned by his suc-

[1] *The Wheat Problem,* by Sir Wm. Crookes, F.R.S., 2nd edition, 1905. The Chemical News Office, 15, Newcastle St., Farringdon St., E.C.

cessor. Writing now, a decade later, I wish merely to point out that Sir William's argument is found valid. He observed that "the actual and potential wheat-producing capacity of the United States is — and will be, for years to come — the dominant factor in the world's bread-supply." Now the recent expert, from whom we have already quoted, declares that "former great wheat exporting countries like the United States, as well as Russia and India, while their production remains as high, are sending far less abroad under the pressure of their own increasing needs. In this connection it may be recorded that a great American corn expert declares that in twenty-five years the United States will want all, or very nearly all, of her wheat production for herself, and will have very little indeed to send us." In 1898 Sir William said "a permanently higher price for wheat is, I fear, a calamity that ere long must be faced." As every one knows, this prophecy is now being fulfilled. Sir William declared that "the augmentation of the world's eating population in a geometrical ratio" is a proved fact. The phrase means, of course, simply that the yearly increase increases. On the other hand, the wheat supply is subject to a yearly increase which does not itself increase — in other words the increase is in an arithmetical ratio. This, a century later, precisely illustrates the principle of Malthus. Sir William also declared that exports of wheat from the United States are only of present interest and that "within a generation the ever-increasing population of the United States will consume all the wheat grown within its borders, and will be driven to import, and, like ourselves, will scramble for the lion's share of the wheat crop of the world."

Next to the United States Russia is the greatest wheat exporter, but the Russian peasant population increases more rapidly than any other in Europe, even though it is inadequately fed, and this source of supply must fail ere very long. As Sir William points out, the Caucasian civilization is indeed founded upon bread. "Other races vastly superior to us in numbers, but differing widely in material and intellectual progress, are eaters of Indian corn, rice, millet and other grains; but none of these grains have the food-value, concentrated health-sustaining power of wheat." As every one knows, Sir William's argument was and is that we must learn how to fix the nitrogen of the atmosphere — that is to say, how to combine it in forms on which the plant can feed. "The fixation of nitrogen is a question of the not far distant future. Unless we can class it among certainties to come, the great Caucasian race will cease to be foremost in the world, and will be squeezed out of existence by races to whom wheat and bread is not the staff of life."

Sir William Crookes was himself the pioneer in the discovery of the electric method of fixing the atmospheric nitrogen, and now, a decade after the delivery of his address, this method is in successful commercial employment in Scandinavia. There is also a method of sowing the bacteria which are capable of fixing nitrogen, and this, according to some, has been already proved practicable. Further, the Mendelians offer us the possibility of new varieties of wheat having more grains to the stalk than we obtain at present. By these methods the output of the land devoted to wheat can be doubled or trebled, but it is evident that even then there will be an impassable limit. We have to face, indeed, the evident but unconsidered fact that *there must be a maximum possible human population for this finite earth,* whether a bread-eating population or any other. I do not propose to speculate regarding this evident truth. If human life is worth living and is the highest life we know, we may desire to obtain that maximum population, but it must be obtained, and its limits observed, by the humane and decent processes which man is capable of putting into practice, and not by the check of starvation.

It is of great interest to the British reader to look at the question briefly from his point of view. At the present time our wheat production is no more than one-eighth of our needs, and in twenty-five years, when the supply from the United States will probably have ceased, we shall require 40,000,000 quarters of wheat per annum. Yet already, in time of peace, careful observers such as the Rt. Hon. Charles Booth and Mr. Seebohm Rowntree declared that thirty per cent. of our own population are living on the verge of starvation. Our available supply of food of all kinds at any moment would last us about three weeks. How many of us realize what a war would mean for this country? Yet in the face of facts such as these, the majority of those who attempt to guide public opinion are urging us to increase our birth-rate and still pin their faith to quantity rather than quality of population as our great need.

THE THEORY OF MALTHUS.—The reader who is interested in general biology will realize, of course, that we are here back to the great argument of Malthus advanced in 1798 in his *Essay on the Principle of Population*. Malthus was a great and sincere thinker, a high and true moralist, and the people who have a vague notion that his name has some connection with immoral principles of any kind, have no acquaintance with the subject. It is of the deepest interest for the history of thought to know that it was the work of Malthus which suggested, independently, both to Charles Darwin and to Dr. Alfred Russel Wallace, that principle of natural selection, the survival of the fittest and their choice for parenthood, the discovery of which constituted one of the great epochs in the history of human knowledge, and which is the cardinal principle underlying the whole modern conception of eugenics or race-culture.

Malthus found in all life the constant tendency to increase beyond the nourishment available. In a given area, not even the utmost imaginable improvement in developing the resources of the soil can or could keep pace with the unchecked increase of population.[1] This applies alike to Great Britain and to the whole world. At bottom, then, the check to population — and this is true of bacteria or men — is want of food, notwithstanding that this is never the immediate and obvious check except in cases of actual famine. There must therefore be a "struggle for existence," and as Darwin and Wallace saw, it follows as a necessary truth that, to use Spencer's terms, the fittest must survive. The

[1] See Chap. III., The *Origin of Species*.

question is whether we are to accept starvation as, at bottom, the factor controlling population (which, in any case, must be and is controlled) or whether we can substitute something better — as for instance, the moral self-control which Malthus recommended. The single precept of this much maligned thinker was "Do not marry till you have a fair prospect of supporting a family"— a fairly decent and respectable doctrine. In the words of Mr. Kirkup, "the greatest and highest moral result of his principle is that it clearly and emphatically teaches the responsibility of parentage, and it declares the sin of those who bring human beings into the world for whose physical, intellectual, and moral well-being no satisfactory provision is made." Who, alas, will declare that even after a century and a decade this great lesson is yet learnt?

It is to be added, first, that though improvement in agriculture is to be commended on every conceivable ground, and though it may in some degree relieve and postpone the difficulty, it is infinitely incapable of abolishing it. Nothing but necessity can check the prolificness of life. To this doctrine, however, there is, as we shall shortly see, a great excepting principle, unrecognized by Malthus, discovered by Herbert Spencer, and of vast and universal importance. Secondly, it is to be noted that emigration — a real remedy for over-population — is so only for a time. It cannot possibly abolish the problem — short of the development of interplanetary communication, if then; and the observer of contemporary politics must be well aware, as Germany, for instance, is well aware already, that its effectiveness as a practical remedy for over-population in some European countries is already being arrested by the invaded states.

The references already made to the work of Sir William Crookes will suffice to show that the teaching of Malthus is of practical importance to us to-day, and not least to the population of Great Britain. I am tempted to quote the actual case in this connection of a young student of biology who applied for Malthus's book at one of the greatest official libraries in this country. He was looked at as a shameless young rascal, and the libarian curtly said, "We have no books of that kind here." I commend this exquisite instance of misapplied and perfectly ignorant British prudery to Mr. Bernard Shaw: not even he could imagine anything to surpass it. No more impeccably decent book than this of "Parson Malthus" has ever been written, and I have no adequate comment for the fact that its nature and contents were not merely wholly unknown but grossly misimagined by this responsible official, and that it could not be obtained in the great library of science in question. This, one may add, was not in the provinces but in London.

We pass in the following chapter to the momentous discovery of Herbert Spencer that the great truth seen by Malthus was not a whole but a half-truth, and that there is a compensating principle, which is at once a source of inspiration and of difficulty to the eugenist. It is in general the principle that as life ascends it becomes less prolific, and its consequences are infinitely more vast than the phrase at first suggests. Had this principle been discovered by a Continental thinker or by a member of a British University instead of by a man who never passed an examination, it would not now need the discussion which we shall have to give it.

CHAPTER VI

THE GROWTH OF INDIVIDUALITY

THE LAWS OF MULTIPLICATION.— Implicit or explicit approval of a falling birth-rate involves opposition to the opinion of the man in the street, the general opinion of the medical profession,[1] the bench of bishops and the social prophet and publicist in general. Nevertheless a fall in the birth-rate is a factor in organic progress, and, in general, the level of any species is in inverse proportion to its birth-rate, from bacteria to the most civilized classes of men in the most civilized countries of to-day. But in truth the uniformed opinion, totally contrary to the whole history of life and to the most obvious comparative facts of the birth-rate amongst and within present day human societies, was utterly disposed of forty years ago in the closing chapter of the greatest contribution yet made to philosophic biology — Herbert Spencer's *Principles of Biology*. The last chapter of that masterpiece is entitled "The Laws of Multiplication." Unfortunately it has not been read by one in ten thousand of those who think themselves entitled to hold, and even to express, opinions about the birth-rate. Spencer's dis-

[1] Including even such an exceptional student as Dr. George Newman, who, in his book on *Infant Mortality*, regards a falling birth-rate as an essential evil, and actually declares without qualification that the factors "which lower the birth-rate tend to raise the infant death-rate."

covery is the complementary half-truth to the discovery of Malthus, and just as the law of Malthus is pessimistic, so the law of Spencer is optimistic. In a word, Malthus assumed — indeed, formally declared — that there was no natural factor of an internal kind, tending to limit the rate of vital fertility. Spencer discovered that there is such a factor, which can and does limit and has been limiting vegetable, animal, and human fertility since the dawn of life.

All reproduction involves an expenditure of energy in some degree on the part of the parent. Now the energy available by any individual is finite. If he expends it all upon reproduction, he himself, or she herself, must cease to exist. This happens in all the lowest forms of life, which multiply by fission or simple splitting. The young bacteria are their subdivided parent. At the other extreme is the case of the individual who retains the whole of his energy for his own development and life, and has no offspring at all. Such consummate bachelor philosophers as Kant and Spencer may be quoted, and the list of childless men of genius might be extended quite indefinitely. This is not to declare this last state to be the ideal, but merely to point out the logical extremes.

Spencer's principle is that there is an "Antagonism," or, as we may rather say, an inverse ratio, between "Individuation" and "Genesis"— between the proportion of energy expended upon the individual and the proportion expended upon the continuance of the race. Thus "Individuation," meaning all those processes which maintain and expand the life of the individual, and "Genesis," meaning all those processes which involve the formation of new individuals — are necessarily antagonistic. Every higher degree of individual evolution is followed by a lower degree of race multiplication, and *vice versâ*. Increase in bulk (*cf.* the elephant) complexity or activity involves diminution in fertility, and *vise versâ*. This is an obvious *à priori* principle.

Should the reader declare that there must be something the matter with an asserted principle of progress which leads in theory or in practice to the production of a childless generation, and therefore the end of all progress, and that this principle suggests that the most completely developed man and woman cannot be parents — then I would join in the chorus of fathers and mothers generally, who would say that, in human parenthood, if not indeed, in sub-human parenthood, the antagonism is reconciled in a higher unity; that the best and most complete development of the individual is effected only through parenthood, in due degree — as Spencer, himself childless, formally declared.

It is impossible here to show how complete is the evidence for Spencer's law, both from the side of logical necessity and from the side of observation. In order to indicate the overwhelming character of the evidence, one would have to transcribe the whole of his long chapter, and to add to it all our modern knowledge of human birth-rate. This cannot be done, but even without it we may venture to say that people who regard a falling birth-rate as in itself, and obviously, a sign of racial degeneration or immorality, or approaching weakness or failure of any kind, can have made no substantial additions to their knowledge of the subject since they themselves formed items in the birth-rate.

Spencer goes on to show, with profound insight, that, in general, greater individuality or, to put it in other words, the more highly evolved organism, "*though less fertile absolutely, is the more fertile relatively.*" The supreme instance of this truth is, of course, the case of man, in whom individuation has reached its unprecedented height, who is *absolutely* the least fertile of all creatures,[1] and yet who is *relatively* the most fertile — unique in his actual and persistent multiplication.

THEIR ACTION IN MAN.— Within the human species the laws of multiplication hold. It is still worth while, after half a century, to quote Spencer's remark as to infertility in women due to mental labor carried to excess — "most of the flat-chested girls who survive their high-pressure education are incompetent to bear a well-developed infant and to supply it with the natural food for the natural period." In all hands people with opened eyes are rightly urging this truth upon us to-day. In the United States the so-called higher education of girls has been proved in effect to sterilize them — and these the flower of the nation's girlhood, and therefore, rightly, the very elect for motherhood. Here is simply an instance of the Spencerian principle in its most unfortunate misdirection by man.

Before leaving Spencer, we must refer briefly to the predictions, based upon the foregoing principles, with

[1] It is not necessary to point out again the exception of the elephant, nor to explain it.

which he concluded his great work. The further evolution of man, he declares, must take mainly the direction of a higher intellectual and emotional development. Hitherto, and even to-day, pressure of population is the original cause of human competition, application, discipline, expenditure of energy — and one may add, the possibility of continued selection. Excess of fertility, then, says Spencer, is the cause of man's evolution, but "man's further evolution itself necessitates a decline in his fertility." The future progress of civilization will be accompanied by increased development of individuality, emotional and intellectual. As Spencer observes, this does not necessarily mean a mentally laborious life, for as mental activity "gradually becomes organic, it will become spontaneous and pleasurable."

Finally the necessary antagonism between individuality and parenthood ensures the ultimate attainment of the highest form of the maintenance of the race —

". . . a form in which the amount of life shall be the greatest possible, and the births and deaths the fewest possible."

If now we look back at the law of Malthus we shall realize the enormous significance of the law of Spencer. In this respect we have the advantage over Malthus that we are aware, as he was not, of the great fact of organic evolution. We discover, then, that an actual consequence of the pressure of population, leading as it does to the struggle for existence and, in the main, the survival of higher types, is that the rate of fertility falls. This conception of the fall in the birth-rate — which, it is maintained, has been a great factor in all organic progress — was entirely absent from the mind of Malthus. In a word, the unlimited multiplication which Malthus observed leads to its own correction. It provides abundance of material for natural selection to work upon, and then the survival-value of individuation, wherever it appears, asserts itself, with the consequence that the rate of multiplication declines. This is actually to be observed to-day. Malthus desired that we should postpone marriage to later ages so as to lower the birth-rate. The increasing necessity and demand for individuation is effecting that which Malthus desired. The average age at marriage has been rising in our own country in both sexes during the last thirty years: and the evidence shows that as civilization advances the age of marriage becomes later and later. Professor Metchinkoff has discussed some aspects of this question in his book, *The Nature of Man*.

THE INTENSIVE CULTURE OF LIFE.—For every student of progress, and not least for the eugenist, Spencer's law is a warrant of hope and a promise of better things to come. It teaches that in the development of higher — that is to say, more specialized — that is to say, more individualized — organic types, Nature is working already and has been working for ages, towards the elimination of the brutal elements in the struggle for existence. This is, of course, what every worker for progress, and every eugenist in especial, desires. Spencer's discovery teaches also that individuality compensates a species for loss of high fertility. The survival-value of individuation is greater than the survival-value of rapid multiplication. *The very fact of progress is the replacement of lower by higher life, the supersession of the quantitative by the qualitative criterion of survival value, the increasing dominance of mind over matter, the substitution of the intensive for the merely extensive cultivation of life.* These various phrases express, I believe, various aspects of one and the same great fact, and I only wish it were possible to include here an exhaustive study of the conception which may be expressed by the phrase "the intensity of life"— as distinguished from its mere extension. There is, I believe, a real and significant analogy, between the introduction of what is called intensive cultivation in agriculture, and the eugenic principle which seeks to replace the extensive by the intensive cultivation of human life.

THE EUGENIC DIFFICULTY.— But it will be already evident to the reader that, though Spencer's law offers hope and warrant to the eugenist, it also poses him with a permanent and ineradicable difficulty which is inherent in natural necessity — viz., the difficulty that, in consequence of the operation of this law, those very classes or members of a society whose parenthood he most desires must be, in general, the least fertile. Throughout the animal world the lesser fertility of higher species is no real handicap to them, as we know; but where the conditions of selections are so profoundly modified as in human society, the case is very different. Furthermore, amongst mankind individuality has often grown, and does grow, to such an extent that parenthood disappears altogether. Indeed, Spencer's law expresses itself — and the eugenist must qualify his hopes by the fact — in the practical infertility of many[1] of the most highly individualized and even unique personalities, that is to say, in the ranks of what we call genius. To this subject we must return.

A notable section in Mr. Galton's great work *Inquiries into Human Faculty,* states very plainly the difficulty for the eugenist involved in Spencer's law, under its more statistical aspect. What are the relative effects of early and late marriages? Mr. Galton proves, mathematically, that in a very few generations a group of persons who marry late will be simply bred down and more than supplanted by those who marry early. Now no one will dispute that the less individualized, the lower types, the more nearly animal, do in general marry earlier, and are more fertile. Here, then, is an anti-eugenic tendency in human society, depending really upon Spencer's law and requiring us to recognize and counteract it by throwing all the weight we can upon the side of progress, which means *increasing to our utmost the survival-value and the effective fertility of the higher types.*

Much more space might be spent upon this gravest of problems for the eugenist — the fact that the very persons from whom he desires to recruit the future on account of their greater individuality are also on that very account the persons who, by natural necessity, tend to be less fertile. The difficulty shows itself in the male sex, but it shows itself still more conspicuously in the female sex, where the proportion of the

[1] Mr. Galton believes their number has been exaggerated.

individual energy devoted to the race, as compared with that devoted to individuation, is necessarily far higher, and must so remain if the race is to persist. Primarily, the body of woman is the temple of life to come — and *therefore*, as we shall some day teach our girls, the holy of holies. Without going further into this matter now, it may be suggested that a cardinal principle of practical importance is involved. It is that the individual development of women, their higher education, their self-expression in works of art and thought and practice, cannot safely be carried to the point at which motherhood is compromised; else the race in question will necessarily disappear and be replaced by any race whatsoever, the women of which continue to be mothers. There are women of the worker bee type whom this argument annoys intensely. No one wants *them* to be mothers.

The proposition that all progress in the psychical world depends upon individuality, just as all organic progress, and indeed, all organic evolution, depends upon the physical individuality which biologists call variation, may suggest to the reader the importance which must attach to our study of talent and genius, and the possibility of aiding their production. Meanwhile, we must look a little further at the general question of individuality or quality *versus* quantity from the international point of view.

Quantity versus quality.— The reader will understand how it is that any one writing from the biological standpoint must view with something like contempt the common assumption that, in international competition, mere statistics of population furnish, as such, final and adequate data for prophecy. Let us remind ourselves once more that, according to these crude criteria, which were really superseded untold æons ago, the dominance of the world must belong in the near future not to Russia, with its balance of more than two million births per annum, rather than to France, with its approximately stationary population, but to the bacteria, the growth of population amongst which, if it be not controlled by the less fertile creature we call man, is of simply inexpressible magnitude. But the world is not, and will not be, ruled by bacteria, their fertility notwithstanding. Indeed, the disease-producing bacteria have already had sentence of death pronounced upon them by the higher intelligence of man, and that sentence will be carried out within a century. Similarly within the bounds of humanity we must recognize the limitations of mere statistics. The population of France, some forty years ago consisted of so many millions of units. The figure does not matter, — let us put it at 30,000,001. Now that 1, so to say, was called Louis Pasteur, and from the point of view of statistics or those who think they can predict history by counting heads, he was only an almost infinitesimal fraction, about one-thirty-millionth part, of the French people. Yet, as Huxley pointed out long ago, his mind sufficed to pay the entire indemnity exacted from France after the Franco-Prussian war. This single unit was worth more than a host of soldiers of the merely mechanical kind. Or take Athens, with its population of 30,000 people, mostly slaves, and consider its influence upon the world. Or, indeed, go where you please, whether to the history of nations or the history of religion or science or art, and ask whether the counting of heads, the ordinary census taking which indeed amounts merely to weighing nations by the ton, is an adequate one. In estimating national capital by the methods of vital statistics alone, we are in a far worse case than he would be who estimated monetary wealth by numbers of coins, without considering whether they were pounds, shillings or pence, whether they were genuine or counterfeit. The illustration is ludicrously inadequate, as every illustration must be, simply because the human case is unique. In the units of a population, which many prophets treat as if they were all of equal value, there are not merely differences to which the difference between a sovereign and a penny offers no parallel; there is not merely an enormous quantity of bogus or counterfeit units, but there is a very large number of units in every population which, so far from adding to the value of the rest, subtract from it, are parasitic upon it. Students of money will find no parallel to this. Yet in the face of facts which ought to be common intellectual property amongst school-children, we find many writers, bishops, socialist economists, moralists, fossil Imperialists, and the rest, pointing merely to the quantitative question of population as if it were everything, though they must surely know that, if international competition were the highest state of mankind, and if the work of Kelvin and Lister had been sold at its real worth by us to the rest of the world, those two men alone, in their services to life, and in the power which they give us over life, would be equal in value to, shall we say, the lower four-fifths of the whole birth-rate during the last generation. All human history teaches, as all animal history teaches in lesser degree, that quality and individuality is everything, that quantity is nothing or far worse than nothing *except in so far as it is quantity of quality*: yet though this lesson is written upon every page of the past, the greater number of our publicists and our public advisers still implicitly deny it. As Mr. Crackanthorpe put it, speaking of the figures for 1907, it is not the defective numbers, but the numbers of defectives, that should give us concern.

MASS VERSUS MIND.—John Ruskin called Darwin "a dim comet, wagging its tail of phosphorescent nothing against the steadfast stars"—a description as delightful as it is foolish. Yet the conception of eugenics, which is indeed a necessary deduction from Darwin's great discovery, finds abundant warrant and support in Ruskin's own wonderful writings, and here I quote, from *Time and Tide*, some sentences which still require to be read and remembered by the majority of our present advisers. He says:—

"And the question of numbers is wholly immaterial, compared with that of character; or rather, its own materialness depends on the prior determination of character. Make your nation consist of knaves, and, as Emerson said long ago, it is but the case of any other vermin—the more, the worse. Or, to put the matter in narrower limits, it is a matter of no final concern to any parent whether he shall have two children, or four; but matter of quite final concern whether those he has shall, or shall not, deserve to be hanged. . . . You have to consider first, by what methods of land distribution you can maintain the greatest number of healthy persons; and secondly whether, if, by any other mode of distribution and relative ethical laws, you can raise their character, while you diminish their numbers, such sacrifices should be made, and to what extent? . . . The French and British public may and will, with many other publics, be at last brought . . . to see farther that a nation's real strength and happiness do not depend upon properties and territories, nor on machinery for their defense, but on their getting such territory as they *have*, well filled with none but respectable persons, which is a way of *infinitely* enlarging one's territory, feasible to every potentate."

Surely it is not necessary, one feels, and yet one knows it is necessary, again to lay down propositions of such shining truth, and one wonders whether they shine so brightly as to blind those who should see them: or what can conceivably be the explanation of such arguments as those of the Bishop of London and others who, in the face of our monstrous infant and child mortality, the awful pressure of population and over-crowding in our great cities, where every year a larger and larger proportion of the population lives, and is born and dies — plead for a higher birth-rate on moral grounds, of all amazing grounds conceivable: and those also who, from the military or so-called Imperial point of view, regarding men primarily as "food for powder," in Shakespeare's phrase, read and quote statistics of population in order to promulgate the same advice?

To the moralist we need make no reply except simply to name the infant mortality, which is at last coming to be recognized everywhere as, perhaps, the most abominable of all our scandals. To the militarist I would quote the case of our ally, Japan. He recalls the war between China and Japan, and its issue, and has some idea, perhaps, of the population ratio of those two Empires. How was it that Providence was on the side of the small battalions? He recalls also the Russo-Japanese war and its issue; and the population ratio of the two Empires in that case. How many other instances does not military history afford of the truth that in the human species mind is the master of matter? One would suppose that a critical historical inquiry had been made, proving that the results of all past wars could have been predicted by the simple method of estimating the total aggregate weight of the combatant nations in flesh and blood and bone! More than this, if the development of the art of warfare means anything, if there has been any such development since the days of fists and stones, it means, as all human development in every sphere means, the increasing dominance of mind over matter, character and initiative over machinery, *dead or alive*. Meanwhile, the estimate of warriors in terms of the scale and the foot rule are still accepted just as if they had not been rendered obsolete forever with the passing of the "dragons of the slime."

As regards the psychical worth of the soldier, is it not recognized, though too commonly forgotten, when we applaud the value of the veteran or of seasoned troops? Physically the veteran is, on the average, inferior to the younger man. It is the psychical that gives him his worth, just as it was patriotism and sobriety that enabled the few sober Japanese to beat the many drunken Russians. It is safe to prophesy that, in all future war, the numerical criterion, which in effect weighs armies by the ton, as if war were merely a tug-of-war, will become less and less important — if, indeed, it is not already negligible: whilst the purely psychical qualities, from generalship and strategy and hygiene to initiative, judgment, accuracy, memory, and down finally to mere brutal red-blooded courage, will determine the issue.

Platitude, of course, but if true, why ignored? Why cannot our military advisers learn, in this respect, from the Navy? Owing to the very nature of the sea as compared with the land, in relation to the merely physical capacities of man, a Navy must be more intelligent than an Army, just as it requires more intelligence to make a boat than to walk; and it is in the Navy that the mechanical factor has been most completely transferred, so that the human machinery is at a discount and the steel machinery made by human mind is much, whilst the value of the psychical in all its aspects dominates and controls the whole. Great Britain, as the foremost naval power in the world, should long ago have left to its ultimate fate amongst other nations the idea that quantity — so many tons of soldiers and so many tons of sailors — affords an estimate of the warring force of a nation: even if the whole history of this little isle and the possession of our present Empire did not teach, as the history of Rome taught and as the history of Athens teaches in another sphere, that not mass but mind makes a nation great.

CHAPTER VII

HEREDITY AND RACE CULTURE

"We cannot but feel that the application of biological results is *only beginning*, and beginning with a tardiness which is a reproach to human foresight. There can be no doubt that it would pay the British nation to put aside a million a year for research on eugenics, or the improvement of the human breed." (Prof. J. A. Thomson, *Heredity*, 1908.)

It is evident that the facts and principles of heredity lie at the very basis of eugenics or race-culture in any of its forms, practical or impractical, scientific or unscientific. Our continual assumption throughout is that *like tends to beget like*, and it is on this ground that we desire to make parenthood the privilege of those whom we regard as *inherently* the best. If there were no such thing as heredity there could be no possibility of race-culture — nor indeed should we be here to discuss it. If a man's children were equally likely to be acorns or babies or tadpoles, the living world would not be the living world that we know.

The potency of heredity is obscured to uncritical examination by the fact that that which is inheritable is that which was innate, inherent or germinal in the parent, as we shall shortly see. We, however, are apt to compare the child with the parent, who has perhaps been much modified by circumstances, so that the resemblance between father and child may seem to be slight. Yet if we could bring back before us that father, as he was, say at the age of two, and compare him with his two year old child, we should perhaps be astonished by the resemblance. But we see the acquirements or acquired characters of the parent; make no distinction between them and his inherent characters; fail to discover these acquired characters in his child;—and discount the importance of heredity. Then, again, the eugenist may be utterly confounded if he estimates the parental value of an individual without reference to this limitation of heredity. Here is a man of culture and accomplishment; his children, then, will presumably tend to be cultured and accomplished. But every kind of advantage that forethought and love and money can afford may have been showered upon that man. So far as native endowment was concerned, he may have indeed been far below mediocrity. Now it is native endowment alone that he can transmit, and our eugenic estimate of him is therefore erroneous and will lead to disappointment. It is impossible to lay too great stress upon the truth that in all eugenic plans or demands or practices we are assuming the fact of inheritance, and that therefore it is our first business to distinguish absolutely between that which tends to be inherited and that which on the other hand, is never inherited.

Yet again, this distinction is of almost incalculable social moment in so far as it affects the process of selection actually occurring in society. This, perhaps, has not been adequately recognized. One may repeat a former statement of this point, which is cardinal for the eugenist.

"Even supposing that we were all identical at birth, yet, since we would come to differ from one another in virtue of different acquirements, due to our adaptation to differing environments, natural selection would ultimately have different individuals from which to select. Those who had made the most advantageous acquirements, such as industry or great knowledge, would tend to survive and prosper, whilst those who had made disadvantageous acquirements, such as laziness or the loss of sight or limbs, would be pushed to the wall. That process, of course, occurs in society at the present day to a greater or less degree, but it has only immediate and temporary or contemporary consequences. For if we recall the assertion that acquirements cannot be transmitted, we shall see that the selection of those who have made advantageous acquirements cannot benefit the next generation, since these acquirements die with their makers. The only process of natural selection which can result in progress is one which consists in the selection of favorable . . . inborn and therefore transmissible characters, such as good digestion, the musical sense, exceptional intelligence, the sympathetic temperament or what not (in so far as these are inborn)—the reason being that such are transmissible and that the children of persons so selected will tend to inherit their parents' good fortune. There is a fictitious way in which we speak of a child inheriting his father's acquirements, as when his father has acquired a fortune; but the child does much better to inherit his father's good sense or good health, which were characters inborn in him. Acquirements, then, are all very well for the day, but it is inborn characters that alone count for the morrow."[1]

It may be added that the time will come when there is a radical "transvaluation," as Nietzsche would say, of the two fashions in which a father "leaves" something to his children. When a question is asked on this head now-a-days, we mean, foolishly enough, to inquire how much money the father left his child, and we say of a man that he has "inherited" a fortune. This kind of "inheritance" may or may not be desir-

[1] Quoted from the author's lectures on *Individualism and Collectivism* (Williams and Norgate, 1906).

able as a social institution, but we can see plainly enough that it may and often does work in an anti-eugenic fashion. The gilded fool is swallowed by the maiden whose native sense would have rejected such a pill without its coat, and so the most pitiable degenerate becomes the father of his like. This point will be alluded to later. The present argument is that when we ask what a father "left" his children, we should really desire to learn what he *gave* them when he was still alive and begot them. These vital, or mortal, characters which they inherit — shall we say good health or insanity — are of incalculably more moment to them as individuals than any monetary fortune, and of incalculably more moment for the future. Yet again is it true that there is no wealth but life, and the best "fortune" or wealth that you can leave your children is sane and vigorous life.

THE CASE OF SLUM CHILDHOOD.— We have already seen that even in the slums the children make a fresh start in a wonderful way, that their stunted growth, their proneness to disease, are mainly due to their environment, which it is therefore our duty to improve. This is *in general* true, and depends evidently upon the fact that the acquired deterioration of the parents — *e.g.*, dental decay — is not transmitted to their children — poisonings apart — so that the children make a fresh start where their parents did. It is necessary to point this out again and again, as the present writer for one has long been weary of doing, because it indicates our immediate duty in this respect, and forbids us to shirk it with any too-comprehensive phrases about "national degeneration." Now who could have predicted that this plain and simple truth would be regarded by some people as constituting a denial — on strict scientific grounds, and as the very latest scientific pronouncement — of the principle of heredity? "The bubble of heredity has been pricked," says Mr. Bernard Shaw.

But popular muddleheadedness does not affect the palpable and universal truth that the *inherent* characters of parents do tend to be inherited by their children: nor yet that these inherent characters differ profoundly in different individuals; nor yet the eugenic argument, which is that for purposes of parenthood, which means for the entire future, some of these should be taken and others left.

"Ye shall know them by their fruits. Do men gather grapes of thorns, or figs of thistles? . . . Wherefore by their fruits ye shall know them." These classical words surely have a special value for the eugenist. As we have said, it is his particular necessity, alike in theory and in practice, to "know" the real nature, the innate, inherent, germinal characters, of the individuals who may or may not be parents: and these, as we have seen, are frequently obscured by the action of environment — as, for instance, in the population of the slums on the one hand, or the man of factitious culture on the other hand. But "by their fruits ye shall know them." In general, the children inherit what was innate in their parents, and in many an instance the surest way in which you could ascertain what the parent really was by nature — what, as we say, Nature "meant" him to be — is by a study of his children. Only, of course, we must take the children very young indeed, before environment has made its mark upon them also, for better or for worse. Thus, when we find the new-born baby of some pallid, half-starved, stunted mother in the slums, to be healthy and vigorous and beautiful,[1] by this fruit we shall know what the mother might and should have been. A healthy baby goes far to demonstrate that the stock is healthy. This is one of the cardinal truths which emerge from the study of infant mortality, and it may be perhaps permitted to warn some students of race-culture of the errors into which they are bound to fall if they do not reckon with what the student of infant mortality is constantly asserting: viz., that the babies of the slums, seen early, before ignorance and neglect have had their way with them, are physically vigorous and promising in certainly not less than ninety per cent. of cases. This primarily demonstrates, of course, the murderous nature of our infant mortality; but it also demonstrates to the eugenist that these classes are perhaps not so unworthy as he may fancy. By their new-born babies ye shall know them. It is under the influence of such considerations that the present writer, for one, is somewhat chary of predictions and proposals based upon the relative fertility of different classes of the community or of the masses as compared with the classes. Directly the eugenist begins to talk in terms of *social* classes (as Mr. Galton has never done), he is skating on thin ice, and if it lets him through, he will find the

[1] As is usually the case, except when the mother is alcoholic or syphilitic.

remains of many of his rash predecessors beneath it.[1]

In fine, then, if we observe the distinction between the innate and the acquired, which is the distinction between the transmissible and the intransmissible, this is so far from denying the fact of heredity at all as in reality to emphasize its potency whilst undoubtedly diminishing its range.

A CRITICISM OF TERMS.— In order that this distinction may be clear and never forgotten, it is well to look to our vocabulary — words being good servants but bad masters. We should certainly have this vocabulary purged altogether of a certain word in common and uncritical employment, especially by the medical profession. This is the thoroughly misleading, indeterminate and useless word "congenital." Not on one occasion in a hundred of its use does any examined meaning attach to it. The word is commonly used as the equivalent of innate, inherent, inborn or germinal. Now nothing is truly innate or inborn save what was present in the germ. But with childish confusion of thought, we persist in attaching quite undeserved importance to the *birth* of those animals which are brought forth "alive"— as if a bird's egg were not alive. Hence we speak of any character present at

[1] If we make a diagram of society, with the social strata labeled, and then proceed to make a eugenic comment upon it, certainly the line dividing the sheep from the goats, *as for parenthood*, would not be horizontal, at any level. Nor would it be vertical — as if the proportions of worth and unworth were the same in all classes. Some would draw it diagonally, counting most of the aristocracy good and most of the lowest strata bad: others would slope it the other way. I should not venture to draw it at all: there are individuals good and bad in all classes and races.

birth as congenital, and then we assume that congenital is synonymous with inherent or germinal. But it is an irrelevant detail that a young mammal happens to leave its mother at the ninth week or month. During the whole period that it spends within its mother, it is to be regarded as an individual organism with its own environment. If that environment so affects it as to strangle a limb, the result is an acquirement, though it may be present at birth. An acquirement is an acquirement, whether it be acquired five minutes or months before, or five minutes or months after, the change of environment which we call birth. Thus a character may be congenital — that is, present at birth — but not inherent or germinal, not inborn at the *real birth,* which was the union of the maternal and paternal germ-cells at conception. Such congenital characters are really acquirements, and — poisonings apart — are not transmissible. In common discussion this distinction is wholly ignored; and two distinct things, fundamentally different in origin and in potency, are lumped together under the blessed word "congenital."

This word is equally foolish and useless in an opposite direction. It constantly leads those who use it to suppose that the inherent characters of an individual are conterminous with his congenital characters or his characters at birth, and that thus any characters which he displays at a later age are acquired. All this comes of the absurdly delusive significance attached to the change of environment called birth, and may doubtless be traced historically to the remotest superstitions which imagined that a baby is not alive until it is born and breathes, or that the soul or breath or *pneuma* or "vital principle" is breathed into it at the moment of birth. We know, however, that a man may display for the first time at the age of twenty or sixty a character which was as truly inherent in his constitution as his nose or his spinal column — perhaps a beard, perhaps a mental character, perhaps a disease, or what not. Now this was not congenital though it was inherent. But as long as the stupid[1] word "congenital" is used as it is, we shall fail to realize that inherent characters may display themselves in an individual at any time after birth as at any time before birth. Thus, to sum up, a character may be congenital or rather *pre-congenital,* yet not inherent but acquired: a character may be post-congenital, yet not acquired but inherent. Now the all-important question as regards heredity is not at what date in the history of an individual a character appears — as, for instance, before birth or after birth; but, whether that character is inherent and therefore transmissible and therefore a possible architect of the future of mankind; or merely an acquirement, with which — the racial poisons apart — heredity has no concern.

It is suggested, then, that the word congenital be expunged from the vocabulary of science, or that, if it be retained, some meaning or other — any will do — be attached to it. If the word is to be retained, and if it be agreed to attach a meaning to it, probably "at birth" would be the most convenient. If this were agreed upon, then the phrase "congenital blindness,"

[1] "For words are wise men's counters, they do but reckon by them; but they are the money of fools" (Hobbes, *Leviathan,* Pt. I. chap. iv.).

now in common use, could be retained, as it would then accurately indicate the nature of the blindness in question, which is due almost invariably, if not invariably, to an infection acquired at the moment of birth.

Yet further. When we say that a man's intelligence or length of limb or whatever it be is hereditary, we mean in ordinary speech that this character can be traced in one or more of his ancestors; and that is, of course, an accurate use of the term. But Shakespeare, for instance, had unremarkable ancestors, so that no one would say that his genius was hereditary; are we, then, to say that it was acquired? Every one would protest at once that a poet is born and not made — than which there is certainly no truer popular saying. What, then, is to be said of it if it was neither hereditary nor acquired? The truth is that language is again at fault. Shakespeare's genius was of inherent or germinal origin — the poet is born and not made: or, more accurately, the poet is conceived and not made, either before birth or after it. Therefore, though Shakespeare did not inherit his mother's genius or his father's genius, neither of them having such a gift to transmit, yet his genius was certainly potential either in the maternal or paternal germ-cell which united to form him, or in both; or at the least arose in consequence of that compromise or rearrangement or settlement, shall we say, which is in effect always agreed upon by the two germ-cells in bi-parental reproduction. Now the two germ-cells are the hereditary material. They were given to Shakespeare by his parents; nay more, they made him. His genius, then, was hereditary in an absolutely correct sense of the word, yet not in the sense of ordinary speech, nor even in the sense in which it is employed by Mr. Galton in his book on *Hereditary Genius*. This confusion of terms is responsible for much confusion of thought. It must the more urgently be cleared up because of the discoveries in heredity initiated by the Abbot Mendel, forty years ago, and now included in the department of the science of heredity which is called Mendelism. We learn from this that highly definite characters may appear in offspring though there was no sign of them in either parent. These, then, are not hereditary in the sense of ordinary speech. Yet, in a more accurate sense of the word they can be proved to be hereditary — nay more, the manner and proportion of their transmission can be predicted in the most exact mathematical terms. These characters were not present in the parent's body; they did not lie open to view in the parent; they were not patent in the parent. They were latent, however, they lay hid, in the parent, or rather in the germ-plasm of which that parent was the host. In many such cases, if we go back a generation further we find that the character in question was patent in a grand-parent. A mother's son may suffer from hæmophilia or the bleeding disease, yet she is not a "bleeder," nor is the boy's father; but her father was a bleeder, and the disease is, of course, hereditary in her son, though neither of his parents displayed a trace of it.

Thus an individual may inherit or may have inherent in the germ-cells from which he was formed characters which were not present in either parent. They were, however, potentially present in the germ-cells of which those parents were the trustees.

But, the reader will say, do we find in the case of every "sport" or "transilient variation," such as Shakespeare, that the new character was, after all, present in some one or other of his ancestors though absent in his immediate parents? The answer is negative, certainly. But genius, to take this case, is a combination of qualities. And the Mendelians are now able to call into existence organisms of new kinds by combination of qualities derived from one parent, or rather from one parental line, with other qualities, formerly apparently incompatible with them, derived from the other parental line. Thus Professor Biffen of Cambridge has called into existence a new kind of wheat such as never existed before — a wheat combining the quality technically called "strength," hitherto lacking in all kinds of wheat capable of being profitably grown in Great Britain, with the power of yielding a large crop and other good qualities found in home-grown wheat. He has also produced a wheat which, together with other desirable qualities, is immune from the disease known as "rust," this immunity having never been found before associated with the other good qualities in question. These advances will not long be limited to the vegetable world merely. Perhaps it requires no very great imagination, after all, to suppose that even something like that combination of qualities which we call genius may some day be produced at will in mankind.

Such a new wheat, then — I will not say such a Shakespeare — owes its unique and unprecedented properties to heredity, and yet there was never anything like it before. Its "genius" is not "hereditary."

The words *innate* and *inborn* are harmless and may be employed, though the apparent allusion to birth is rather unfortunate. We mean, however, by innate or inborn qualities, qualities which were potential in the germ. The genius of Shakespeare was innate or inborn. It was present potentially at his real birth, the union of the parental cells. It preceded his "birth" in the ordinary sense of the word: Shakespeare, when only *in embryo,* was a Shakespeare *in embryo.*

Better still is the word *inherent,* which, of course, literally means "sticking in." By anything inherent we mean that which was there from the first as part and parcel of, as indeed essential to, the entity to which we refer. Now inherent characters are always inherent in the accurate sense that they inhere in the germ-cells, which are the inherited material. As these germ-cells make us or as we are made out of them, it follows, of course, that all our potentialities whatsoever, our ultimate fates in every particular, partly depend upon inheritance.[1]

Nature and *nurture* are antithetic terms of Shakespearean origin which are in frequent use and much favored by Mr. Galton. That which comes by nature is the inborn, inherent, or germinal; and that is due to

[1] It might be supposed that the words "inherent" and "inherited" were allied etymologically. This is not so. "Inherit" is derived from "heir," and this from a verb meaning "to take." In natural inheritance the heir inherits what is inherent in the germ-cells which make him. Says Professor Thomson: "The organization of the fertilized ovum is the inheritance"—*and the heir,* we may add.

nurture which is the result of the converse of the germinal with the environment — a man's accent for instance.

Perhaps, in some ways, *germinal* is the most useful word of all, though inherent is so convenient and familiar, as well as being accurate etymologically, that it has been employed throughout this book. Not only is the word germinal strictly accurate, but also it suggests the idea of the germ-plasm, and has the particular virtue of avoiding all reference to the change of environment to which young mammals are subjected and which is called birth.

There remains the terminological difficulty that, as I have tried to show, the individual may display characters which were potential in the germ, inherent and necessarily inherited, though they did not appear in the parent nor yet in any ancestor. We have to face the paradox, then, that in natural inheritance a parent can transmit what he has not got, though this does not apply to the unnatural inheritance of property in human society. Now what word is there which shall indicate the origin or at least the time and conditions of origin of such characters as these? They are germinal, yet they are — in some cases — not wholly present in either of the germ-cells which united to form the new individual in question. They are present however, in the new single cell from which this individual, like every living organism, takes its origin.[1] The terms "congerminal" or "conceptional" might be employed.

[1] Unless indeed it be an organism so lowly as only to consist of one cell throughout.

"Acquired character," even, is a bad term. It replaced "functionally-produced modification," which was long employed by Spencer. The blacksmith's biceps answers to this phrase. It is this and other such modifications that are non-transmissible. Alcoholic degeneration is not a "functionally-produced modification," but it is an "acquired character," as is lead poisoning. These do produce results in offspring — naturally enough. If the older phrase were still the one employed, we should see that the Weismannian argument as to non-transmission does not apply to *such* "acquired characters."

The word "reversion," also, not to say "atavism," may well be dropped. Its attempted jurisdiction by Professor Thomson has led to severe and conclusive Mendelian criticism. The "reversion" of fancy pigeons to the blue ancestor is simply due to the coming together of Mendelian units long separated. The "reversion" of the feeble-minded is not reversion but the result of poisoning. Primitive man was not feeble-minded, nor is the ape. Science has no further use for the word: its suggestions and implications are all now known to be unwarranted or erroneous.

MATERNAL IMPRESSIONS.— We are now, at last, after our attempt to clear up the vocabulary of heredity, in a position to consider certain doctrines and popular beliefs which bear very directly upon race-culture. Realizing, for instance, that "congenital" means nothing; realizing as perhaps some of us have not so clearly realized before, *when* exactly it is that the new human being comes into existence, we shall be prepared to understand how definite and indisputable are the denials which science offers to certain popular ideas.

Thus, for instance, in the interests of race-culture or, to be more particular, in the interests of her unborn baby, the expectant mother may faithfully follow the example of Lucy in *Richard Feverel*.[1] Does this have its intended effect? The answer is an unqualified negative. Consider the case. The baby is at this time already a baby, though rather small and uncanny, floating in a fluid of its own manufacture. Its sole connection with its mother is by means of its umbilical cord — that is to say, blood vessels, arterial and venous. There is no nervous connection whatever: absolutely nothing but the blood-stream, carried along a system of tubes. This blood is the child's blood, which it sends forth from itself along the umbilical cord to a special organ, the placenta or after-birth, half made by itself and half made by the mother, in which the child's blood travels in thin vessels so close to the mother's blood that their contents can be interchanged. Yet the two streams never actually mix. The child's blood, having disposed of its carbonic acid and waste-products to the mother's blood, and having received therefrom oxygen and food, returns so laden to the child. Pray how is the mother's reading of history to make the child a historian? If, after birth, a small operation were performed, so that some of the mother's blood should run along an artificial tube

[1] The reader will remember the chapter, "A Berry to the Rescue." "Says Lucy demurely 'Now you know why I read history, and that sort of books . . . I only read sensible books and talk of serious things . . . because I have heard say . . . dear Mrs. Berry! don't you understand now?'"

into one of her baby's veins the effective connection between the two organisms would in a sense be actually closer than it was before birth when, as has been said, the two streams are always kept apart. Should we expect such an operation to serve the child for education? If the mother then acquired a scar should we expect it to give the child a similar scar?

We see now why the learning of geometry on the part of the mother before its birth will not set her baby upon that royal road to geometry of which Euclid rightly denied the existence — any more than after its birth. Such a thing does not happen, and there is no conceivable means by which it could happen — unless we are to call in telepathy. All maternal hopes and efforts of this kind are utterly misguided: as misguided as if the father entertained similar hopes. Let the devoted mother acquaint herself not with what historians are pleased to call history, but with the history of the developing human mind and body, so that she may be a fit educator of her child when it is born.

Let her also realize that her blood is everything to her child. It is food and air and organ of excretion. If she introduces alcohol into her blood in any considerable quantity she is feeding her child on poisoned food. Surely the reader must see the distinction between a case like this and the supposed transmission of historical knowledge or even historical aptitude from mother to baby by the diligent perusal of histories. Yet though the distinction is so palpable and evident, there are extremists who believe and even print their beliefs that the denial of the one (supposed) possibility, which is palpably inconceivable, logically carries with it a denial of the other possibility, which is indeed a palpable necessity. Or, to state the criticism in another way, there are those who, if we protest that the introduction of poisons into the mother's organism must surely involve risk to the child who is nourished by her blood, will retort "Oh, well, I suppose you believe that if you learn a number of languages before your next child is born, he or she will be a linguist!"[1]

HEREDITARY GENIUS.— Mr. Galton's world-famous work on *Hereditary Genius* was published in 1869 and reprinted with a most valuable additional chapter in 1892. It has long been out of print, however, and for the definite purpose of attempting to arouse the reader's interest in it so that he may somehow or other obtain a copy to read, I may here go over one or two points, chosen to that end. The argument, of course, is that ability is hereditary.[2]

This, in the judgment of most unbiased people, Mr. Galton conclusively proved: and we do not at all realize to-day how repugnant and revolutionary this doctrine appeared to popular opinion some forty years ago. Mr. Galton has, however, followed up his cita-

[1] Contrast Mr. Galton, the propounder of the now accepted view:—

"As a general rule, with scarcely any exception that cannot be ascribed to other influences, such as bad nutrition or transmitted microbes, the injuries or habits of the parents are found to have no effect on the natural form or faculties of the child." (*Hereditary Genius*, Prefatory Chapter to the Edition of 1892, p. xv.)

[2] In the later edition Mr. Galton discusses the question of the title, and says that if it could now be altered, it should appear as *Hereditary Ability*. We may note that, as the author says himself, "The reader will find a studious abstinence throughout the work from speaking of genius as a special quality."

tion of facts on more than one occasion since,[1] and those who now deny his view belong to that very large majority of any population which finds itself able to pronounce confidently upon the value of an author's work without the labor, found necessary by less fortunate people, of reading it.

The following quotation states the question of national eugenics in final form: —

"As an example of what could be sought with advantage, let us suppose that we take a number, sufficient for statistical purposes, of persons occupying different social classes, those who are the least efficient in physical, intellectual, and moral grounds, forming our lowest class, and those who are the most efficient forming our highest class. The question to be solved relates to the hereditary permanence of the several classes. What proportion of each class is descended from parents who belong to the same class, and what proportion is descended from parents who belong to each of the other classes? Do those persons who have honorably succeeded in life, and who are presumably, on the whole, the most valuable portion of our human stock, contribute on the aggregate their fair share of posterity to the next generation? If not, do they contribute more or less than their fair share, and in what degree? In other words, is the evolution of man in each particular country, favorably or injuriously affected by its special form of civilization?

"Enough is already known to make it certain that the productiveness of both the extreme classes, the best and the worst, falls short of the average of the nation as a whole. Therefore, the most prolific class necessarily lies between the two extremes, but at what intermediate point does it lie? Taken altogether, on any reasonable principle, are the natural gifts of the most prolific class, bodily, intellectual, and moral, above or below the line of national mediocrity? If above that line, then the existing con-

[1] The reader may note "A eugenic investigation: Index to achievements of near kinsfolk of some of the Fellows of the Royal Society," *Sociological Papers*, 1904, pp. 85–99 (Macmillan); also *Noteworthy Families* (John Murray, 1906).

ditions are favorable to the improvement of the race. If they are below that line, they must work towards its degradation."

The main body of the book deals with inquiries in special cases — the judges of England between 1660 and 1865, statesmen, commanders, authors, men of science, poets, musicians, painters, divines, senior classics of Cambridge, oarsmen and wrestlers.

The concluding chapters should be printed in gold. Only one or two notes can here be made. Mr. Galton believes that the dark ages were largely due to the celibacy enjoined by religious orders on their votaries: —

"Whenever a man or woman was possessed of a gentle nature that fitted him or her to deeds of charity, to meditation, to literature or to art, the social condition of the time was such that they had no refuge elsewhere than in the bosom of the Church. But the Church chose to preach and exact celibacy, and the consequence was that these gentle natures had no continuance, and thus, by a policy so singularly unwise and suicidal that I am hardly able to speak of it without impatience, the Church brutalized the breed of our forefathers. She acted precisely as if she had aimed at selecting the rudest portion of the community to be, alone, parents of future generations. She practiced the arts which breeders would use, who aimed at creating ferocious, currish, and stupid natures. No wonder that club law prevailed for centuries over Europe; the wonder rather is that enough good remained in the veins of Europeans to enable their race to rise to its present very moderate level of natural morality."

Yet further: —

"The policy of the religious world in Europe was exerted in another direction, with hardly less cruel effect on the nature of future generations, by means of persecutions which brought thousands of the foremost thinkers and men of political aptitudes to the scaffold, or imprisoned them during a large part of their manhood, or drove them as emigrants into other lands. In every one of these cases the check upon their leaving issue was very considerable. Hence the Church, having first captured all the gentle natures and condemned them to celibacy, made another sweep of her huge nets, this time fishing in stirring waters, to catch those who were the most fearless, truth-seeking, and intelligent, in their modes of thought, and therefore the most suitable parents of a high civilization, and put a strong check, if not a direct stop, to their progeny. Those she reserved on these occasions, to breed the generations of the future, were the servile, the indifferent, and, again, the stupid. Thus, as she — to repeat my expression — brutalized human nature by her system of celibacy applied to the gentle, she demoralized it by her system of persecution of the intelligent, the sincere, and the free. It is enough to make the blood boil to think of the blind folly that has caused the foremost nations of struggling humanity to be the heirs of such hateful ancestry, and that has so bred our instincts as to keep them in an unnecessarily long-continued antagonism with the essential requirements of a steadily advancing civilization."

For this final quotation no apology is needed: —

"The best form of civilization in respect to the improvement of the race, would be one in which society was not costly; where incomes were chiefly derived from professional sources, and not much through inheritance; where every lad had a chance of showing his abilities, and, if highly gifted, was enabled to achieve a first-class education and entrance into professional life, by the liberal help of the exhibitions and scholarships which he had gained in his early youth; where marriage was held in as high honor as in ancient Jewish times; where the pride of race was encouraged (of course I do not refer to the nonsensical sentiment of the present day, that goes under that name); where the weak could find a welcome and a refuge in celibate monasteries or sisterhoods, and lastly, where the better sort of emigrants and refugees from other lands were invited and welcomed, and their descendants naturalized."

THE STUDY OF PSYCHICAL INHERITANCE.— This early work of Mr. Galton has been followed by much more on the same lines. Contemporary psychology, however, is *just beginning* to indicate the lines on which new inquiry is needed. The naïve assertions of the actuary as to the inheritance of, say, "conscientiousness," are not useful to the psychologist, who has some idea of the structure and history of that most complex social product we call conscience. The psychologists must analyze out for us those elementary units of the mind upon which experience and the social state, education and suggestion act, to make human nature as we know it. The reader may be directed to Dr. McDougall's recent work on *Social Psychology* — written at the present writer's suggestion — for an outline analysis of what is really inherent, and therefore alone transmissible, in the human mind — certain instincts and impulses, together with native varieties in capacity of memory, and so on. Recently the Mendelians have entered this field, and they have the advantage of realizing the importance of dealing with real primary units. Their law seems to apply to the musical sense in man and to the brooding instinct in the hen.[1] The line of study here suggested is earnestly commended to the psychologists for their *indispensable* help.

Eugenics and parties.— Let us once again consider the fashion in which men and women are classified to the eugenic eye. We have already realized that the most essential division *of fact* is that between those who will and those who will not be parents. The most essential division *of ideal* is of those who are worthy and those who are not worthy to be parents. It is the object of eugenics to make the real and the ideal divisions coincide. And let us here say with

[1] These researches have not yet been published.

all possible force that before such classifications as these all others are trivial and nearly all others impudent. The eugenist has nothing to do with the low game called party politics: terms like socialism and so forth mean very little for him. He may or may not be a socialist, but if he be, at least he does not subscribe to what, so far as I can judge, is the first article in the creed of socialism — that all evil is of economic origin; he knows that there is much evil of germinal origin. As for conservatism and liberalism, he might have some use for these terms if the creed of conservatism were that there is no wealth but life, which must be conserved; and the creed of liberalism that life has not yet reached its zenith, and there must be liberty for all progressive variations of body and mind and thought and practice. As it is, all these things are somewhat nauseating. If and when there is a thinking party, and that party will have the eugenist, he will doubtless join it. Meanwhile he appeals to that great and growing section of the community which knows party-politics for the humbug and sham that it is, and the House of Commons as a lethal chamber for souls.

Similarly, the eugenic classification of mankind cuts right across the ordinary social classification. The parasite and the parent of parasites must be branded, whether he be at the top or the bottom of the social scale. The quality of the germ-plasm which men and women carry is the supremely important thing. Its architecture is the architect of all empires. Year by year we shall more surely be able to infer the nature and the worth of the germ-plasm in particular cases, though its host may have been veneered or, on the other hand, repressed; and year by year the basal facts of heredity will furnish ever surer criteria for the theory and practice of a New Imperialism which knows, for instance, what militarism did for Rome and Napoleon for France, and which will some day sweep all the money changers out of the Temple of Life.[1]

[1] In the later chapters of a former book, "Health, Strength, and Happiness" (Grant Richards, London; Mitchell Kennerley, New York, 1908), I have discussed various aspects of heredity from the eugenic point of view more fully than has been possible here.

CHAPTER VIII

EDUCATION AND RACE CULTURE

"Education is but the giving or withholding of opportunity." — BATESON.

IT is true that education can seem to accomplish miracles; that in a single generation the results of an ideal education would be amazing. It is true, also, that in certain epochs of history, when wise counsels have prevailed, great results have been attained. It is true that at present scarcely a man or woman amongst us, if any, has reached the full stature which would have been attained under an ideal system of education. It is true, finally, that no system of race-culture can ignore education or be effective without it. Though the general question of education is not the specific question of the present volume, yet there is only too good reason for some brief allusion to the subject here, especially since it bears on the question of the measure of importance which we ascribe to heredity.

MODERN EDUCATION — THE DESTRUCTION OF MIND. — When we observe in such contrasted cases as those of Herbert Spencer and Wordsworth, for instance, that absence of early education, especially in the first septennium, has co-existed with the subsequent efflorescence of the mightiest genius, we may almost be inclined to inquire whether genius could not in effect be made to order even in the very next generation by the simple device of suspending the process which we are pleased to call education. Doubtless that is scarcely so, though every one who has any knowledge of the subject is well assured that mere suspension of the present destructive process might suffice to produce a population that would wonder at its ancestors.

A simple analogy will show the disastrous character of the present process, which may be briefly described as "education" by cram and emetic. It is as if you filled a child's stomach to repletion with marbles, pieces of coal and similar material incapable of digestion — the more worthless the material the more accurate the analogy: then applied an emetic and estimated your success by the completeness with which everything was returned, more especially if it was returned "unchanged," as the doctors say. Just so do we cram the child's mental stomach, its memory, with a selection of dead facts of history and the like (at least when they are not fictions) and then apply a violent emetic called an examination (which like most other emetics causes much depression) and estimate our success by the number of statements which the child vomits on to the examination paper — if the reader will excuse me. Further, if we are what we usually are, we prefer that the statements shall come back "unchanged"— showing no signs of mental digestion. We call this "training the memory."

Such a process as one has imagined in the physical case would assuredly ruin the physical digestion for life. In the mental case, which is not imaginary but actual, a similar result ensues. It is thus unfair to the

Anglo-Saxon germ-plasm to credit it with the abundant stupidity of its products. Much of this stupidity is factitious and artificial. We shall continue to produce it so long as by education or drawing forth we understand intrusion or thrusting in, and so long as the only drawing forth which we practice is by means of the emetics we call examinations. The present type of education is a curse to modern childhood and a menace to the future. The teacher who cannot tell whether a child is doing well without formally examining it, should be heaving bricks, but such a teacher does not exist. In Berlin they are now learning that the depression caused by these emetics, for which the best physical parallel is antimony, often lead to child suicide — a steadily-increasing phenomenon mainly due to educational over-pressure and worry about examinations.

Short of such appalling disasters, however, we have to reckon with the existence of this enormous amount of stupidity, which those who fortunately escaped such education in childhood have to drag along with them in the long struggle towards the stars. This dead weight of inertia lamentably retards progress.

Our factitious stupidity is injurious both in the governing and the governed. As Professor Patrick Geddes once remarked to the present writer, there are three kinds of governments: the government of the future — as yet only ideal, which believes that there are ideas and that they may be worth acting upon: the second is instanced by the Russian government, which believes that there are ideas, but fears and suppresses them: the third by the British government, which denies that there are ideas at all, and prefers the method of "muddling through"— to use a Cabinet Minister's contented phrase — though truth is one and error infinite, though there are a million ways of going wrong for one of going right. This characteristic is not to be attributed to any germinal stupidity of the ruling classes in England. If it were we should of course look upon the decadence of their birth-rate with the utmost gratitude. It is a factitious product of their education. If you have been treated with marbles and emetics long enough, you may begin to question whether there is such a thing as nourishing food; if you have been crammed with dead facts, and then compelled to disgorge them, you may well question whether there are such things as nourishing facts or ideas.

Not less disastrous is this factitious stupidity amongst the governed. It produces, of course, the kind of man with whom we are all familiar. Having at great labor been taught to read, he is incapable of reading anything but rubbish. He never thinks for himself, and if he does you wish he had not, so inadequate is his machinery and so deplorable the result. He believes in politicians. He is, as we have said, so much dead weight for the reformer, whose energy is diverted from the discovery of new truth by the need of directing the eyes of stupidity to the old, though it shines as the sun in his strength.

Therefore, let not the reader suppose that in the advocacy of eugenics or race-culture we have become blinded to the possibilities offered us by reasonable education even of the very heterogeneous material offered us by heredity.

THE LIMITS OF EDUCATION — INDIVIDUAL AND RACIAL.— Yet it must be maintained that, though we cannot do without education, and though something infinitely better than we practice at present will be necessary if the ideal of race-culture is ever to be realized, yet education alone, however good, can never enable us to achieve our end. It must be maintained, in the first place, that education is limited in its powers by the inherent nature of the educated material — it is a process of *drawing out*, and you cannot draw out what is not there: and secondly, that its value, so far as the nature of individuals is concerned, is confined to the individuals in question and is not reproduced or maintained in their children. Thus education alone would have similar material to act upon from age to age, would have to make a fresh beginning in each generation, and its results, however good, relatively, would still be limited and finite. We shall do well, perhaps, to obtain and retain an adequate definition of education. No true conception of education was possible, notwithstanding the derivation of the word, so long as the child's mind was likened to a piece of "pure white paper" for us to write upon: or an empty box waiting to be filled. The *tabula rasa* of Locke is, we now know, the last thing in the world to resemble a child's mind. Indeed, if any such figure be demanded, the child's mind is a piece of mosaic — made of ancestral pieces — and education is the process of realizing what is so given.

Or, if a child's mind is a portmanteau, to educate is not to pack but to unpack it. We understand, at least, that education never can begin at the beginning, nor anywhere near it — that, as Professor MacCunn says in his admirable book, *The Making of Character*, "the page of the youngest life is so far from being blank that it bears upon it characters in comparison with which the faded ink of palæography is as recent history."

We are learning, too, though none but the very few know this, that the process by which the "faded ink" is made visible must not be credited with having done the writing: any more than the fire to which you hold a paper written upon with ink that fire makes visible. Still less do we realize that what really seems to be the product of education is often the result of an inherent mechanism now developed, which was not yet formed when we began the educational process. One reason why the baby cannot walk is that it has not the nervous apparatus. A child may walk at the first attempt, if that attempt be delayed until the machinery is developed. A child may similarly speak sentences at the first attempt. Very commonly we start teaching a child something, which after some years, it learns. We have done nothing but interfere. The learning is none of our doing: merely the mental apparatus is now evolved — and lo! the result. At birth the sucking apparatus is perfect. If we could, doubtless we should start teaching the unborn infant to suck long before the machinery was ready — and should applaud ourselves for its facility at birth; only that probably this facility would be impaired by our efforts, as many capacities of later development are damaged by our interference. What we understand, or misunderstand, by education should begin approximately when the child is seven. The first seven years of life should really have the term of childhood confined to them, for there is a natural term so indicated. The growth of the brain is a matter of the first seven years almost wholly. It grows relatively little after that period; and until that is completed the physical apparatus of mind is not ready for educational interference. Without any such interference, and with merely the provision of conditions, physical and mental, for its spontaneous development, the brain of the seven year old will suffice for surprising things — so surprising that if their evolution were possible under any system of schooling practiced before that date, we should applaud it as ideal. Probably there is no such system — much less any that will improve on the spontaneous process.

EDUCATION THE PROVISION OF AN ENVIRONMENT.— We are prepared, then, to realize the limits to the action of education upon the individual. We shall not confuse this great and many-sided thing with such of its factors as instruction or schooling. It is not intrusion but education: "the guidance of growth," to use Sir James Crichton-Browne's phrase. This guidance, this process of unpacking, educing or realizing, is accomplished by the action of circumstances or the environment. Environment is a large word and is invariably abused when it is used in less than the large sense. Here it includes, for instance, air and food, mother-love and the schoolmaster. I therefore define education as *the provision of an environment.* This definition prepares us to understand the limitations of the process. If we think of education as a packing or cramming process, we shall err in this respect; we shall expect limitless results from education provided that one packs early and tightly and carefully enough. It is this erroneous conception which rules us and daily betrays us in practice. If, however, we think of education as the provision of an environment, capable of creating nothing, but merely of causing the expression or the repression of potential characters inherent in the individual educated, then we shall begin to recast our methods on the lines determined by this truth. Yet, further, we shall begin to understand the cardinal truth, one of the many platitudes which we have yet to appreciate, that "you cannot make a silk purse out of a sow's ear."

HEREDITY AND ENVIRONMENT.—Let us consider the question in general terms. The characters of any living thing are determined by two factors — heredity and environment. The old phrases were character and circumstances, but they were less than useful since character is modified by circumstances. Now one of the most important questions in the world, and not the least for the eugenists, is as to the relative importance of these two factors. The technical terms may not be in our mouths, but we discuss this instance or that of the question in point almost every day of our lives. One part of the business of philosophy and of science is not only to answer questions but to ask them correctly. This question is always wrongly asked, and therefore cannot be answered, or is incorrectly answered. We persist in using the mathematical idea of addition, and we seek to show that, say, seventy per cent. of the result is due to the innate factor and thirty per cent. to the acquired. But the truth is that so long as we begin with this idea we may prove what we please. If we keep our attention fixed upon the environmental or educational factor we can easily and correctly demonstrate that in certain circumstances Mozart would have been stone-deaf and Shakespeare a gibbering idiot — hence, but incorrectly, we argue that environment is practically everything. *Per contra*, we can easily and correctly demonstrate that no education in the world could enable a door-mat or a cabbage or ourselves to write *Don Giovanni* or *Hamlet* — hence, but incorrectly, we argue that the material to be operated upon is everything. We have to learn, however, that the analogy *is not one of addition but of multiplication.* Neither inheritance nor environment, as such, gives anything. The environmental factor may be potentially one hundred — an ideal education — but the innate or inherited factor may be nothing, as when the pupil is a door-mat or a fool. The result then is nothing. Darwin had the trombone played to a plant, but he did not make a Palestrina. No academy of music will make a beetroot into a Beethoven, though I daresay a well-trained beetroot might write a musical comedy. The point is that one hundred multiplied by nothing equals nothing. Similarly, the innate factor may be one hundred, as in the case of a potential genius, but he may be brought up upon alcohol and curses amongst savages, and the result again is nothing. Keep the idea of multiplication in the mind, and the facts are seen rightly. No matter how big either factor be, if it is multiplied by nothing it yields nothing, or if it be multiplied by a fraction, as in the ordinary education of a genius, it yields less than it should. But in this controversy people persist in assuming that inheritance or education gives definitely so much which is there anyhow, whereas, really, it only supplies a potential figure which may realize infinity or nothing, according to what it is multiplied by. With all deference, I submit this as a real answer to these endless disputes.

But further, granted that neither factor in itself produces any actuality, which is normally the weightier of the two factors? We must make the qualification, "normally," because such a thing as disease or poison, included in the environmental factor, will dominate the result, completely overshadowing the importance of whatever heredity gave. Such things apart, however, we may be thoroughly assured that heredity is the weightier of the two factors. The more we study education, the more we recognize its true nature. Indeed the more we realize its ideal, the more do we realize its limitations. The more we study education the more important does heredity appear. If the reader has not had the opportunities of observing children for himself let him refer to such a book as Mr. Galton's *Inquiries into Human Faculty,* and he will begin to realize how large is the factor given by inheritance and how relatively small is the factor given by education.

EDUCATION CAN EDUCATE ONLY WHAT HEREDITY GIVES.— Heredity, as the eugenist must never forget, gives not actualities but only potentialities. It depends upon circumstances whether they shall become actualities. That, however, we all know. No one supposes that education is superfluous or impotent. We do, however, persistently forget the converse truth that education, on the other hand, makes no definite contribution, but merely multiplies — or alas, divides — the potentialities given by inheritance. These potentialities constitute a limiting condition which no education can transcend. Education can educate only what heredity gives. Long ago Helvetius thought that the differences between men were due to differences in education. But it is not so. We make, of course, the most ridiculous claims for education. The remark wrongly attributed to the Duke of Wellington, that "the battle of Waterloo was won on the playing-fields of Eton," is an instance in point. Recently, when Francis Thompson, the poet, died, the local newspaper of his birthplace said that it should be proud to have produced him. We may laugh at this conception of the genesis of genius, but we all talk in this fashion. A genius was educated at Eton, and we say that Eton produced him. The truth is, of course, that Eton failed to destroy him. (One says Eton for convenience, but the name of any accepted school will do.) If Eton produced him, why does it not produce thousands like him? There is plenty of material: but it is not the right material.

We should cease to speak, in our pride for our own *Alma Mater* or our own methods, as if education created genius or anything else. Men are born unequal. To realize the nature of education is not only to avoid the popular assumption that an ideal education will do everything for us, forgetting that no amount of polishing will make pewter shine like silver; it is not only to send us back to the principle of selection in recognition of the power of inheritance; it is not merely to dispose of the idea that men are born inherently equal; but it is also to combat the idea that education is a leveling process. On the contrary, it accentuates the differences between men. You may confuse the unpolished pebble and the diamond, but not when education has done its utmost for both. If education were a process of addition to what inheritance gives, it would almost level men: the addition of a large sum to figures such as 1, 2, and 3, would almost obliterate their original disproportion. But the analogy is with multiplication, as I have suggested: and the larger the sum by which 1, 2 and 3 are multiplied, the greater is the disparity between the products. This is, perhaps, one of the truths of vast importance which the common run of contemporary socialism implicitly denies; though it is of course abundantly recognized by such a socialist as that master-thinker Professor Forel. The socialist's panacea, ideal education for all, is much to be desired, and will accomplish much, as we began by admitting; but it is not a panacea. Those who believe it to be such do not understand the nature of education nor its limitations. They should remember the remark of

Epictetus, "the condition and characteristic of a fool is this: he never expects from himself profit nor harm, but from externals." The dogma of the unthinking socialist — who exists, though he is doubtless rarer than the unthinking individualist — is that all evil is of economic origin: correct your economics and your education and you obliterate evil. But it is not so. As Lowell said, "A great part of human suffering has its root in the nature of man, and not in that of his institutions." When by means of eugenics we can give education the right materials to work upon, we shall have a Utopia, and as for forms of government they may be left for fools to contest. Forel, incomparably the greatest socialist thinker of the day, sees this. He makes his Utopian predictions not so much as to mere externals, like clothing and language, but as regards the kind of man and woman: and, unlike some writers, he entitles himself to paint these pictures, for in that great eugenic treatise *Die Sexuel Frage,* he tells us how to realize them by pedagogic reform working upon the materials provided by human selection. A paragraph may be quoted from Forel:—

> "Malgré tout l'enthousiasme qu'on doit montrer pour une pédagogie rationelle, il ne faut jamais oublier qu'elle est incapable de remplacer la sélection. Elle sert au but immédiat et rapproché, qui est d'utiliser le mieux possible le matérial humain tel qu'il existe maintenant. Mais, par elle-même, elle n'améliore en rien la qualité des germes à venir. Elle peut néanmoins, grâce à l'instruction donnée à la jeunesse sur la valeur sociale de la sélection, la préparer à mettre cette dernière en œuvre."

and another from Spencer:—

"We are not among those who believe in Lord Palmerston's dogma, that all children are born good. On the whole, the opposite dogma, untenable as it is, seems to us less wide of the truth. Nor do we agree with those who think that, by skillful discipline, children may be made altogether what they should be. Contrariwise, we are satisfied that though imperfections of nature may be diminished by wise management, they cannot be removed by it. The notion that an ideal humanity might be forthwith produced by a perfect system of education, is near akin to that implied in the poems of Shelley, that would make mankind give up their old institutions and prejudices, all the evils in the world would at once disappear; neither notion being acceptable to such as have dispassionately studied human affairs."

RUSKIN ON EDUCATION AND INEQUALITY.— Three great paragraphs may be quoted from Ruskin's *Time and Tide*:—

". . . Education *was desired by the lower orders because they thought it would make them upper orders*, and be a leveler and effacer of distinctions. They will be mightily astonished, when they really get it, to find that it is, on the contrary, the fatallest of all discerners and enforcers of distinctions; piercing, even to the division of the joints and marrow, to find out wherein your body and soul are less, or greater, than other bodies and souls, and to sign deed of separation with unequivocal seal.

"171. Education is, indeed, of all differences not divinely appointed, an instant effacer and reconciler. Whatever is undivinely poor, it will make rich; whatever is undivinely maimed, and halt, and blind, it will make whole, and equal, and seeing. The blind and the lame are to it as to David at the siege of the Tower of the Kings, "hated of David's soul." But there are other divinely-appointed differences, eternal as the ranks of the everlasting hills, and as the strength of their ceaseless waters. And these, education does not do away with; but measures, manifests, and employs.

"In the handful of shingle which you gather from the sea-beach, which the indiscriminate sea, with equality of fraternal foam, has only educated to be, every one, round, you will see little difference between the noble and the mean stones. But the jeweler's trenchant education of them will tell you another story.

Even the meanest will be the better for it, but the noblest so much better that you can class the two together no more. The fair veins and colors are all clear now, and so stern is nature's intent regarding this, that not only will the polish show which is best, but the best will take most polish. You shall not merely see they have more virtue than the others, but see that more of virtue more clearly; and the less virtue there is, the more dimly you shall see what there is of it.

"172. And the law about education, which is sorrowfulest to vulgar pride, is this — that all its gains are at compound interest; so that, as our work proceeds, every hour throws us farther behind the greater men with whom we began on equal terms. Two children go to school hand in hand, and spell for half an hour over the same page. Through all their lives, never shall they spell from the same page more. One is presently a page a-head, two pages, ten pages — and evermore, though each toils equally, the interval enlarges — at birth nothing, at death infinite."

So much for one relation of this question to Socialism. Quite lately (*The New Age*, April 11th, 1908) Mr. Havelock Ellis has summed the matter up as follows:—

"Education has been put at the beginning, when it ought to have been put at the end. It matters comparatively little what sort of education we give children; the primary matter is what sort of children we have got to educate. That is the most fundamental of questions. It lies deeper even than the great question of Socialism *versus* Individualism, and indeed touches a foundation that is common to both. The best organized social system is only a house of cards if it cannot be constructed with sound individuals; and no individualism worth the name is possible, unless a sound social organization permits the breeding of individuals who count. On this plane Socialism and Individualism move in the same circle."

We cannot agree with Socialism when, as we think, it assumes that all evil is of economic or of educational origin. The student of heredity finds elements of evil abundant in poisoned germ-plasm and not absent from the best. Surely, surely, the products of progress are not mechanisms but men; and surely no economic system as such can be the only mechanism worth naming — which would be one that made men. The germ-plasm is such a mechanism, indeed; and hence its quality is all important.

But if Socialism, sooner than any other party, is going to identify itself with the economic principle of Ruskin that "there is no wealth but life"; and if in its discussion of the conditions of industry it will concern itself primarily with the culture of the racial life, which is the vital industry of any people (and basis enough for a New Imperialism, or at least a New Patriotism, that might be quite decent); if so, then it seems to me that we must look to the socialists for salvation. But books which describe future externals, books which assume that education is a panacea, forgetting that education can educate only what heredity gives, turn us away again when we are almost persuaded. The *economic* panacea must fail (at least as a panacea); the *educational* panacea must fail; the *eugenic* panacea may not fail.

Education, then, cannot achieve our ideal of race-culture. No matter how good our polishing, we must have silver and diamonds to work upon, not pewter and pebbles. When we have the right material to work upon, our labor will not be wasted, or far worse than wasted, as it now too often is.

Education is a Sisyphean task.— But the belief in education as in itself an adequate instrument of race-culture chiefly depends upon the popular doctrine as to its influence upon the race. It is supposed, in a word, that if you educate the parents, the child will begin where the parents left off. This is the doctrine of Lamarck, who said that if the necks of the parent giraffe were educated or drawn out, the baby giraffe would have this anatomical acquirement transmitted to it, and, so to speak, when it grew up, would be able to begin feeding on the leaves of trees at the level where its parents had to leave off. In the course of its life its own neck would become elongated or educated, and its children would outstretch both itself and their grand-parents. This doctrine of the transmission of acquired characters by heredity, as we have seen, is, at the present day, repudiated by biologists. It is generally believed by the medical profession and by the public, notwithstanding the fact that, for instance, the skin of the heel of every new baby is almost as thin and delicate as it is anywhere else, though for unthinkable generations all the ancestors of that baby on both sides have greatly thickened the skin of both heels by the act of walking.

It is quite evident that, if the Lamarckian theory were true, education would be a completely adequate instrument of race-culture, incomparable in its rapidity and certainty. It would not reform the world in a single generation because, as we have seen, its results would be limited by the inherent nature of its material; but since those results would involve the vast amelioration of the material upon which it worked in the second generation, mankind would be little lower than the angels in a century. The good habits acquired by one generation would be innate in the next. If the father learned one language in addition to his own, the child would start with the knowledge of two, waiting only for opportunity, and could accumulate more and hand them on to its child. "My father's environment would be my heredity." If we desired muscular strength we could in two generations produce a race amongst whom Sandow would be a puny weakling. We should not need to discuss any question of selection for parenthood. Without any such process we could answer Browning's prayer and "elevate the race at once"—physically, mentally and morally.

But the Lamarckian theory does not correspond with facts. The results of education, physical, mental or moral, are limited to the individuals educated. The children do *not* begin where the parents left off, but they make a fresh start where the parents did. Thus even though we had and employed an ideal method of education, we should make no permanent improvement by its means alone in the breed of mankind, any more than the breeder of race-horses could attain his end by the same means. In each generation the same problem, the same difficulties, the same limitations inherent in the nature of the new material, would have to be faced. We must learn from the horse-breeder, who knows that the blood of a single horse, Eclipse, runs in the veins of the great majority of winners since his time.

It is exceedingly difficult to dispossess the popular mind of the Lamarckian idea, the more especially as members of the medical profession, who are regarded as authorities on heredity, contentedly accept this idea themselves. Yet the advocates of eugenics or race-culture have to recognize that, so long as the Lamarckian idea obtains, their crusade will fail to find a hearing. We believe that nothing can really be accomplished in the way of race-culture until public opinion — that "chaos of prejudices," as Huxley called it — is marshalled on our side. But the popular notion of heredity is a most formidable obstacle. The Lamarckian idea seems to provide a method for the improvement of a species which cannot be surpassed for simplicity, rapidity and certainty. It even excludes the possibility of mistakes. You cannot go wrong if you simply educate every one to the utmost. Doubtless some persons are more suited for parenthood than others, but only let education be wise and universal, and any question of selection by marriage or otherwise will be superfluous. A thousand difficulties offered by public sentiment, by convention, by the churches, by the large measure of uncertainty which attends the working of heredity, could be ignored, if race-culture were simply a matter of education.

Nevertheless, these difficulties have to be faced by the eugenist. The popular misconception of heredity — instanced by Sir James Simpson's belief, not inexcusable sixty years ago, that the education of a future mother will enlarge her child's brain — must be removed. It can scarcely be doubted that the sway of the Lamarckian idea will soon be diminished, and then, at last, those who are interested in the future will discover that only by the process of selection for parenthood, which has brought mankind thus far, can further progress be assured.

REAL FUNCTIONS OF EDUCATION FOR RACE-CULTURE. —Nevertheless education has a true function for race culture in addition to the obvious fact of its necessity in order to realize the inherent potentialities of the individual. One of its functions is to provide a level of public opinion and public taste such that the finer specimens of each generation shall receive their due reward and shall not be crushed out of existence or superverted. There is a passage in Goethe which suggests the true function of education, and makes us suspect that, so far as many kinds of genius and talent are concerned, our immediate business is perhaps less to endeavor to produce them by breeding — if that be possible — than to make the most of them when they are vouchsafed us. Says Goethe: —

> "We admire the Tragedies of the ancient Greeks; but to take a correct view of the case, we ought to admire the period and the nation in which their production was possible rather than the individual authors; for though these pieces differ in some points from each other, and though one of these poets appears somewhat greater and more finished than the other, still, taking all things together, only one decided character runs through the whole.
>
> "This is the character of grandeur, fitness, soundness, human perfection, elevated wisdom, sublime thought, pure, strong intuition, and whatever other qualities one might enumerate. But when we find all these qualities, not only in the dramatic works which have come down to us, but also in lyrical and epic works — in the philosophers, orators, and historians, and in an equally high degree in the works of plastic art that have come down to us — we must feel convinced that such qualities did not merely belong to individuals, but were the current property of the nation and the whole period."

EDUCATION AS TO THE PRINCIPLE OF SELECTION.— Further, the hope may be warranted that, though education, as such, will not achieve the ideal of true race-culture, and though it has never hitherto averted the ultimate failure of all civilizations, yet the case may be different to-day, in that our acquired or traditional progress, transmitted by the process of education accumulating from age to age — not in our blood and bone and brain, but mainly in books, whereby the non-transmission of the results of education is circumvented in a sense — has reached the point at which the laws of racial or inherent progress have been revealed to us, as to none of our predecessors.[1] Having the knowledge of these laws it is possible that we may avert our predecessors' fate by putting them into force. If we do not, we must ultimately become "one with Nineveh and Tyre." Fifty years have now elapsed since the principle of natural selection was demonstrated for all time by the genius of Darwin. We must not be guilty of starting to tell the story of organic evolution and leaving out the point. So long as we supposed that man was created as he is, the idea of racial progress was an absurdity. It is the correct thing now-a-days to decry the possibility of human perfection. This possibility is rightly to be decryed if it be assumed that ideal education of the present material or anything like it will realize perfection. We have seen that it would not. It is the principle of selection, in which Darwin has educated us, that must be taught to all mankind, and thus edu-

[1] See the last sentence of the quotation from Forel on p. 149.

cation may indeed become the factory of an effective race-culture.

THE POWER OF INDIVIDUAL OPINION.— Since ultimately opinion rules the world, it is for us to create sound opinion. That is the purpose of this book. But every individual may be a center of eugenic opinion, and the time has assuredly come for attempting to realize this ideal though a thousand years should pass before the facts of heredity are completely ascertained and understood. The main principles are of the simplest character, and can be readily imparted to a child. Especially does the responsibility fall upon parents and those who are in charge of childhood.

The young people of the next and all succeeding generations must be taught the supreme sanctity of parenthood. The little boy who asks what he is to become when he grows up, must be taught that the highest profession and privilege he can aspire to is responsible fatherhood; the little girl may less frequently ask these questions, the answer to which has been imparted to her by her own Mother-Nature — as the doll instinct, so little appreciated or utilized, sufficiently demonstrates; but she likewise must be taught reverence for Motherhood. As childhood gives place to youth, what may be called the eugenic sense must be cultivated as a cardinal aspect of the moral sense itself; so that even personal inclination — at the controllable and self-controllable stage which precedes "head over ears" affection — will wither when it is directed to some one who, on any ground, offends the educated eugenic sense. There is here a field for moral education of the highest and most valuable kind, both for the individual and for the race. Is there any other aspect of duty which can claim a higher warrant? Is there any hitherto so wholly ignored?

The preceding paragraph is re-printed from a brief account of its objects written for the Eugenics Education Society, as a Society which amongst other purposes exists "to further eugenic teaching at home and in the schools and elsewhere." The difficulties of teaching this subject to children are more apparent than real. I may freely confess that though I have been speaking, writing, and thinking about eugenics for six years, I did not realize the importance of eugenic education until I heard the views of some of the women who belong to this Society, and even then I was at first sceptical as to its practicability. The subject has been entirely ignored by the pioneers of this matter. But if we turn to such a work as Forel's masterpiece we begin to realize that the eugenic education of children is the real beginning at the beginning, that it is in fact indispensable, and must be antecedent to all legislation in the direction of positive eugenics, though not to certain forms of legislation in the direction of negative eugenics.[1] In the earlier chapters of his great work Professor Forel offers the parent and the guardian abundant, detailed and accurate guidance as to the lines and methods of this teaching. It is urgently necessary for both sexes, but more especially for girls, who may suffer incredibly from the cruel prudery ordained by Mrs. Grundy, the only old woman to whom the word "hag" should be applied.

[1] For definition of these terms see p. 199 *et seq*

We must remove the reproach of Herbert Spencer nearly fifty years ago in words which may well be quoted: —

"The greatest defect in our programs of education is entirely overlooked. While much is being done in the detailed improvement of our systems in respect both of matter and manner, the most pressing desideratum, to prepare the young for the duties of life, is tacitly admitted to be the end which parents and schoolmasters should have in view; and happily, the value of the things taught, and the goodness of the methods followed in teaching them, are now ostensibly judged by their fitness to this end. The propriety of substituting for an exclusively classical training, a training in which the modern languages shall have a share, is argued on this ground. The necessity of increasing the amount of science is urged for like reasons. But though some care is taken to fit youth of both sexes for society and citizenship, no care whatever is taken to fit them for the position of parents. While it is seen that for the purpose of gaining a livelihood, an elaborate preparation is needed, it appears to be thought that for the bringing up of children, no preparation whatever is needed. While many years are spent by a boy in gaining knowledge of which the chief value is that it constitutes "the education of a gentleman"; and while many years are spent by a girl in those decorative acquirements which fit her for evening parties; not an hour is spent by either in preparation for that gravest of all responsibilities — the management of a family. Is it that this responsibility is but a remote contingency? On the contrary, it is sure to devolve on nine out of ten. Is it that the discharge of it is easy? Certainly not; of all functions which the adult has to fulfill, this is the most difficult. Is it that each may be trusted by self-instruction to fit himself, or herself, for the office of parent? No; not only is the need for such self-instruction unrecognized, but the complexity of the subject renders it the one of all others in which self-instruction is least likely to succeed."

THE LINES OF EUGENIC EDUCATION.—The teaching of the main facts of heredity must come first in order to the end of eugenic education. The vegetable world is at our service in this regard, the products of horticulture with their beauty and grace and novelty are illustrations one and all of what heredity means and what the due choice of parents will effect. There need be no personal allusions at this stage; the thing can be presented in an impersonal biological setting. And as heredity produces these wonderful results in plants, so also does it in the animal world. Numberless domestic forms are at our service. You take your children and your dog to the Zoological gardens, and show the resemblance between wolf and dog. What easier, then, than to point out that by consistent choosing for many generations of the least ferocious wolves, you may make a domesticated race?[1]

The mind of any child that has fortunately escaped education will make the transition for itself from subhuman races to mankind, and instances will occur, say, where extreme short-sightedness or deafness appears in children whose parents were similarly afflicted, and were perhaps closely related. At yet a later age a boy or girl may learn the doom which often falls upon the children of drunkards.

And then may it not be possible, when a little boy asks what he is to be when he grows up, to suggest that the highest profession to which he can be called, for which he may strive to make himself worthy, is fatherhood? And when the racial instinct awakes, would it be wrong, improper, indecent, to teach that it has a purpose, that no attribute of mind or body has a higher purpose, that this is holy ground? Or is it

[1] By some such means we may hope that man too may some day become domesticated without losing his fertility!

better that by silence, both as to the fact and as to its meaning, we should make it unmentionable, indecent, dishonorable? The Bible is used now-a-days as an instrument of political immorality, but if and when it should be employed for the function of other great literature, there is a passage sufficiently relevant to our present argument.[1]

Perhaps we are wrong in regarding and treating the racial instinct as if it were animal and low, a thing as far as possible to be ignored, repressed, treated with silent contempt in education and elsewhere. We may be wrong in practice because the method is not successful, because the development of this instinct is inevitable and little short of imperious in every normal child if that child is ever to become a man or a woman, and because our silence does not involve the silence of less responsible persons who are less likely even than we ourselves to teach the young inquirer that this thing exists for parenthood, and is therefore holy and to be treated as such.

Perhaps we are wrong in principle also, since that which exists for parenthood, and without which the continuance and future terrestrial hope of mankind is impossible, cannot be animal and low, unless human life, even at its best attained or attainable, be animal and low. Our business rather is to treat this great fact in a spirit worthy of the purpose for which it exists; and therefore, as part of that process of education by which we desire to make the young into reasonable, moral and fully human beings to teach explicitly, without unworthy shame, that this thing exists

[1] Corinthians xii, 22, 23, 24.

for the highest of purposes, that nothing which the future holds for boy or girl can conceivably be higher or happier than worthy parenthood, however commonplace that may appear to common eyes, and that accordingly this instinct is to be guarded, treated, used, honored as for parenthood, a fact which immediately raises it from the egoistic to the altruistic plane. We have to learn and to teach that worthy parenthood is the highest end which education can achieve — highest alike on the ground of its services to the individual and its services to the future, and the relation of the racial instinct to parenthood being what it is, we have to look upon it in that light, at once austere and splendid.

In the teaching of girls, only a false and disastrous prudery offers any great obstacle. The idea of motherhood is essentially natural to the normal girl. It is the eugenic education of boys that is more difficult, and the possibility of which will be questioned in some quarters, especially by those who regard the type of boy evolved in semi-monastic institutions, devoid of feminine influence, as a normal and unchangeable being. Co-educationists, however, are teaching us to revise that opinion, and will yet demonstrate, perhaps, that the inculcation of the idea of fatherhood is not so impossible nor so alien to the boy nature as some would suppose. If such a duty involved upon the present writer, he would feel inclined, perhaps, to present his teachings in terms of patriotism. He would urge that "there is no wealth but life"; that nations are made not of provinces or property but of people; that modern biology is teaching historians to explain such phenomena as the fall of Rome in terms of the quality of the national life; that therefore, individuals being mortal, parenthood necessarily takes its place as the supreme factor of national destiny; that the true patriotism must therefore concern itself with the conditions of the quality of parenthood — much less with its quantity; that the patriotism which ignores these truths is ignorant and must be disastrous: that we must turn our attention therefore from flag waving to questions of individual conduct; that if alcohol and syphilis, for instance, can be demonstrated to be what I would call racial poisons, the young patriot must make himself aware of their relation to parenthood, and must act upon his knowledge of that relation. It can thus be demonstrated that righteousness exalteth a nation not only in the spiritual but also in the most concrete sense.

To this we shall come. We may even recognize eugenic education as the most urgent need of the day, as the most radical and rational, perhaps even the most hopeful, of the methods by which the cleansing of the city, and much more, is to be achieved. We must create a eugenic aspect for the moral sense. We can associate this alike with individual and civic duty, and with those very ideals to which, as we all know, the young most readily respond. Thus I believe it shall be said of us in the after time that we have raised up the foundations of many generations.

And so, finally, the unselfish significance of marriage might conceivably be taught, alike to boys and girls, and especially in the case of undoubtedly good stocks might we inculcate, as Mr. Galton has pointed out, a rational pride in ancestry — that is to say, a rational pride in the quality of the germ-plasm which has been entrusted to us. And so may be cultivated a eugenic aspect of the moral sense — which is immeasurably more plastic than any but the student of moral ideas knows — and, thus endowed, the young man or woman will be prepared for the possibility of marriage. It is perfectly conceivable that in days to come the argument — in any case false — that affection never brooks control, may become wholly irrelevant, when there arises a generation in whose members there has been cultivated or created the eugenic sense. It is conceivable that, just as to-day the mere possibility of falling in love is arrested by any of a thousand trivial considerations, so misplaced affection may be incapable of arising because its possible object affronts the educated eugenic sense. The natural basis for such education already exists. But the natural eugenic sense still works mainly on the physical plane, and although we owe to it the maintenance of our present modest standard of physical beauty, we aim at higher ideals — and will one day thus attain them.

CHAPTER IX

THE SUPREMACY OF MOTHERHOOD

"The dregs of the human species — the blind, the deaf mute, the degenerate, the imbecile, the epileptic — are better protected than pregnant women."— BOUCHACOURT.

"I hold that the two crowning and most accursed sins of the society of this present day are the carelessness with which it regards the betrayal of women, and the brutality with which it suffers the neglect of children."— RUSKIN.

A CHAPTER must be included here concerning a question which can never safely be ignored in any consideration of race-culture, but the importance of which, as I think I see it, is recognized by no one who has concerned himself at all with this subject, from Mr. Francis Galton himself downwards. We must all be agreed, Mr. Galton declares, as to the propriety of breeding, if it be possible, for health, energy and ability, whatever else may be doubtful. To this I would add that, whether we are agreed or not, we must breed for motherhood, and that, even if we do not, we shall have to reckon with it. The general eugenic position, I fancy, is that the requirements which we should make of both sexes, the mothers of the future as well as the fathers, are essentially identical: but it seems to me that we have not yet reckoned with the vast importance of motherhood as a factor in the evolution of all the higher species of animals, and its absolute supremacy, inevitable and persistent whether recognized or ignored, in the case of man. Any system of eugenics or race-culture, any system of government, any proposal for social reform — as, for instance, the reduction of infant mortality — which fails to reckon with motherhood or falls short adequately appraising it, is foredoomed to failure and will continue to fail so long as the basal facts of human nature and the development of the human individual retain even approximately their present character. Whatever proposals for eugenics or race-culture be made or carried out, the fact will remain that the race is made up of mortal individuals; that every one of these begins its visible life as a helpless baby, and that the system which does not permit the babies to survive, *they* will not permit to survive. This is a general and universal proposition, admitting of no exceptions, past, present or to come. It applies equally to conscious systems of race-culture, to forms of marriage, to forms of government, to any other social institution or practice or character that can be named or conceived. Upon every one of these the babies pronounce a judgment from which there is no appeal, and the execution of which is never long postponed. The baby may be a potential Newton, Shakespeare, Beethoven or Buddha, but it is at its birth the most helpless thing alive, the potentialities of which avail it not one whit. It is in more need of care, immediate and continuous, than a baby microbe or a baby cat, whatever the unpublished glories of which its brain contains the promise; and in the total absence of any apparatus, mechanical, legal, or scientific, which can provide the mother's breast and the mother's love, individual motherhood, in its exquisitely complementary aspects, physical and psychical, will remain the dominant factor of history so long as the final judgments upon every present and the final determinations for every future lie in the hands of helpless babyhood — which will be the case so long as man is mortal. When, if ever, science, having previously conquered disease, identifies the cause of natural death and removes them, then motherhood and babyhood may be thrown upon the rubbish heap; but until that hour they are enthroned by natural law and can be dethroned only at the cost of certain and annihilative vengeance.

It is the master paradox that at his first appearance the lord of the earth should be the most helpless of living things. Consider a new-born baby. "Unable to stand, much less to wander in search of food; very nearly deaf; all but blind; well-nigh indiscriminating as to the nature of what is presented to its mouth; utterly unable to keep itself clean, yet highly susceptible to the effects of dirt; able to indicate its needs only by alternately turning its head, open-mouthed, from side to side and then crying; possessed of an almost ludicrously hypersensitive interior; unable to fast for more than two or three hours, yet having the most precise and complicated dietetic requirements; needing the most carefully maintained warmth; easily injured by draughts; the prey of bacteria (which take up a permanent abode in its alimentary canal by the eleventh day) — where is to be found a more complete picture of helpless dependence?" How comes it that this creature is to be lord of the earth, and a member of the only species which succeeds in continually multiplying itself?

MOTHERHOOD AND INTELLIGENCE.— We have maintained that the vital character which is of supreme survival-value for man is his intelligence, and this, as we know, is his unique possession. It is very largely for intelligence, therefore, that race-culture or eugenics proposes, if possible, to breed. But if there be certain conditions which must be complied with before intelligence can possibly be evolved, eugenics will come to disaster should it ignore them. These conditions do exist, and have hitherto been entirely ignored by all students of this question. Let certain great facts be observed.

Why is the human baby the most helpless of all creatures? Since it is to become the most capable, should it not, even in its infant state, show signs of its coming superiority? What is the meaning of this paradox?

The answer is that, so far as physical weapons of offense and defense are concerned, these have disappeared because intelligence makes them superfluous or even burdensome. But the peculiar helplessness of the human infant depends not upon its nakedness in the physical sense but upon its lack of very nearly all instinctive capacities. It is this absence of effective instincts which distinguishes the baby from the young of all other creatures. Why should its endowment in this respect be so inferior?

It is because of the fact that, if instinct is to give rise to intelligence, it must be plastic. A purely instinctive creature reacts to certain sets of circumstances in certain effortless, perfect and fixed ways. The reactions are the whole of its psychical life. They need no education, being as perfectly performed on the first occasion as on the last, and in many instances being performed only once in the whole history of the creature in question. But, on the other hand, they are almost incapable of education, and even in the cases where they lack absolute perfection at first, they only require the merest modicum of opportunity in order to acquire it. Perfect within their limits, they are yet most definitely limited. They never achieve the new, they are utterly at fault in novel circumstances, and they are wholly incapable of creating circumstances.

A creature cannot be at once purely instinctive and intelligent. An instinctive action is simply a compound reflex action, a highly adapted automatism: now automatism and intelligence are necessarily inversely proportional. It is possible for an intelligent creature to acquire automatisms, which are popularly described as instinctive. They are not instincts, however, but the acquired equivalents of instincts: "secondary automatisms." If they are used to replace intelligence, the individual, in so far, sinks from the human to the sub-human level. Their proper function is to leave the intelligence free for higher purposes more worthy of it than, say, the act of dressing oneself.

In order that an intelligent creature should be evolved it was necessary that instinct should become plastic. Intelligence could not be superposed upon a complete and final instinctive equipment. You cannot determine your own acts if they are already determined for you by your nervous organization. The incomparable superiority of intelligence depends upon its limitless and creative character, in virtue of which, as Disraeli puts it, "men are not the creatures of circumstances; circumstances are the creatures of men." But whilst intelligence can learn everything, it has everything to learn, and the most nearly intelligent creature whom the earth affords thus begins his independent life almost wholly bereft of all the instruments which have served the lower creatures so well, whilst, on the other hand, he is provided with an utterly undeveloped, and indeed, at that time non-existent, weapon which, even if it did exist, he could not use. Hence the unique helplessness of the human baby: one of the most wonderful and little appreciated facts in the whole of nature — effectively hidden from the glass eyes of the kind of man who calls a baby a "brat," but, to eyes that can see, not only the master paradox from the philosophical point of view but also a fact of the utmost moment from the practical point of view.

THE EVOLUTION OF MOTHERHOOD.— It directly follows that motherhood is supremely important in the case of man. It is the historical fact that its importance in the history of the animal world has been steadily increasing throughout æonian time. The most successful and ancient societies we know, those of the social insects, which antedate by incalculable ages even the first vertebrates, could not survive for a single generation without the motherhood or foster-motherhood to which the worker females sacrifice their lives and their own chances of physical maternity.

The development of maternal care may be steadily traced throughout the vertebrate series — *pari passu* with evolution of sexual relations towards the ideal of monogamy, which is ideal just because of its incomparable services to motherhood. But whilst motherhood is of the utmost service for lower creatures, ending always to lessen infant mortality — if it may be so called — and to increase the proportion of life to death and birth, it is of supreme service in the case of man because of the absolute dependence upon it of intelligence, the solitary but unexampled weapon with which he has won the earth. Hence in breeding for intelligence we cannot afford to ignore that upon which intelligence depends. Even if we could produce genius at will, we should find our young geniuses just as dependent upon motherhood as the common run of mankind. Newton himself was a seven months' baby, and the potentialities of gravitation and the calculus and the laws of motion in his brain could not save him: motherhood could and did.

Even our least biological reformers must admit that purely physical motherhood, up to the point of birth, can scarcely be omitted in any schemes for social reform or race-culture. Some of them will even admit that purely physical motherhood, so far as the mother's breasts are concerned, cannot wisely be dispensed with. The psychical aspects of motherhood, however, many of these writers — I do not call them thinkers — ignore. In relation to infant mortality — which is the most obvious symptom of causes productive of vast and widespread physical deterioration amongst the survivors, and which must be abolished before any really effective race-culture is possible — it is worth noting that motherhood cannot safely be superseded. I do not believe in the *crèche* or the municipal milk *depôt* except as stop-gaps, or as object-lessons for those who imagine that the slaughtered babies are not slaughtered but die of inherent defect, and that therefore infant mortality is a eugenic process. In working for the reduction of this evil we must work through and by motherhood. In some future age, displaying the elements of sanity, our girls will be instructed in these matters. At present the most important profession in the world is almost entirely carried on by unskilled labor, and until this state is put an end to, it is almost idle to talk of race-culture at all. But under our present system of education, false and rotten as it is in principles and details alike, it is necessary for us to send visitors to the homes of the classes which, in effect, supply almost the whole of the future population of the country, and to establish schools for mothers on every hand.

PSYCHICAL MOTHERHOOD.— I confess myself opposed to the principle of bribing a woman to become a mother, whether overtly or covertly, whether in the guise of State-aid or in the form of eugenic premiums for maternity. It may sound very well to offer a bonus for the production of babies by mothers whom the State or any eugenic power considers fit and worthy. But though the bonus may help motherhood in its physical aspects, the importance of which no one questions, I do not see what service it renders to motherhood in its psychical aspects — which are at least equally important. What is the outlook for the baby when the bonus is spent? In fact, with all deference to Mr. Galton, and with such deference as may be due to the literary triflers who have discussed this matter, I am inclined to think that a cardinal requisite for a mother is love of children. Ignorant this may be, and indeed at first always is, but if it is there it can be instructed. The woman who does not think the possession of a baby a sufficient prize is no fit object, I should say, for any other kind of bribe or lure. The woman who "would rather have a spare bedroom" than a "baby" is the woman whom I do not want to have a baby. Thus I look with suspicion on any proposals which assume that the psychical elements of motherhood are of little moment in eugenics. I see no sign or prospect that they can be dispensed with, and I think eugenics is going to work on wrong lines if it proposes to ignore them. Even if you turn out Nature with a fork she will yet return — *tamen usque recurret*.

In this question we should be able to derive great assistance from biography. Real guidance, I believe, is obtained from this source, but only a pitiable fraction of that which should be obtained. Scientific biography is yet to seek, and it is the ironical fact that when Herbert Spencer, in his *Autobiography*, devoted a large amount of space to the discussion of *both* his parents and their relatives, the literary critics were bored to death. Nevertheless, we cannot know too much about the ancestry, on both sides, and the early environment of great men. At present it is always tacitly assumed that a great man is the son of his father alone. The biographer would probably admit, if pressed, that doubtless some woman or other was involved in the matter, and that her name was so and so — if any one thinks it worth mentioning. On the score of heredity alone, however, we derive, men and women alike, with absolute equality from both parents; and we cannot know too much about the mothers of men of genius. Such knowledge would often avail us materially in cases where the paternal ancestry offers little explanation of the child's destiny.

We do owe, however, to great men themselves many warm and unqualified tributes to their mothers, not on the score of heredity, but on the score of the psychical aspects of motherhood. This, indeed, is one of the great lessons of biography which some eugenists have forgotten. It is all very well to breed for intelligence, but intelligence needs nurture and guidance, and that need is the more urgent, the more powerful and original the intelligence in question. The physical functions of motherhood from the moment of birth onwards can be effected, no doubt, though at very great cost, by means of incubators and milk laboratories, and so forth. But there is no counterfeiting or replacing the psychical component of complete maternity, and a generation of the highest intelligence borne by unmaternal women would probably succeed only in writing the blackest and maddest page in history.

THE EUGENIC DEMAND FOR LOVE.— Mr. Galton desires that we breed for physique, ability, and energy. But we also need more love, and we must breed for that. Nothing is easier or more inevitable once we make human parenthood conscious and deliberate. When children are born only to those who love children, and who will tend to transmit their high measure of that parental instinct from which all love is derived, we shall bring to earth a heaven compared with which the theologians' is but a fool's paradise.

The first requisite, then, for the mothers of the future, the elements of physical health being assumed, is that they should be motherly. They may or may not, in addition, be worthy of such exquisite titles as "the female Shakespeare of America," but they must have motherliness to begin with. For this indispensable thing there is no substitute. It must certainly be granted, and the fact should not be ignored, that the hidden spring of motherliness in a girl may be revealed only by actual maternity, and the frivolous damsel who used to think babies "silly squalling things" may be mightily transformed when the silly squalling thing is her own — and the Fifth Symphony sound and fury signifying nothing compared with its slightest whimper. I will grant even that the maternal instinct is so deeply rooted and universal that its absence must be regarded as either a rare abnormality or else as the product of the grossest mal-education in the wide sense. But the reader will not blame me for insisting at such length upon what, as he would think, no one could deny, when he discovers that these salient truths are denied, and that in what should be the sacred name of eugenics, they are openly flouted and defied.

Before we go on to consider these perversions of a

great idea, it may briefly be observed that, though fatherhood is historically a mushroom growth compared with motherhood, and though its importance is vastly less, yet as a complementary principle, aiding and abetting motherhood, and making for its most perfect expression, fatherhood played a great part in animal evolution, in the right line of progress, ages before man appeared upon the earth at all, and that its work is not yet done. To this subject we must return. Meanwhile it is well to note the dangers with which eugenics is at present threatened in the form of certain proposals which, if for a time they became popular — and they have elements making for popularity — would inevitably throw the gravest discredit upon the whole subject.

EUGENICS AND THE FAMILY.— Certain remarkable tendencies invoking the name of eugenics are now to be observed in Germany. These have considerable funds, much enthusiasm, journalistic support, and even a large measure of assistance in academic circles. In pursuance of the idea of eugenics there is a movement the nature of which is indicated by the following quotation from a private letter:—

"I wonder if your attention was drawn to the German projects of the reform of the Family. They all aim at improving the German race and rendering decisive its superiority over all others. The means seem to be too revolutionary. The more modern wish the establishment of the matriarchal family (*ein nach Mutterrecht*), the more logical require universal polygamy and polyandry, an individualization of Society. Others hope to increase the production of German geniuses by the 'hellenic friendship.' [!] The three movements are strongly organized, command large pecuniary means, a phalanx of original and prolific writers, and enthusiastic devotion to their cause. More

even than the support of Courts and aristocracy is, in my eyes, that of the Universities. It is there that the destinies of Germany have always been shaped, and if they are determined to reform the Family in that way, it will be done. . . . The Herren Professoren are terribly in earnest, yet they say things which even to the least prejudiced minds appear ridiculous and even vulgar. Still, their projects have some relation to Eugenics, and to Sociology in general."

This sufficiently indicates the dangers run by the eugenic principle at the hands of those who see in it an instrument of protest and rebellion against established things. We dare not repudiate the sacred principles of protest and rebellion, which have been the conditions of all progress, but believing in motherhood as we must, believing it to be authorized by nature herself and not by any human conventions, we must deplore any tendencies such as the two last cited. For us in this country, however, a more immediate interest attaches to the views of a much admired and discussed writer who claims to be a social philosopher of the first order, and whose claims must now be examined.

The opinions of Mr. Bernard Shaw on the question of eugenics may be quoted from his contribution to the subject published in *Sociological Papers* 1904, pp. 74, 75, in discussion of Mr. Galton's great paper. Mr. Shaw begins by saying: "I agree with the paper and go so far as to say that there is now no reasonable excuse for refusing to face the fact that nothing but a eugenic religion can save our civilization from the fate that has overtaken all previous civilizations." And further:—

"I am afraid we must make up our minds either to face a considerable shock to vulgar opinion in this matter or to let eugenics alone. . . . What we must fight for is freedom to breed the race without being hampered by the mass of irrelevant conditions implied in the institution of marriage. If our morality is attacked, we can carry the war into the enemy's country by reminding the public that the real objection to breeding by marriage is that marriage places no restraint on debauchery, so long as it is monogamic. . . . What we need is freedom for people who have never seen each other before and never intend to see one another again, to produce children under certain definite public conditions, without loss of honor."

The conception of individual fatherhood here stated involves a deliberate reversion to the order of the beast: it excludes individual fatherhood from any function in aiding motherhood or in serving the future. It involves, of course, the total abolition of the family. It denies and flouts the very best elements in human nature. It assumes that the best women will find motherhood worth while without the interest and sympathy and help and protection of the father. It does not, however, condemn or exclude the psychical functions of motherhood, since so far as this quotation goes it might be assumed that the mother would be permitted to live with her own child. On this point, however, Mr. Shaw offered us further guidance in his controversy with myself in the *Pall Mall Gazette,* in December, 1907. One or two of his *dicta* must here be quoted — they followed upon my remark, "Anything less like a mother than the State I find it hard to imagine":—

"When the State left the children to the mothers, they got no schooling; they were sent out to work under inhuman conditions, under-ground and over-ground for atrociously long hours, as soon as they were able to walk; they died of typhus fever in heaps; they grew up to be as wicked to their own children as their parents had been to them. State socialism rescued them from the worst of that, and means to rescue them from all of it. I now publicly challenge Dr. Saleeby to propose, if he dares, to withdraw the hand of the State and abandon the children to their mothers as they fall. . . . All I need say is that before Dr. Saleeby can persuade me to sacrifice the future of human society to his maternalism, he will have to tackle me with harder weapons than the indignant enthusiasm of a young man's mother worship."

Mr. Shaw's teaching constitutes a brutal and deliberate libel upon the highest aspects of womanhood. For his own purposes he attributes to the mothers all the abominations which, as every one knows, have lain and in some measure still lie, at the door of the State. The man who has this opinion of motherhood is complacently ignorant of the elements of the subject. His charge is denied by every one who has worked as doctor or nurse or visitor or missionary amongst the poorer classes, and knows that the mothers there met are of the very salt of the earth.

It is well to state plainly here that these utterly irresponsible *dicta* have absolutely no relation or resemblance whatever to the opinions or proposals of Mr. Francis Galton himself, who desires to effect race-culture through marriage, and whose whole propaganda is based upon this assumption. This we shall afterwards see. Meanwhile we may note Mr. Galton's own words: "The aim of eugenics is to bring as many influences as can be reasonably employed, to cause the useful classes in the community to contribute *more* than their proportion to the next generation." Mr. Galton would be the first to assert that influences designed to supersede motherhood and to abolish everything but the physical aspect of fatherhood, would not be reasonable but insane in the highest degree.

The idea of race-culture without fatherhood or motherhood, except in the mere physiological sense, constitutes a denial of the greatest facts in evolution, as we have seen. It ignores everything that is known and daily witnessed regarding the development of the individual, and the formation of character, without which intelligence is a curse. There is not the slightest fear that any such reversion to the order of the beast is possible, absolutely forbidden as it is by the laws of human nature. There is, however, reasonable ground for apprehension, especially when the recent developments in Germany are remembered, that the public may obtain its notions of eugenics in a highly-garbled form.[1]

It must be asserted as fervently and plainly as possible that, if the idea of race-culture is even in the smallest degree to be realized, it must work through motherhood and fatherhood not less in their psychical than in their physical aspects. It is time to have done with the gross delusions of Nietzsche regarding the nature and course of organic evolution. Morality is not an invention of man but man the child of morality,

[1] Mr. G. K Chesterton, one of the most amusing of contemporary phenomena, has lately said, "The most serious sociologists, the most stately professors of eugenics, calmly propose that for the good of the race people should be forcibly married to each other by the police." Readers unacquainted with Mr. Chesterton's standard of accuracy and methods of criticism, might be misled by this inexcusable nonsense.

and it is not by the abolition of motherhood, in which morality originated, nor of fatherhood, its first ally, that the super-man is to be evolved: but by the attainment of those lofty conceptions of the function, the responsibility and the privilege of parenthood which it is the first business of eugenics to inculcate.

As for marriage, invaluable though at its best it be for the completion and ennoblement of the individual life, its great function for society and for the race is in relation to childhood. Thus considered, the dictum of Professor Westermarck may be understood, that children are not the result of marriage but marriage the result of children. This, in other words, is to say that marriage has become evolved and established as a social institution because of its services to race-culture. This great subject must next occupy our attention.

CHAPTER X

MARRIAGE AND MATERNALISM

OUR present concern is the relation of marriage to race-culture, and for this purpose we must investigate an epoch ages before the institution of human marriage, ages before mankind itself. We must first remind ourselves of what may be called the trend of progress from the first in respect of that reproduction upon which all species depend, all living individuals being mortal.

At first, in the effort for survival and increase, life tried the quantitative method. If we take the present day bacteria as representatives of the primitive method, we see that not quality nor individuality but quantity and numbers are the means by which, in their case, life seeks to establish itself more abundantly. We express our own birth-rate in its proportion per year, to one thousand living: but twenty thousand bacteria injected into a rabbit have been found to multiply into twelve thousand million in one day. "One bacterium has been actually observed to rear a small family of eighty thousand within a period of twenty-four hours." "The cholera bacillus can duplicate every twenty minutes, and might thus in one day become 5,000,000,000,000,000,000,000, with the weight, according to the calculations of Cohn, of about 7,366 tons. In a few days, at this rate, there would be a mass of bacteria as big as the moon, huge enough to fill the whole ocean."

If now we trace the history of life up to man, we find in him — as we have seen — the lowest birth-rate of any animal in proportion to his body weight, the longest ante-natal period, the longest period of maternal feeding, and by far the lowest infant mortality and general death-rate. A chief fact of progress has been, in a word, the supersession of the quantitative by the qualitative criterion of survival-value. Immeasurably vast vital economy and efficiency have thus been effected. The tendency of progress, in short — a tendency coincident with the evolution of ever higher and higher species — is to pass from the horrible Gargantuan wastefulness of the older methods towards the evident but yet lamentably unrealized ideal — that every child born shall reach maturity. This great historical tendency, which will ultimately involve the restriction of parenthood to the fit, fine and relatively few, has occurred under the impartial rule of natural selection simply and solely because it has endowed with survival-value the successive species in which it has been demonstrated.

THE RISE OF PARENTHOOD.— Consistently with this fact and with the argument of the previous chapter is the tendency towards the lengthening of infancy, a very characteristic condition of the evolution of the higher forms of life. This lengthening and accentuation of infancy makes for variety of development and, as we have seen, is supremely instanced in man, where it depends upon the transmutation of fixed instincts into the plastic thing we call intelligence. Thus, to quote the words of Dr. Parsons,[1] "we find that as infancy is prolonged in the progress of species, the care given to offspring by parents is increased. It extends over a longer period and it is directed more and more towards the total welfare of offspring. The need of a potentially many-sided and enduring kind of parental care is filled through the social group we call the family."

Apart from these immensely significant creatures, the social insects, we find well-marked though primitive signs of motherhood amongst the fishes, and in a few cases, such as the stickleback, the beginnings of fatherhood. But it is not until we reach the mammals, and especially the monkeys and apes, that we find a great development of motherhood, far more prolonged and far more important than the more frequently extolled parental care found amongst the birds.

Very interesting, however, in the case of the fishes is the fact observed by Sutherland that "as soon as the slightest trace of parental care is discovered the chance of survival is increased and the birth-rate is lowered." As a general summary these words of Dr. Parsons will serve:—"Diminution of offspring is a threefold gain to a species. (1) It lessens the vital drain upon the parent. (2) It enables the size and capacity of the limited number of offspring to be increased. (3) In the case of the higher developments of parental care after birth, it concentrates the advantage of that care upon a few instead of

[1] *The Family*, p. 20.

scattering it, thereby weakening its influence, upon many."

Now how are these facts connected with that relation between the parents which we call marriage, temporary or permanent, foreshadowed or perfected? *It may be submitted that the racial function or survival-value of marriage in all its forms, low or high, animal or human, consists in its services to the principle of motherhood, these services depending upon the help and strength which are afforded to motherhood by fatherhood.*

ANIMAL MARRIAGE.—Let us now look very briefly at the facts of animal marriage from this point of view. The phrase, animal marriage, may possibly offend the reader, but is there any reason to be offended at the suggestion that the principle of marriage actually has a warrant older even than mankind? It has lately been pointed out by a distinguished naturalist, Mr. Ernest Thompson Seton, that animals, like men, have long been groping, so to say, for an ideal form of marriage. We now know, as will be shown, that, contrary to popular opinion, promiscuity does not prevail amongst the lowest races of men. Equally false is the popular notion that promiscuity prevails amongst most of the lower animals. Promiscuity, it is true, does occur, but so also does strict monogamy, "and promiscuous animals, such as rabbits and voles, while high in the scale of fecundity, are low in the scale of general development." Says Mr. Seton: " It is commonly remarked that while the Mosaic law did not expressly forbid polygamy, it surrounded marriage with so many restrictions that by living up to the spirit of them the Hebrew ultimately was forced into pure monogamy. It is extremely interesting to note that the animals, in their blind groping for an ideal form of union, have gone through the same stages, and have arrived at exactly the same conclusion. Monogamy is their best solution of the marriage question, and is the rule among all the higher and more successful animals."

The moose, Mr. Seton tells us, has several wives in one season but only one at a time. The hawks practice monogamy lasting for one season, "the male staying with the family, and sharing the care of the young till they are well-grown." The wolves consort for life, but the death of one leaves the other free to mate again. There is a fourth method "in which they pair for life, and, in case of death, the survivor remains disconsolate and alone to the end. This seems absurd. It is the way of the geese." The point especially to be insisted upon as regards animal marriage is its evident service to their race-culture, in accordance with the principle here laid down that *marriage is of value because it supports motherhood by fatherhood*, and that its different forms are of value in proportion as they do so more or less effectively. We may note also, as a corollary to this, that marriage must be more important in proportion as the young of a species are helpless and in proportion as their helplessness is long continued. The importance of marriage for man, therefore, must necessarily be higher than for any of the lower animals.

HUMAN MARRIAGE.— We must turn now to human marriage, and the principle which we must remember is that of survival-value. We are discussing a natural phenomenon exhibited by living creatures. This is what so few people realize when they speak of marriage. They cannot disabuse themselves of the idea that it is a human invention, and especially an ecclesiastical invention. Thus, on one hand, it is supported by persons who base its claims on mystical or dogmatic grounds; whilst, on the other hand, it is attacked by those who are opposed to ecclesiasticism or religion of any kind, and attacked in the name of science — in which, if the fact could only be recognized, is found every possible warrant and sanction, and indeed imperative demand, for this most precious of all institutions. Here we must endeavor to look upon it as an exceedingly ancient fact of life, vastly more ancient than mankind; and judging it and explaining it we must apply Nature's universal criterion, which is that of its survival-value or service to race-culture. Let us then glance very briefly at the actual facts of human marriage — conceived as an institution by which the survival-value of fatherhood is added to that of motherhood.

The pioneer student of marriage from the standpoint of science was Herbert Spencer, who, with great labor, supported the conclusion that monogamy is the highest, best and latest form of marriage. But in the absence of the great mass of evidence which is now before us, Spencer too readily assumed the truth of the popular notion that promiscuity was the primitive state, and taught that human marriage has developed from this through polygamy towards the ideal of monogamy. The work of Professor Westermarck, however — Spencer's chief follower in this path — has shown, and later writers have abundantly confirmed it, that this primitive promiscuity never existed. There is no nation or race or clan of man now extant, however primitive or barbaric, that has not definite marriage laws; there is no society on earth, however rude, that does not punish the unfaithful wife. Furthermore, polygamy, the only historical rival of monogamy, is now known to have played a quite trivial part in history, not merely compared with monogamy, but as compared with that which it was supposed to have played. Even in countries which we call polygamus to-day, polygamy is the relatively rare exception and monogamy is the rule. On this most important question it is well, however, to quote the words of Professor Westermarck himself:—

> "The great majority of peoples are, as a rule, monogamous, and the other forms of marriage are usually modified in a monogamous direction." "As to the history of the forms of human marriage, two inferences regarding monogamy and polygyny may be made with absolute certainty; monogamy, always the predominant form of marriage, has been more prevalent at the lowest stages of civilization than at somewhat higher stages; whilst, at a still higher stage, polygyny has again, to a great extent, yielded to monogamy." "We may thus take it for granted that civilization, up to a certain point, is favorable to polygyny; but it is equally certain that in its highest forms it leads to monogamy." "But, though civilization up to a certain point is favorable to polygyny, *its higher forms invariably and necessarily lead to monogamy.*"

It is the principle of survival-value that explains the dominance of monogamy at all stages of human society — with the single exception of continuously and wholly militant societies, in which polygamy obtained in consequence of the great numerical excess of women. It is the fate of the children, in which everything is involved, that has determined the history of human marriage. Furthermore, we may see here one more illustration of the truth that quality is ousting quantity in the course of progress, and that a low birth-rate represents a more advanced stage than a high birth-rate. The birth-rate under polygamy is undoubtedly high, but polygamy does not make for the survival and health of the children, and the infant mortality is gigantic. As I have said elsewhere, "the form of marriage which does not permit the babies to survive, *they* do not permit to survive. There is the beginning and the end of the whole matter in a nutshell. It is not a question of the father's taste and fancy, but of what he leaves above ground when the worms are eating him below. . . . No system yet conceived can compare for a moment with monogamy in respect of the one criterion which time and death recognize, the fate of the children."

In a word, the wholly adequate and only possible explanation of the historical fact of the dominance of monogamy is its supreme survival-value. It has competed with every other kind of sex relation and has been selected by natural selection because of its supreme service for race-culture — the most perfect conceivable addition of fatherhood to motherhood.

Plato and motherhood.— Thus eugenics must repudiate not only the ideas of Mr. Shaw on this subject, but the teaching of Plato, from whom Mr. Shaw's ideas on this particular subject are apparently derived.

It is in the fifth book of his *Republic* that the pioneer eugenist lays down his ideas for race-culture. He realized, indeed, the importance, after birth, of the nurture of children —" it is of considerable, nay, of the utmost importance to the State, when this is rightly performed or otherwise;" and he refers also to their nurture while very young, " in the period between their generation and their education, which seems to be the most troublesome of all." His method involved a complete community of wives and children amongst the guardians of the State, and on no account were the parents to know their own children nor the children their parents. The best were to be chosen for parents, on the analogy of animal race-culture by man. The children of inferior parents were to be killed. The others were to be conveyed to the common nursery of the city, but every precaution was to be taken that *no mother should know her own child.* This practice was to be the cardinal point of the Republic and " the cause of the greatest good to the city."

We see here, then, that the very first proposals for race-culture involved the destruction of marriage and the family, and a total denial of the value of the psychical aspects of motherhood and fatherhood alike. Plato's first critic, however, his own great pupil Aristotle, devoted the best part of his work, the *Polities,* to showing that the suggestions of Plato were not only wrong in themselves, but would not secure his end. Aristotle showed, in the words of Mr. Barker, that " the destruction of the family, and the substitution in its place of one vast clan, would lead but to the destruction of warm feelings, and the substitution of a sentiment which is to them as water is to wine. . . . So with the system of common marriage, as opposed to monogamy. The one encourages at best a poor and shadowy sentiment, while it denies to man the satisfaction of natural instinct and the education of family life; the other is natural and right, both because it is based on those instincts, and because it satisfies the moral nature of man, in giving him objects of permanent yet vivid interest above and beyond himself." The truth of this matter is that the rest may reason and welcome — but we fathers know.

MARRIAGE A EUGENIC INSTRUMENT.— It has definitely to be stated, then, that the abolition of marriage and the family is in no degree whatever a part of the eugenic proposal. We desire to achieve race-culture by and through marriage, on the lines which indeed many lower races of men successfully practice at the present day. We must make parenthood more responsible, not less so. It will afterwards be shown that the suggested incompatibility between marriage and the family, on the one hand, and race-culture or eugenics on the other, does not exist. It will be shown that we have in marriage not only the greatest instrument of race-culture that has yet been employed — half-consciously — by man, but also an instrument supremely fitted, and indeed without a rival, for the conscious, deliberate, and scientific intentions of modern eugenists. The applicability of marriage for this purpose will be shown by reference to actual facts. Mr. Galton himself has shown how effectively an educated public opinion can employ marriage for the purposes of race-culture, its services to which have indeed led to its evolution. It has furthermore to be added that only the formation of public opinion can ever lead to the ideal which we desire. This opinion already exists in some degree as regards one or two transmissible diseases, and, though without adequate scientific warrant, as regards the marriage of first cousins. In these respects it is not without some measure of effectiveness and the fact is of the utmost promise.

"Marriage," said Goethe, "is the origin and the summit of all civilization." Perhaps it would be more accurate to say *the family* rather than *marriage*. The childless marriage may be and often is a thing of the utmost beauty and value to the individuals concerned, but it is certainly not the origin of civilization, and if it be its summit it is also its grave. The eugenic support of marriage, therefore, depends upon a belief in the family, and that form of marriage will commend itself which provides the best form of family. From the point of view of certain eugenists, polygamy would be desirable in many cases, as extending the parental opportunities of the man of fine physique or intellectual distinction. The problem remains, however, as to the nurture of the children so obtained, and historical study returns us a very clear answer as to the relative merits of the polygamous family and the monogamous family. It is this last that pre-eminently justifies itself on the score of its services to childhood and therefore to the race. Its survival is a matter of absolute certainty, because of its survival-value. Neither Plato nor Mr. Shaw, nor any kind of collectivist legislation will permanently abolish it.

THE PRINCIPLE OF MATERNALISM.— The merits of monogamy can be defined in terms of the principle which I would venture to call maternalism — the principle of the permanent and radical importance of motherhood and whatever institutions afford it the greatest aid.

Maternalism would point, I think, to the supreme paradox that the dominant creature of the earth is born of woman, and born the most absolutely helpless of all living creatures whatsoever, animal or vegetable; it would note that this utter dependence upon others, mother or foster-mother, is not only the most unqualified known, but the longest maintained; it would observe that of all the human beings now alive, all that have lived, all that are to be, not one could survive its birth for twenty-four hours but for motherhood; it would note that only motherhood has rendered possible the development of instinct into that intelligence which, itself dependent upon motherhood for the possibility of its development, has dependent upon it the fact that the earth is now man's and the fulness thereof; and to the advocates of all the political-isms that can be named, and the small proportion of them that can be defined, it would apply its specific criterion. Do you regard the safeguarding and the ennoblement of motherhood as the proximate end of all political action, the end through which the ultimate ends, the production and recognition of human worth, can alone be attained; do you realize that marriage is invaluable *because* it makes for the enthronement of motherhood as nothing else ever did or can; do you realize that, metaphors about State maternity notwithstanding, the

State has neither womb nor breasts, these most reverend and divine of all vital organs being the appanage of the individual mother alone?

The maternalist principle being assumed, and the value of monogamy on the ground that it supports motherhood by fatherhood, the forthcoming discussion as to the possibilities of race-culture will assume the persistence of monogamy and will center upon the possibility of selecting or rejecting, for the purposes of race-culture, those who are available for entrance into the marriage state. The reader who has not studied social anthropology — and this is true of nearly all the critics of eugenics, very few of whom have studied anything — will be astounded, I believe, to discover the practically unlimited extent to which public opinion, whether or not formulated as law, has always been capable of controlling marriage, and therefore, race-culture.

Proposed definition of marriage.— Recognizing the existence of subhuman marriage, we may be at a loss to define marriage as distinguished from sex-relations in general. It is that form of sex-relation which involves or is adapted to *common parental care* of the offspring — the support of motherhood by fatherhood.

PART II

THE PRACTICE OF EUGENICS

N'abandonnons pas l'avenir de notre race à la fatalité d'Allah; créons-le nous-mêmes.— Forel.

"It is surprising how soon a want of care, or care wrongly directed, leads to the degeneration of a domestic race; but except in the case of man himself, hardly any one is so ignorant as to allow his worst animals to breed.

"With savages, the weak in body or mind are soon eliminated, and those that survive commonly exhibit a vigorous state of health. We civilized men, on the other hand, do our utmost to check the process of elimination; we build asylums for the imbecile, the maim and the sick; we institute poor laws; and our medical men exert their utmost skill to save the life of every one to the last moment. . . . Thus the weak members of civilized societies propagate their kind. No one who has attended to the breeding of domestic animals will doubt that this must be highly injurious to the race of man."— Darwin, *The Descent of Man*, 1871, Pt. i., chap. v.

CHAPTER XI

NEGATIVE EUGENICS

HITHERTO we have mainly concerned ourselves with broad aspects of theory, endeavoring to prove that conscious race-culture is a necessity for any civilization which is to endure, and to show how alone it can be effected. But evidently for a great many of the practical proposals that might be, and for not a few that have been, based upon these views, public opinion is not ripe. We may be thankful to believe that for some it will never be ripe: it would be rotten first. Marriage, for instance, we hold sacred and essential: we find intolerable the idea of the human stud-farm; we are very dubious as to the help of surgery; we are much more than dubious as to the lethal chamber. It is necessary to be reasonable, and, in seeking the superman, to remain at least human. Now if we were to achieve any immediate success we must clearly divide our proposals, as the present writer did some years ago, with Mr. Galton's approval, into two classes: *positive eugenics* and *negative eugenics.* The one would seek to encourage the parenthood of the most desirable, the other to discourage the parenthood of the least desirable. Positive eugenics is the original eugenics, but, as the writer endeavored to show at the time, negative eugenics is one with it in principle. The two are complementary, and are both practiced by Nature: natural selection is one with natural rejection. To choose is to refuse.

In regard to positive eugenics I, for one, must ever make the criticism that I cannot believe in the propriety of attempting to bribe into parenthood people who have no love of children: we have to consider the parental environment of the children we desire, as well as their innate quality. Thus, positive eugenics must largely take the form, at present, of removing such disabilities as now weigh upon the desirable members of the community, especially of the more prudent sort.

For instance, it was recently pointed out by a correspondent of the *Morning Post* that in Great Britain, despite the alarm caused by the decreasing marriage-rate, no one has protested against —

". . . the tax which the propertied middle classes have to pay on marriage. . . . To take a few instances. Two persons each having £160 a year marry. Previous to marriage they were exempt from income tax; after marriage they pay £6 per annum. Two persons each having £400 a year pay £18 before and £30 after marriage. Similarly the additional income tax payable on marriage by people each having £600 a year is £9, by those having £1,200 a year £30, and by those having £2,000 a year £50. It is difficult to see how our legislators arrived at this result unless they started to average the incomes of married people and then forgot to divide by two. . . . If, as I contend, a man and his wife should be counted as two people, not one, should not children also be counted in any scheme of graduated taxation, and an income be divided by the number of persons it has to support in order to fix the rate at which the tax is to be charged? It is ridiculous to suppose that a man with a wife and six children is as well off on £1,000 a year as a bachelor with the same income. It is, I believe, acknowledged that the moderately well-off professional classes marry later and have fewer children than the wage-earners, and I think there can be no doubt that the special burden they have to bear is a material influence contributing to this result. Thus, while we are deploring the decadence of the race, the State is doing what it can to discourage marriage in a class whose children would in all probability prove its most valued citizens."

But it is in negative eugenics that we can accomplish most at this stage, and in so doing can steadily educate public opinion, the professional jesters notwithstanding. There is here a field for action which does not demand a great revolution in the popular point of view; and, further, does not require us to wait for certainty until the facts and laws of heredity have been much further elucidated. The services which a conscious race-culture, thus directed, may even now accomplish, can scarcely be over-estimated; and even if we cannot reach the public heart at once we can reach the public head by means of the public pocket — which will benefit obviously and greatly when these proposals are carried out. As Thoreau observes, for a thousand who are lopping off the branches of an evil there is but one striking at its roots. If we strike at the roots of certain grave and costly evils of the present day, we shall abundantly demonstrate that this is a matter of the most vital economy.

THE DEAF AND DUMB.— We might begin with the case of the *deaf and dumb*, since the facts here are utterly beyond dispute. The condition known as deaf-mutism is congenital or due to innate defect in about one-half of all the cases in Great Britain. Says Dr. Love,[1] "In every institution examples may be found of deaf-mute children who have one or two deaf par-

[1] *Encyclopædia Medica*, vol. ii., Article "Deaf-Mutism."

ents or grandparents, and of two or more deaf-mute children belonging to one family." A recent report from Japan is of a similar order, and the evidence might be multiplied indefinitely. The obvious conclusion that the inherently deaf should not marry "is generally conceded by those who work amongst the deaf, but the present arrangements for the education of the deaf, and their management in missions and institutes for the deaf during the period of adolescence, is eminently fitted to encourage union between the congenitally deaf. If not during the school period, at least during the period of adolescence, everything should be done to discourage the association of the deaf and dumb with each other, and the danger of their meeting with those similarly afflicted should be constantly kept before the congenitally deaf by those in charge of them." Dr. Love quotes the following newspaper report: "At an inquest yesterday, on Will Earnshaw, 59, a St. Pancras saddler, it was stated that the relatives could not identify the body, as the wife and sister were blind, deaf and dumb, and that the four children were deaf and dumb. The deceased was deaf and dumb, and was so when he was married."

THE FEEBLE-MINDED.—The case of the *feeble-minded* is of course parallel. The problem would be at once reduced to negligible proportions if all cases of feeble-mindedness were dealt with as they should be. These unfortunate people might lead quite happy lives, the utmost be done for their feeble capacities, the supreme demands of the law of love be completely but providently complied with. The feeble-minded girl might be protected from herself and from others

— her fate otherwise is often too deplorable for definition — and the interests of the future be not compromised. These two words were written whilst awaiting the long overdue Report of the Royal Commission on this subject — which abundantly confirms them. The proportion of the mentally defective in Great Britain is now 0.83 per cent.: and it is doubtless rising yearly. Only by the recognition and application of negative eugenics can this evil be cured. I have elsewhere [1] discussed the supposed objection which will be raised in the name of "liberty" by persons who think in words instead of realities. The right care of the feeble-minded involves the greatest happiness and liberty and self-development possible for them. The interests of the individual and the race are one. What liberty has the feeble-minded prostitute, such as our streets are filled with?

THE INSANE.—As regards obvious *insanity,* the same principles of negative eugenics must be enforced. It is probably fair to say that the whole trend of modern research has been to accentuate the importance, if not indeed the indispensableness, of the inherent or inherited factor in the production of insanity. Yet, on the other hand, the trend of treatment of the insane has undoubtedly been towards permitting them more liberty, sometimes of the kind which the principles of race-culture must condemn. It is well, of course, that we should be humane in our treatment of the insane. It is well that curative medicine should do its utmost for them, and it seems well, at first sight, that the pro-

[1] In a lecture, "The Obstacles to Eugenics," delivered before the Sociological Society, March 8, 1909.

portion of discharges from asylums on the score of recovery should be as high as it is. But at this point the possibility of the gravest criticism evidently arises. I have no intention whatever of exposing the question of race-culture to legitimate criticism by laying down dogmatically any doctrines as to the perpetual incarceration of insane persons, including those who have been, but are not now, insane. Pope was of course right when he hinted at the nearness of the relation between *certain forms* of genius and certain forms of insanity. It may well be that if we could provide a fit environment we might welcome the children of some of those, highly and perhaps uniquely gifted in brain, who, under the stress of the ordinary environment of modern life, have broken down for greater or longer periods. On the other hand, there are forms of insanity which, beyond all dispute, should utterly preclude their victims from parenthood. As a result of recent controversies it seems on the whole probable, if not certain, that the apparent persistent increases in the proportion of the insane in civilized countries generally during many years past, is a real increase, and not due simply to such factors as more stringent certification or increase of public confidence in lunatic asylums. If, then, there be in process a real increase in the proportion of the insane, who will question that no time should be lost in ascertaining the extent — undoubtedly most considerable — to which the principles of negative eugenics can be invoked in order to arrest it?

As regards *epilepsy* and *epileptic insanity* there can be no question. There is, of course, such a thing as acquired epilepsy, and we may even assume for the sake of the argument that no inherent and therefore transmissible factor of predisposition is involved in such cases. Yet, wholly excluding them, there remains the vast majority of cases in which epilepsy and epileptic insanity are unquestionably germinal in origin, and therefore transmissible. The principle of negative eugenics cannot too soon be applied here.

The criminal.— When we come to consider the question of *crime* the cautious and responsible eugenist is bound to be wary — chiefly, perhaps, because such a vast amount of sheer nonsense has been written on this subject. The whole question, of course, is the old one, is it heredity or environment that produces the criminal? If and when it is the environment, race-culture has nothing to do with the question, since the merely acquired criminality is, as we know, not in any degree transmissible. If the criminal, however, is always or ever a "born criminal," then the eugenist is intimately concerned. At the one extreme are those who will tell us that the idea of crime is a purely conventional one, that the criminal is the product of circumstances or environment, and that we, in his case, would have done likewise. The remedy for crime, then, is education. It is pointed out, however, that education merely modifies the variety of crime. You have less murder but more swindling, and so forth. Then, on the other hand, there are those who declare that criminality is innate, and that if we are to make an end of crime we must attach surgeons to our gaols; or at any rate must extend the principle of the life-sentence.

Doubtless, the truth lies between these two extremes. In the face of the work of Lombroso and his school, exaggerated though their conclusions often be, we cannot dispute the existence of the born criminal, and the criminal type. There are undoubtedly many such persons in modern society. There is an abundance of crime which no education, practiced or imaginable, would eliminate. Present day psychology and medicine, and, for the matter of that, ordinary commonsense, can readily distinguish cases at both extremes — the *mattoid* or semi-insane criminal at one end, and the decent citizen who yields to exceptional temptation at the other end. Thus even though there remain a vast number of cases where our knowledge is insufficient, we could accomplish great things already if the born criminal, the habitual criminal and his like were rationally treated by society, on the lines of the reformatory, the labor colony, indeterminate sentences, and such other methods as aim, successfully or unsuccessfully, at the reform of the individual, whilst meanwhile protecting the race. Here, as in some other cases, the nature of the environment provided for their children by certain classes of the community may be taken into account when we decide whether they are to be prohibited from parenthood. Heredity or no heredity, we cannot desire to have children born into the alcoholic home; heredity or no heredity, we cannot desire to have children born into the criminal environment. In Great Britain we are no longer to manufacture criminals in hundreds by sending children to prison. It remains to be seen, after the practical disappearance of the made criminal, what proportion of crime is really due to the born criminal. He, when found, must certainly be dealt with on the lines indicated by our principles.[1]

So far we have considered exclusively diseases and disorders of the brain, the question of alcoholism being deferred to a special chapter. When we come to other forms of defect or disease we find a long graduation of instances: at the one extreme being cases where the fact of disastrous inheritance is palpable and inevitable, whilst at the other extreme are kinds of disease and defect as to which the share of heredity is still very uncertain. In some instances, then, the eugenist is bound to lay down the most emphatic propositions as, for instance, that parenthood on the part of men suffering from certain diseases is and should and must be regarded and treated as a crime of the most heinous order: whilst in other instances all we can say is that here is a direction in which more knowledge is needed.

Some particular cases may be referred to.

The diseases known as Daltonism or color-blindness, and hæmophilia or the "bleeding disease," are certainly hereditary. The sufferers are usually male, but the disease is commonly transmitted by their daughters (who do not themselves suffer) to their male descendants. As regards color-blindness, the defect is evidently insufficient to concern the eugenist, but hæmophilia is a serious disease the transmission of

[1] Since these words were written there has been passed the "Prevention of Crimes Act," which is the first attempt in this country to apply the elementary truths of the subject in legislation. As an essentially eugenic proposal it is to be heartily welcomed.

which should not be excused. It may seem hard to assert that the daughter of a hæmophilic father should not become a mother, she herself being free from all disease. But it has to be remembered that the possibility of this hardship depends upon the fact that a hæmophilic man has become a father, as he should not have done.

This point, as to the amount of hardship involved in the observance of negative race-culture, has always to be kept in mind. If negative eugenics were generally enforced upon a given generation some persons would, of course, suffer in greater or less degree from the disabilities imposed upon them. But their number would depend upon the neglect of eugenics by previous generations, and *thereafter the number of those upon whom our principles pressed hardly would be relatively minute.*

EUGENICS AND TUBERCULOSIS.—It would not be correct to say that the old view of consumption regarded it as hereditary. In this and a hundred other matters, medical, astronomical, or what we please, if we go back to the Arabic students, or further, to the Greeks, we are lucky enough to find sound observation and reasoning. Many quotations might be cited to show that the infectious nature of tuberculosis was recognized long ago, just as the revolution of the earth around the sun was recognized a millenium and a half before Copernicus. But the view of our more immediate fathers was that tuberculosis is a hereditary degeneration, and the medical profession proclaimed with no uncertain sound the hopeless and paralyzing doctrine that an almost certain doom hung over the children of the consumptive. Then, in memorable succession, came Villemin, Pasteur, and lastly Koch, with his discovery of the bacillus in 1882. The doctrine was then altered in its statement. There was, of course, no choice in the matter, since it was easy to show that not one new-born baby in millions harbors a tubercle bacillus; so all-but-miraculous and, rightly considered, beautiful are the ante-natal defenses. It was taught, then, that we inherit a predisposition from consumptive parents, that the bacillus is ubiquitous, and that variations in susceptibility determine the incidence of the disease in one and not in another. It was lightly assumed (simply through what may be called the inertia of belief) that these variations in susceptibility were hereditary; but we are wholly without evidence that the hereditary factor counts for anything substantial, even assuming that it appreciably exists at all. These differences, so far from being inherent, are *most palpably* acquired. Under-feeding, alcohol, and influenza, let us say, will adequately prepare any human soul. Furthermore, we are learning that the bacillus is nothing like so ubiquitous as used to be supposed. Tuberculosis is now sometimes described as a dwelling disease. It might probably be described with still more accuracy as a bed-room disease, or a bed-room and public-house disease. It has been evident for many years past that the more we learned about tuberculosis the less did we talk about heredity; and in one of the most recent authoritative pronouncements [1] upon the subject, the lecturer did not even allude to heredity at all. Many readers will be up in

[1] Dr. Bulstrode's Lecture to the Royal Institution, May 15, 1908.

arms at once with apparently contrary instances; and much labor may be spent in the mathematical analysis of statistical data — as that of cases where a father and a child have tuberculosis. But suppose the father kissed the child? What have you proved regarding heredity? No mathematics can get more out of the data than is in them.

The statistics designed to measure the degree of inheritance in this disease labor under the cardinal fallacy of assuming that where father and son suffer, the case is one of inheritance, and then proceed to measure the average extent of his inheritance. These statistics are so much waste paper and ink — assuming what they claim to prove. They do not allow for the fact that the child is very frequently exposed in grave measure to infection by the parent; they ignore wholly, indeed, the entire question of exposure to infection, both as regards its extent in time and the virulence of the infection in question. At the present day, discussions as to the inheritance of consumption and tuberculosis in general are not fit for practical application: and a practical disservice is rendered by those who seek to divert public attention from the removable environmental causes upon which the disease mainly depends. We know, for instance, that the incidence of tuberculosis is directly proportional to over-crowding: this being universally true, we must work to abolish over-crowding and to provide fresh air for every one by day and by night. When that is done, alcoholism disposed of, and our milk-supply purified, we may turn to the question of heredity: but the incidence of the disease will then present merely trivial instead of the present appalling proportions.

It is not asserted that inherent variations in susceptibility to this disease are not existent. The case would be unique if it were so. But it *is* asserted that the more we learn of the disease the less importance we attach to this factor, and the more surely do we see that the three syllables constituting the word "infection" substantially suffice to dispose of all the confident dogmas with which we are too familiar. One is almost tempted to quote a forcible phrase of Mill's, and say that, given this point of view, "once questioned, they are doomed." The only method of accurately studying the question of inherited predisposition would be by comparative study of the resistance of new-born infants as measured by their "opsonic index"— which may be (very roughly) described as the measure of the power of the white cells of the blood to eat up tubercle bacilli.[1] Nor will even this method be free from fallacy.

The present writer believes that eugenics is going to save the world; that there is no study of such urgent and practical importance as that of heredity; that if we get the right people born and the wrong people not born, forms of government and such questions will be left even without fools to contest regarding them. Thus he has every bias in favor of emphasizing the hereditary factor in tuberculosis. The fact will at least not discredit the foregoing views, which are in

[1] This suggestion, first made by the present writer in March, 1908, and in the paper referred to is, I believe, to be the subject of an official inquiry.

absolute accord with those of Dr. Newsholme, our leading authority, in his recent work upon the subject. Nothing need here be said about cancer, the best and most recent evidence tending to show that the disease is not hereditary.

The foregoing may briefly suffice to illustrate the general proposition that negative eugenics will seek to define the diseases and defects which are really hereditary, to name those the transmission of which is already certainly known to occur, and to raise the average of the race by interfering as far as may be with the parenthood of persons suffering from these transmissible disorders. Only thus can certain of the gravest evils of society, as, for instance, feeble-mindedness, insanity, and crime due to inherited degeneracy, be suppressed: and if race-culture were absolutely incapable of effecting anything whatever in the way of increasing the fertility of the worthiest classes and individuals, its services in the negative direction here briefly outlined would still be of incalculable value, To this policy we shall most certainly come: but here, as in other cases, I trust far more in the influence of an educated public opinion than in legislation; though there are certain forms of transmissible disease, interfering in no way with the responsibility of the individual, the transmission of which should be visited with the utmost rigor of the law and regarded as utterly criminal no less than sheer murder.

In the next chapter, recognizing marriage as the human mode of selection, we must consider it in its relation to eugenics, both positive and negative.

CHAPTER XII

SELECTION THROUGH MARRIAGE

HISTORICAL EVIDENCE OF CONTROL OF MARRIAGE: WESTERMARCK'S EVIDENCE.— To begin with the most recent refutation of the doctrine that marriage selection is uncontrollable, one may quote from the inaugural lecture delivered by Dr. Westermarck in December, 1907, on his appointment as Professor of Sociology in the University of London. He said:—

"For instance, when the suggestion has been made that the law should step in and prevent unfit individuals from contracting marriage, the objection has at once been raised that any such measure would be impracticable. Now we find that many savages have tried the experiment and succeeded. Mr. Im Thurn tells us that among the wild Indians of Guiana, a man, before he is allowed to choose a wife, must prove that he can do a man's work and is able to support himself and his family. In various Bechuana and Kaffir tribes, according to Livingstone, a youth is prohibited from marrying until he has killed a rhinoceros. Among the Dyaks of Borneo no one can marry until he has in his possession a certain number of human skulls. Among the Arabs of Upper Egypt a man must undergo an ordeal of whipping by the relatives of his bride, in order to test his courage; and if he wishes to be considered worth having, he must receive the chastisement, which is sometimes exceedingly severe, with an expression of enjoyment.

"I do not say that these particular methods are worthy of slavish imitation, but the principle underlying them is certainly excellent, and especially the fact that they are recognized and enforced by custom shows that it has been quite possible among many people to prohibit certain unfit individuals from marrying.

The question naturally arises whether, after all, something of the same kind may not be possible among ourselves."

MR. GALTON'S EVIDENCE.— But Mr. Galton himself, with his characteristic thoroughness, and in full recognition of the fact that this young science must meet ignorant as well as other objections, read before the Sociological Society[1] a paper entitled "Restrictions in Marriage," with special reference to the objection "that human nature would never brook interference with the freedom of marriage. . . . How far have marriage restrictions proved effective, when sanctified by the religion of the time, by custom and by law? I appeal from armchair criticism to historical facts." Mr. Galton then proceeds to quote seven forms of restriction in marriage which have actually been practiced — monogamy, endogamy, exogamy, Australian marriages, taboo, prohibited degrees and celibacy. He shows how powerful under each of these heads is the influence of "immaterial motives" upon marriage selection, how they may all become hallowed by religion, accepted as custom and enforced by law. "Persons who are born under their various rules, live under them without any objection. They are unconscious of their restrictions as we are unaware of the tension of the atmosphere." In many cases the establishment of monogamy and the prohibition of polygamy "has been due not to any natural instinct against the practice, but to consideration of social well-being." It was penal for a Greek to marry a barbarian, for a Roman patrician to marry a plebeian, for a Hindoo of one caste to marry one of another

[1] *Sociological Papers* (Macmillan, 1905), p. 3.

caste, and so forth. Similar restrictions have been enforced in multitudes of communities, even under the penalty of death." Cases from ancient Jewish law are quoted, and, to take a very different case, that of the marriage rule amongst the Australian bushmen, it is shown that "the cogency of this rule is due to custom, religion and law, and is so strong that nearly all Australians would be horrified at the idea of breaking it." Passing further on, one need offer no excuse for quoting, regarding marriage in general, the following words of the founder of eugenics:—"*The institution of marriage as now sanctified by religion and safeguarded by law in the more highly civilized nations, may not be ideally perfect, nor may it be universally accepted in future times, but it is the best that has hitherto been devised for the parties primarily concerned, for their children, for home life, and for society.*"

Mr. Galton then proceeds to show how extensive are the restrictions in marriage already recognized and practiced amongst ourselves and quite contentedly accepted. He proves also that our objection to marriage within prohibited degrees depends mainly upon what he calls immaterial considerations, and adds "it is quite conceivable that a non-eugenic marriage should hereafter excite no less loathing than that of a brother and sister would do now." Then, in allusion to the possibility "of a whole-hearted acceptance of eugenics as a national religion . . . the thorough conviction by a nation that no worthier object exists for man than the improvement of his own race," Mr. Galton shows from the history of conventual life what abundant evidence there is "of the power of religious authority in directing and withstanding the tendencies of human nature towards freedom in marriage." This paper was discussed by no less than twenty-six authorities, British and Continental, and in his reply Mr. Galton observes that not one of them impugns his main conclusion "that history tells how restrictions in marriage, even of an excessive kind, have been contentedly accepted very widely, under the guidance of what I called immaterial motives." Lastly, we may quote Mr. Galton's admirable distinction between the two stages of love, "that of slight inclination and that of falling thoroughly into love, for it is the first of these rather than the second that I hope the popular feeling of the future will successfully resist. Every match-making mother appreciates the difference. If a girl is taught to look upon a class of men as tabooed, whether owing to rank, creed, connections or other causes, she does not regard them as possible husbands and turns her thoughts elsewhere. The proverbial 'Mrs. Grundy' has enormous influence in checking marriages she considers indiscreet."

Surely all the foregoing suffices to show, first, that eugenics or race-culture is compatible with marriage, and secondly, that it is compatible with the love of the sexes — two conclusions of the most cardinal and fundamental importance. This importance it is, and the obstinate stupidity of critics of a kind, which must excuse me for having devoted so much space to propositions which the thoughtful reader would naturally have arrived at for himself.

THE PRESENT INFLUENCE OF MARRIAGE ON RACE-CULTURE.— We must turn now from the past to the present aspect of the question, viz., the actual relation of marriage to eugenics at the present day. Its nature is very much disputed. On the one hand, there are those who see in our present methods what has elsewhere been called reversed selection — that is to say, an anti-eugenic process, involving the mating of the least desirable. On the other hand, there are many conservative critics who, starting from a general opposition to any new thing, such as eugenics, maintain that we are doing very well as we are, and that, without any conscious interference, as they call it — as if there were no such interference — selection by marriage is actually working for the eugenic end. Dr. Maudsley, for instance, is "not sure but that nature in its own blind impulsive way does not manage things better than we can by any light of reason:" an astounding opinion from the veteran pioneer who has devoted so many decades to successfully modifying natural processes by the light of his own splendid reason!

This most important question, as to what is actually happening within the limits of marriage, may legitimately be regarded as substantially equivalent to the question of the extent and nature of selection, for good or for evil, as it occurs in society to-day. If we remember that an overwhelming proportion of children are born in wedlock, that the death-rate of illegitimate children is gigantic, whilst the illegitimate birth-rate is generally falling, we shall be fully entitled to assume that the answer to the one question is the answer to the other; in a word, if under the present conditions of selection for marriage we find a eugenic tendency or an anti-eugenic tendency or a mere neutrality, the answer will be, *on the whole*, the approximate answer to the larger question as to the present state of selection for parenthood and therefore of our racial prospects, marriage or no marriage. The conclusion which we shall maintain is that *both forms of selection occur in society to-day* — the selection of the desirable and the selection of the undesirable. We shall go ludicrously wrong if we agree, with one party, that society in general to-day exhibits reversed selection; or, with the second party, that everything is going on admirably on the whole; or with the third party, which jumbles the whole mass of facts and tendencies, and declares that there is no process of selection of any kind occurring in society to-day — an opinion which, in the face of disease, the enormous premature death-rate, and the fact that whilst vast numbers of women are unmarried, the choice of women for marriage does not occur by lot, beggars comment; is a girl with a birth-mark covering half her face, or a nose destroyed by transmissible disease, as likely to marry as a "beauty"? If not, surely we are actually select to-day for beauty and therefore for whatever beauty depends upon — for instance, health. But really it cannot be necessary to deal seriously with the proposition that no selection occurs in society to-day.

Let us attempt to state clearly the point at issue. There is granted, in the first place, that by far the greater part of all parenthood, in civilized and uncivilized communities alike, occurs within the limits of marriage; to which may be added that, owing to the excessive death-rate of illegitimate children, the proportion of effective parenthood, so to say, that occurs within the limits of marriage is even larger; and this intervention of marriage, and any selection that may be involved in it, steadily recurs from generation to generation. Thus even those born outside wedlock will nevertheless be selected for parenthood, on their own part, mainly by the selective factors in marriage.

Selection by marriage has the last word.— It follows, then, though the fact is almost constantly ignored by eugenic writers, that selection by marriage in effect has the last word. Thus supposing that all other forms of selection, depending upon, for instance, the various causes of death amongst the immature, were what we call reversed selection; or supposing that, as is actually the case, society permitted large numbers of so-called unfit to survive,— even so, marriage selection (if it meant that many or most of these were rejected by it) would control and correct the dangerous tendency. On all hands, scientific and unscientific, we have writers telling us of the disastrous multiplication of the unfit. Such multiplication does occur and is disastrous. Yet hitherto they have failed to recognize that if — to take an extreme case — all these unfit are rejected by marriage selection — that is to say, do not themselves become parents — this alarming multiplication is, after all, not a persistent factor in racial change, but merely the throwing up or throwing aside in each generation of a certain number of undesirables *whose breed gets no further.*

Of course there would be much less urgent need for eugenics if this last were wholly and happily the case. Our object, indeed, is to make it the case: but so long as selection by marriage exists — and its occurrence is palpably indisputable — *it is a serious flaw in the common argument to assume that the production and preservation of undesirables necessarily involves their own parenthood in due course.* It is necessary that strict statistical inquiry be made on this point. It would show, I believe, that the marriage-rate *and the birth-rate* amongst the *grossly* unfit is much lower than that of the general community, or, in other words, that the influence and value of selection by marriage (which, as we have shown, is in effect selection for parenthood, the only selection that ultimately matters) has not yet been fully appreciated. I very strongly incline to the view that if this protective factor were not constantly at work, the "multiplication of the unfit" would long ago have led to the destruction of every civilized nation on the earth: they would have swamped us long ago. Indeed, the proposition may be laid down that, supreme and indispensable as are the services of marriage to race-culture, in its protection of motherhood, and the support of motherhood by fatherhood, probably the services of marriage as in effect the working of sexual selection, are worthy of being rated almost, if not quite, as high.

Sexual selection is certainly true of mankind.— Before adducing the outlines of the evidence in favor of marriage as an instrument of selection, it may be well to point out that here we are really discussing what Darwin called "sexual selection," modified by the psychology and peculiar characters of mankind. We must protect ourselves from the critics who will remind us that sexual selection is very largely discredited to-day, rather more than a generation after Darwin's enunciation of it in *The Descent of Man* (1871). The controversy regarding sexual selection as the producer of feathers and markings and song, and so forth, amongst the lower animals, is fortunately quite irrelevant to our present discussion, which is concerned with mankind. We can afford to note with equanimity the observation that, in lower species, no mature female goes unmated, for instance; the fact remains that in the case of mankind a very considerable percentage of women remain unmarried. The case is similar as regards the male sex. In short, one may declare that, whether or not sexual selection is possible, or occurs, or accomplishes anything, in the case of lower animals, it palpably and patently is possible, and does occur, amongst mankind, and especially amongst civilized peoples, in the form of selection by or for marriage — which, as we have seen, is in effect selection for parenthood. Let us first note the statistical evidence regarding marriage-selection of health and energy.

Spencer on marital longevity.— We are all aware that married people live longer, on the average, than unmarried people, the conclusion being, "of course," that marriage is good for the health. But some are taken and others left in this respect, and if, for any conceivable reason, health is a factor making for selection by marriage, that may be a real explanation, in whole or in part, of the longer life of married people. Considering the risks to life involved in motherhood, the superior longevity of married as compared with unmarried women would be incomprehensible except on some such assumption. Yet it is the fact, so imperfect still is the entry of the idea of selection into the popular and even the expert mind, that the superior longevity of married people is still constantly asserted to mean that marriage makes for long life; every year, when the statistics are printed, this argument may be seen in the newspapers, and I remember encountering it in the *Encyclopædia Britannica,* to my utter astonishment. This uncritical conclusion was disposed of by the author of the phrase "the survival of the fittest"—appropriately enough —more than thirty years ago. If the reader will turn to Herbert Spencer's *Study of Sociology* (a masterpiece which may be commended to the publishers for the purpose of indexing—twenty editions without an index are too many) he will find in Chapter V. a discussion of this question. It is an astonishing thing that though Spencer conclusively exposed it a generation ago, the childish fallacy is still apparently as flourishing as ever. He shows how the greater healthfulness of married life was supposed to be proved by Dr. Stark from comparison of the rates of mortality among the married and among the celibate. Then no less an authority than M. Bertillon went into the matter and contributed a paper called "The Influence of Marriage"—thus begging the question in its very title—to the Brussels Academy of Medicine. He showed that, from twenty-five to thirty years of age, several continental countries being taken into the reckoning. "The mortality per thousand is 4 in married men, 10.4 in bachelors, and 22 in widows. This beneficial influence of marriage is manifested at all ages, being always more strongly marked in men than in women." The absurdity of the apparent conclusion regarding widows is surely, as Spencer says, too obvious for discussion. But, for the rest, Spencer goes on to show that, in reality, "marriage and longevity are concomitant results of the same cause" — in other words, "that superior quality of organization which conduces to long life also conduces to marriage. It is normally accompanied by a predominance of the instincts and emotions prompting marriage; there goes along with it that power [1] which can secure the means of making marriage practicable; and it increases the probability of success in courtship." Spencer shows how "of men whose marriages depend upon getting the needful income" those who will succeed are in general "the best, physically and mentally — the strong, the intellectually capable, the morally well-balanced." It shows also how "women are attracted towards men of power — physical, emotional, intellectual; and obviously their freedom of choice leads them, in many cases, to refuse inferior samples of men; especially the mal-formed, the diseased, and those who are ill-developed, physically and mentally. So that, in so far as marriage is determined by female selection, the average result on men is that

[1] "In any scheme of eugenics, energy is the most important quality to favor; it is, as we have seen, the basis of every action, and it is eminently transmissible by descent." — GALTON.

while the best easily get wives, a certain proportion of the worst are left without wives."

Very likely the stupid conclusion into which so many distinguished men have been betrayed will survive for many years yet amongst less distinguished people, but at any rate we may free our minds from it here, and may recognize in the figures to which I have referred, and which are of the same order to-day, the statistical proof of what any observer, however casual, might have inferred from what he sees even amongst his own friends only — that marriage is, as it probably always has been, a selective agent of much value in preserving and augmenting the desirable inherent qualities of the race. It is, of course, the object of race-culture or eugenics to strengthen the hands of marriage in this respect to the utmost possible degree.

WOMAN AS PRACTICAL EUGENIST.— We must especially note one most important matter, radically affecting race-culture, which is referred to by Herbert Spencer in the passage cited, and has been greatly insisted upon by Dr. Alfred Russel Wallace, the co-discoverer with Darwin of the principle of natural selection. The matter in question is the possibliity of race-culture through the choice of their husbands by women. Not long ago Dr. Wallace[1] described selection through marriage as the "more permanently effective agency through which the improvement of human character may be achieved." This, in his opinion, can only be perfectly achieved "when a greatly improved social system renders all our women economically and socially free to choose; while a rational and complete

[1] *Fortnightly Review,* January, 1908.

education will have taught them the importance of their choice both to themselves and to humanity. It will act through the agency of well-known facts and principles of human nature, leading to a continuous reduction of the lower types in each successive generation, and it is the only mode yet suggested which will automatically and naturally effect this." Thus "for the first time in the history of mankind his Character — his very Human Nature itself — will be improved by the slow but certain action of a pure and beautiful form of selection — a selection which will act, not through struggle and death, but through brotherhood and love."

Dr. Wallace is a socialist, and he believes that only through socialism can we achieve "that perfect freedom of choice in marriage which will only be possible when all are economically equal, and no question of social rank or material advantage can have the slightest influence in determining that choice." As I have said elsewhere, I would call myself neither a socialist nor an anti-socialist, but if the labels are necessary, a eugenist and maternalist. As such, I can only say that this argument for socialism — that it is the necessary condition of eugenics or race-culture — is, for me, incomparably the best argument for that creed; and if it were proved that only through socialism could the utmost be made of women's choice of husbands, then no other argument against socialism could have any appreciable weight at all. The fundamental and permanent argument against certain of the highly various and incompatible doctrines which, for our confusion, are commonly lumped together as socialism, is that they would arrest the process by which Nature rewards worth and permits it to perpetuate itself. If, then, it can be shown, as may or may not be the case, that only through socialism can male worth be most effectively chosen and male unworth be rejected for fatherhood, the supreme — that is, the eugenic — argument against socialism becomes the conclusive argument in its favor.

THE FIELD OF CHOICE.— But, however this may be, there can be no question that the eugenic purpose, as well as the happiness and elevation of individuals in the present, will be greatly served by whatever measures increase, to the utmost extent possible, the opportunities for choice in marriage afforded to women and also to men. One of the most amazing and satisfactory facts about marriage as at present practiced is, I think, the large proportion — often estimated at seventy-five per cent.— of unions which, apart from any eugenic question, turn out happily, in Great Britain, at any rate. What makes this fact more amazing is the almost incredible limitation of the field of choice within which both sexes are still confined as a whole. If the reader will consider the cases most familiar to him or her, it will surely be admitted that the considerable success of marriage takes on an astonishing aspect when the present strait conditions of choice are taken into account. I am convinced that few more radical and far-reaching, because eugenic, reforms can be conceived than any which, in accordance with Dr. Wallace's argument, tend to widen the field of choice, and that not for one sex only but for both. He would be a rash man who ventured to allot superior value to the selection of a man by woman rather than of woman by man, or *vice versâ*. Quite apart from any deeper and more difficult reforms, such as Dr. Wallace alludes to, I am sure that even the mere widening of the field of choice, as such, is the most desirable. To take an instance, which the reader may very likely think trivial and absurd, I have witnessed in my brief career as a hockey player, two unions most happy and eugenic in every way, which entirely depended upon the existence of the amusement called mixed hockey — whereat the contracting parties met one another! It is not asserted that these two cases suffice for world-wide generalization. They are merely cited as instances which set at least one hockey player thinking, even on the field — the field of choice. It is a great argument, because it is a eugenic argument, in favor of community of sports and amusements amongst young people of, both sexes, that it does widen the field of choice in marriage, and that in doing so it also tends to favor those factors of selection which the eugenist would desire to see selected: and this especially as compared with the ball-room. I think that the reader will agree that the conditions, the "atmosphere," the costume, and the other features of what young people call a "dance," whilst undoubtedly serving the purpose of marriage and widening somewhat a field of choice which might otherwise be ludicrously and impracticably restricted, compare most unfavorably with the conditions of even the mixed hockey field, which, decried though they often be, are to my mind immeasurably healthier on every conceivable ground than those of the ball-room, and not least of all on the eugenic ground of the prominence gained by most desirable qualities, of which mere strength and energy and neuro-muscular skill are quite the least, whilst unselfishness, capacity for self-control, patience, real gallantry — as when a male "full-back" refrains from hitting the ball with all his might against the toes of a girl "forward" — the sporting spirit and other true and radical virtues, are the greatest. It is undoubtedly the case that the personal factors, physical and psychical which determine the mutual attraction of young people, have dependent upon them the whole of human destiny. In society to-day, what one may call the incidence of parenthood, upon which all the future necessarily depends, *is* determined by nothing other than the humanized form of what Darwin called "sexual selection." Therefore it is not trivial but supremely important to discuss the conditions under which the selection obtains.[1]

It has already been suggested that in order to enhance the eugenic value of marriage we should endeavor to widen the field of choice, at present ludicrously restricted by custom, class, religion, economic position, and so forth. The increased locomotion of to-day will be of real eugenic service to the race in this respect, I believe.

Then it has been hinted that young people should meet one another under conditions which make prom-

[1] "As the German philosopher Schopenhauer remarks, the final aim of all love intrigues, be they comic or tragic, is really of more importance than all other ends in human life. What it all turns upon is nothing less than the composition of the next generation. . . . It is not the weal or woe of any one individual, but that of the human race to come, which is at stake." — DARWIN, *Descent of Man*, p. 893.

inent the psychical and put the merely physical or animal into the background — *e.g.* on the hockey field or the ice (or in the "literary circle") rather than in the ball-room. This proposition accords, of course, with what has been said elsewhere as to that great factor of progress which I define as the enhancement of the survival-value of the psychical as against that of the physical. (Note the obvious sequence — survival-value, selection-value, marriage-value, parenthood-value, progress- value.) This proposition and the last might both be worked out, I believe, in considerable detail and not without profit.

Arguing on the same lines, we may agree that even such a small matter, usually considered wholly domestic, as the length of engagements, is of eugenic or racial importance. The eugenist, I think, must welcome long engagements simply because, though they may involve a reduced marriage-rate and a reduced birth-rate — the latter partly in consequence of the reduced marriage-rate, and partly because of the later age at marriage — they tend by the mere operation of time, as we say, to enhance the importance of the psychical and to reduce the importance of the physical factors which determine sexual attraction.

To these three points a fourth, of great importance, must be added. It is that we should favor, as far as possible, those factors of choice for marriage which are inherent, and therefore transmissible, as against those which are acquired, accidental, and therefore not transmissible, *and therefore* of no racial or eugenic importance. This, of course, is the point made by Dr. Wallace in the article quoted above — or at any rate it is involved in the point he makes. I simply mean that every time a marriage is brought about by, for instance, money, the eugenic value of marriage is at least nullified and may become actually anti-eugenic. Again I say, *if* socialism be necessary in order that selection for marriage shall be determined by the possession of personal qualities of racial value rather than the power of the purse, which has always been a racial curse, then the sooner socialism is established the better.

THE EUGENIC VALUE OF CONTEMPORARY MARRIAGE. — The first purpose of this chapter has been to show that in marriage, wherever, and in so far as, it is determined by the mutual attractiveness of young people, there exists a eugenic factor in society to-day; and since the race is in effect recruited by the married people, this aspect of marriage deserves the closest study and attention. I commend this subject, *the eugenic value of contemporary marriage,* to the small but rapidly increasing number of students who realize that eugenics or race-culture will be the supreme science of the future, and who are now devoting themselves to its foundations. No more important and urgent inquiry can be undertaken at this stage. Which, for instance, is the more eugenic the English system or the French?

The second purpose has been to show that one may believe in and work for eugenics or race-culture without proposing to overthrow all human institutions, or to adopt the methods of the stud-farm, or to initiate a vast campaign of surgery, or sensational and drastic legislation, or even, yet, the employment of marriage certificates. One or all of these things may have their place, now or hereafter; or may, on the other hand, be far worse than futile. But most assuredly it is possible now for the individual parent of marriageable children, for the clergyman, the leader of fashion, the doctor, not to start but to strengthen such by no means impotent eugenic forces as already exist in society, without outraging sentiment or custom — indeed, without attracting public attention to their action at all.

Eugenics has already suffered much at the hands of its so-called friends. It is to be hoped that a real service may be discharged by this attempt to show that on the highest, most accurate and scientific eugenic grounds, we may recognize, claim and welcome every father and mother who desire that the son or daughter whom they care for shall marry for psychical and not for physical love. Every such parent is a eugenist, in effect, though his sole motive may be the welfare of his individual child.

At present we interfere with marriage on every imaginable ground, many utterly trivial, many worse. We encourage or discourage on economic grounds; we recognize many taboos, of caste, creed, color. It is not for us, certainly, acting as we do, to be offended at the suggestion that we should use our influence to affect marriage on the highest conceivable ground — the life of mankind to come. What we really need is not so much the abolition of Mrs. Grundy as her conversion to the eugenic idea. It is the business of those who believe that eugenics is the greatest ideal in the world to make a eugenist of Mrs.

Grundy, as we shall some day: and then it will be realized how potent for good public opinion may become, once it is rightly educated.

Says Mr. Galton, in his latest contribution to the subject:—

> The power of social opinion is apt to be rather under-rated than over-rated. Like the atmosphere which we breathe and by which we live, social opinion operates powerfully without our being conscious of its existence. Everyone knows that governments, manners, and beliefs which were thought to be right, decorous, and true at one period have been judged wrong, indecorous, and false at another; and that views which we have heard expressed by those in authority over us in our childhood and early manhood tend to become axiomatic and unchangeable in mature life.
>
> Speaking for myself only, I look forward to local eugenic action in numerous directions, including the accumulation of considerable funds to start young couples of "worthy" qualities in their married life, and to assist them and their families at critical times. The gifts to those who are the reverse of "worthy" are enormous in amount; it is stated that the charitable donations in the year 1907 amounted to £4,868,050. I am not prepared to say how much of this was judiciously spent, or in what ways, but merely quote the figures to justify the inference that many of the thousands of persons who are willing to give freely at the prompting of a sentiment based upon compassion, might be persuaded to give largely also in response to a more virile sentiment, based on the desire of promoting the natural gifts and the National Efficiency of future generations.
>
> In circumscribed communities especially, social approval and disapproval exert a potent force. Its presence is only too easily read by every one who is the object of either, in the countenances, bearing, and manner of those with whom they daily meet and converse. Is it then, I ask, too much to expect that when a public opinion in favor of Eugenics has once taken sure hold of such communities and has been accepted by them as a quasi-religion, the result will be manifested in sundry and very effective modes of action which are as yet untried and many of them even unforeseen?

BREACH OF PROMISE" AND RACE-CULTURE.— It may be added that perhaps we shall have to learn to reconsider our ill-judged and stupid censoriousness, directed against young people who get engaged but then become tired of one another — as they accurately say, discover that they are not suited for one another. Not only is it obvious that we are fools in denouncing this discovery of impermanence in their attraction, happily made before marriage, whilst we ignore the disasters of its lamentably *postmature* discovery, after marriage: but also it should be obvious that the eugenic end is negatively served whenever what would have been an unfortunate union is broken off in time. Our imbecile standard of honor, and the law of breach of promise, which is outrageously abused, at present condemn the man, for instance, who finds that he has made a mistake, whilst passively applauding him who, finding his mistake, thinks it his duty to make it irreparable. Far better would it be that the man incapable of forming an attachment made of the non-material ties which last, should not marry at all. The man who cannot see, or seeing, cannot find it in his heart to love, the spiritual beauties of womanhood, is just the man who can be safely omitted in the eugenist's scheme for fatherhood.

The plea of insanity is, in English law, no protection against a claim for damages for breach of promise to marry, unless it be proved insanity at date of contract in the defendant. A valid contract once made, it is no excuse for non-performance that insanity has been discovered in the family of the other party. This wicked law must be altered.

THE NEED FOR FURTHER STUDY.— In his study of this subject the student will naturally turn to Mr. Havelock Ellis's volume entitled *Sexual Selection in Man.*[1] This, of course, has its own scientific value as a statement of facts, notwithstanding its intensely nauseating character. But anything less relevant to what most of us understand by psychology, it would be difficult to imagine. The book considers *seriatim*, touch, smell, hearing, and vision as the bases of so-called love. It thus deals with "sensology" not psychology. Indeed, to the best of one's recollection, after very close and careful reading, there is no allusion to the human mind in it anywhere. If men and women were simply animals, this book would doubtless cover the ground, and perhaps the word "psychology" would even be justified in connection with it. From end to end men and women are consistently treated as animals and no more. Since, however, the human species is possessed of psychical characters which distinguish it from the lower animals, it is not unreasonable to suppose that a volume which really dealt with sexual selection in man would, to say the least of it, recognize the existence of those characters — even if only to reject them as irrelevant to the subject under discussion.

The foregoing remarks do not imply that the purely anatomical and sensory factors are irrelevant to the selection of parents in any generation, and for methodological purposes it might be of value to abstract from the factors of sexual selection in human society such things as odor and contour. But it would be ur-

[1] *Studies in the Psychology of Sex*, vol. iv. (F. A. Davis Co., Philadelphia, 1905.)

gently necessary in the course of such a study, if it were to be other than extremely misleading, to observe that this selection of factors was made for purposes of convenience and that the relation of their importance to that of other factors was a matter for further and by no means casual consideration.

We may certainly agree with Mr. Havelock Ellis that sexual selection occurs in human society, and may welcome his volume as supporting that assertion. There follows the extremely interesting and indeed urgent necessity of ascertaining what the factors of this selection really are, what is their relative potency and what is their capacity for modification. We may further inquire whether they tend to be eugenic. A contribution to this subject is furnished by Mr. Ellis when he shows that width of pelvis is a female character commonly admired by men. Since a wide pelvis is one which can accommodate and safely give birth to a large fœtal head, there is here, as a practically solitary case, a bearing on the eugenic issue: large heads mean, in general, large brains, and it would be ill for the white races if men admired hips as narrow as those of, for instance, the negress, whose pelvis could not find room for the average head of a purely white baby, and who suffers terribly in many cases where the father is white, especially if the child be a boy.

Meanwhile we must wait for studies of this great question from various points of view, notably for a study of the economics of sexual selection as it obtains in human society. Yet further, we require a detailed study of the influence of legislation, custom and public opinion upon sexual selection — on the lines of

Mr. Galton's paper on "Restrictions in Marriage." Mr. Havelock Ellis has more than adequately dealt with the nervous physiology of sexual selection; there remain the psychology and sociology of it — these latter comprehending, one may suppose, ninety-nine per cent. of the whole subject. In the preceding pages allusion has been made to one or two of the more salient aspects of this matter.

CHAPTER XIII

THE RACIAL POISONS: ALCOHOL [1]

In the first chapter of our second part, which deals with the practice of eugenics, there were introduced, defined, and briefly illustrated the terms *positive eugenics,* and *negative eugenics.* Of these the latter, as the more urgent and the more completely and immediately practicable, claims our special attention; though the present writer, notwithstanding that he has devoted to it the greater part of his eugenic work, is bound to protest that the positive increase of ability and worth is never to be regarded as of secondary importance. The two methods are, of course, complementary in practice, as they are one in principle — to select is to reject, to choose is to refuse. The preceding chapter, on selection (and rejection) through marriage, has dealt with the conditions under which both aims are to be pursued. In the following pages we must discuss a specially urgent and practicable and indisputable portion of negative eugenic practice: none the less urgent because of the contemporary emergence and future world-importance of sober nations, such as Japan and Turkey. The term

[1] Part of the matter of this chapter was included in a paper entitled "Racial Hygiene or Negative Eugenics, with special reference to the extirpation of Alcoholism," read before the Congress of the Royal Institute of Public Health, at Buxton, 1908.

racial poisons, introduced by the present writer in the year 1907, is self-explanatory. After dealing with the most important of these poisons, we shall proceed, in the next chapter, to discuss some others. The racial poisons constitute a special department of eugenics which has not hitherto been considered by the pioneers of this subject, but for which I press the claim of the utmost gravity and moment, and which I conceive to be certainly a part, and a most important part, of our manifold yet single subject.

The argument of this chapter is that parenthood must be forbidden to the dipsomaniac, the chronic inebriate or the drunkard, whether male or female; and this whether Lamarck or Galton and Weismann be right, or whether, as we may believe with Galton and Weismann themselves, the controversy between the two parties is wholly irrelevant to the question in hand. This conclusion, that on no grounds whatever, theoretical or practical, can we continue to permit parenthood on the part of the drunkard, is one temperance reform, perhaps the only one, on which disagreement is absolutely impossible. It is, further, the most radical that can be named within the sphere of practical politics, and it is conspicuously practicable. It has hitherto been lamentably neglected by workers and reformers of all schools. Indeed, at the time of writing, the London County Council, governing the greatest city in the world, is pursuing a course of action in this regard, which will be detailed later, and which, as will appear, is imbecile, scandalous and shameful in the last degree.

ALCOHOL AND HEREDITY.— According to Dr. Archdall Reid, "alcohol, year after year, eliminates from the race a great number of people so constituted that intoxication affords them keen delight, leaving the perpetuation of the race in great measure to those on whom intoxication confers little or no delight. . . . Now since alcohol weeds out enormous numbers of people of a particular type, it is a stringent agent of selection — an agent of selection more stringent than any one disease." The factor that really makes the drunkard "is certainly inborn, and therefore as certainly transmissible to offspring. The man who has it is cursed with the 'alcohol diathesis,' with the 'predisposition to drunkenness.' Thus most savages are keenly capable of enjoying drink, and their offspring inherit the capacity." Féré has shown that "it is one of the characteristics of the degenerate that they are prone to have recourse to the poisons, like alcohol and morphia, which hasten their decadence and elimination." Thus, as Dr. W. C. Sullivan points out, alcohol "might certainly be adjudged a salutary evil if its incidence were limited to individuals whose extreme inferiority of organization renders them wholly undesirable and useless to the community. *But this is very far from being the case.*" [1]

The whole crux of the question lies in this last sentence. Alcohol certainly destroys many degenerate stocks, and that is good, though it would be better to do what we shall do some day — hasten and ameliorate the process by forbidding parenthood to the degenerate. *But does alcohol also make degenerates;*

[1] Italics mine.

does it even make more degenerates than it destroys? A somewhat similar difficulty arises in the case of infant mortality. The causes of infant mortality destroy many children inherently unfit, diseased or weakly. But we are not justified in keeping up our infant mortality, if we find, as we do, that for every diseased child whom they destroy they damage many. With this parallel in our minds let us ask ourselves whether or not alcohol can really create degenerates.

A man was born sober — in most cases, but not always,[1] as we shall see — and any changes produced in his body by alcohol are "acquired." Therefore, rejecting Lamarck, are we to reject the doctrine that the effects produced by alcohol on parents are transmitted to offspring?

The controversy between Lamarck and Weismann has *absolutely nothing to do with the question.* Let us consider what would be a case of Lamarckian transmission in the sense which the modern student of heredity denies. The birth of a child with a scar on its scalp, to a father who had acquired a similar scar before the child was conceived, would be such a case: and this does not happen. Or suppose that instead of a scar on the scalp the father has an inflammatory change, not so dissimilar to a scar, produced by alcohol in the membranes covering his brain. Then it would be a case of Lamarckian transmission if the membranes of his baby's brain were similarly affected;

[1] To-day many of the children who make our destiny are born drunk, owing to maternal intoxication during labor. I have myself attended the birth of such children, both in Edinburgh and in York.

and this does not happen. Such is the kind of transmission of which exhaustive experiment and observation fail to find a conclusive instance anywhere.

But what has such a supposition to do with the theory, as definitely supported by observation and experiment as the other is not, that if a man saturates his body with alcohol carried by his blood, he injures all the tissues which are nourished by that blood, including the racial elements of his body with the rest: and therefore that his child may be degenerate?

What says Weismann himself? In *The Germ-Plasm*, p. 386, under the heading "The influence of temporary abnormal conditions of the parents on the child," he writes as follows:—

> "Although I do not consider that the cases which come under the above heading have anything to do with heredity, I should not like to leave them entirely on one side.
>
> "It has often been supposed that drunkenness of the parents at the time of conception may have a harmful effect on the nature of the offspring. The child is said to be born in a weak bodily and mental condition, and inclined to idiocy, or even to madness, etc., although the parents may be quite normal both physically and mentally.
>
> "Cases certainly exist in which drunken parents have given rise to a completely normal child, although this is not a convincing proof against the above-named view; and in spite of the fact that most, or perhaps even all, the statements with regard to the injurious effects on the offspring will not bear a very close criticism,[1] I am unwilling to entirely deny the *possibility* that a harmful influence may be exerted in such cases. These, however, have nothing to do with heredity, but are concerned with an *affection of the germ by means of an external influence.*"

[1] This was written in 1892, before the accumulation of the modern evidence on the subject.

Weismann goes on to quote cases showing how germ-cells may be injured by various agents, and continues: —

"It does not appear to me impossible that an inter-mixture of alcohol with the blood of the parents may produce similar effects on the ovum and sperm cell. According to the relative quantity of alcohol either an exciting or a depressing influence might be exerted, either of which would lead to abnormal development. . . .

"*New* predispositions can certainly never arise owing to such deviations from the normal course of development, and therefore a modification of the process of heredity itself is out of the question. It is, however, conceivable that more or less considerable abnormalities may affect the course of development, and either cause the death of the embryo, or else produce more or less marked deformities. The question as to whether such deformities really result in consequence of the drunken condition of the parents can only be decided by observation."[1]

This is all that Weismann has to say on the subject, since, not referring to functionally-produced modifications,[2] it does not concern his theory of heredity at all: yet it is upon this theory that the most palpable facts of the racial influence of alcohol are denied. Weismann's own remarks are quite open to criticism, as, for instance, where he denies that new predispositions can arise in the manner indicated. This is possibly only a question of words, and Weismann is perhaps merely denying that alcohol can produce progressive

[1] "Alcohol taken into the stomach can be demonstrated in the testicle or ovary within a few minutes, and, like any other poison, may injure the sperm or the germ element therein contained. As a result of this intoxication of the primary elements, children may be conceived and born who become idiots, epileptics, or feeble-minded. Therefore it comes about that even before conception a fault may be present."—McAdam Eccles, F.R.C.S., in the *British Journal of Inebriety*, April, 1908.

variations. Also his remarkably brief discussion of the subject seems to concern itself mainly with the influence of alcohol on the germ-cells *just before their union*. He has not a word to say regarding the influence on the germinal tissues of years of soaking in alcohol. It suffices, however, to make the point which is quite clearly made, that the Weismannians are going absurdly beyond their book in denying what, indeed, the book of Nature demonstrates.

Let us turn now to the experimental side of this question. An American botanist, Dr. T. D. MacDougal, read an address on "Heredity and Environic Forces" at the Chicago Meeting of the American Association for the Advancement of Science in 1907. His experiments require confirmation, but may be provisionally accepted. He has permanently modified the germ-plasm of plants under the influence of various chemicals. There is here a vast field for experiment with alcohol. I quote one paragraph indicating the remarkable results of these experiments. The reader will see their bearing on our present question, and will also see that they do not for a moment affect Weismann's denial of the doctrine that by cutting off rats' tails you can produce a race of tailless rats, or that by learning a language you can save your future children the trouble of doing so for themselves:—

"It was found that the injection of various solutions into ovaries of Raimannia was followed by the production of seeds bearing qualities not exhibited by the parent, wholly irreversible, and fully transmissible in successive generations. One of the seeds produced by a plant of *Œnothera biennis* which had been treated with zinc sulphate differed so widely from the parental form that it could be distinguished from it by a novice. This new form has been tested to the third generation, and transmits all its characteristics fully."

ALCOHOL A PROVED RACIAL POISON.— But the reader will rightly desire some kind of experimental proof that alcohol itself can act as a cause of racial degeneration. We may first refer to the chapter on alcoholism and human degeneration in Dr. W. C. Sullivan's *Alcoholism, a Chapter in Social Pathology* [1] for a recent *résumé* of the subject. Without actually quoting Weismann, Dr. Sullivan begins by showing that, as we have seen, the doctrinal objection of Dr. Reid and others to the theory of alcoholic degeneration is quite irrelevant —"the effects attributed to parental alcoholism are not in the category of transmitted acquirements at all; they are the results, expressed in defect and deviation of development, of a deleterious influence exerted on the germ-cells, either directly through the alcohol circulating in the blood, or indirectly, through the deterioration of the parental organism in which these cells are lodged, and from which they draw their nutriment." Later Dr. Sullivan points out that the racial effects of alcoholism in man are similar to those obtained by experimental intoxication in the lower animals. Combemale, for instance, found that pups begotten of a healthy bitch by an alcoholized dog, were congenitally feeble and showed a marked degree of asymmetry of the brain. Recent experiments have shown the same thing as regards other poisons, but it is especially to be noted that

[1] London: James Nisbet and Co. 1906.

in the experiments cited the mother was healthy. They prove that *paternal* alcoholism alone (all questions of the nourishment of the growing child before birth, for instance, thus being excluded) can determine degeneration. Mr. Galton[1] himself long ago quoted the case "of a man who after begetting several normal children, became a drunkard and had imbecile offspring"; and another case has been recorded "of a healthy woman who, when married to a drunken husband, had five sickly children, dying in infancy, but in subsequent union with a healthy man, bore normal and vigorous children." Other intoxications show similar results though they are not *yet* of grave racial importance. For instance, "a man who had had two healthy children acquired the cocaine habit, and while suffering from the symptoms of chronic poisoning engendered two idiots." Brovardel and others have discovered that the expectant mother who is a morphino maniac may give birth to a child who shows all the phenomena of the morphia habit. Demme has traced the appalling contrast between the offspring in ten sober families and in ten families where one or both parents suffered from chronic alcoholism. Dr. Sullivan himself, realizing the obviously greater importance of maternal alcoholism, since here we have the action of poisoned food — the maternal blood — upon the child before birth, made an inquiry of his own. He found that

[1] Will our modern extremists be good enough to remember that Mr. Galton is the prime author of the doctrine that functionally-produced modifications are not inherited?

". . . of 600 children born of 120 drunken mothers 335 (55.8 per cent.) died in infancy or were still-born, and that several of the survivors were mentally defective, and as many as 4.1 per cent. were epileptic. Many of these women had female relatives, sisters or daughters, of sober habits and married to sober husbands; on comparing the death-rate amongst the children of the sober mothers with that amongst the children of the drunken women of the same stock, the former was found to be 23.9 per cent., the latter 55.2 per cent., or nearly two and a half times as much. It was further observed that in the drunken families there was a progressive rise in the death-rate from the earlier to the later born children."

Dr. Sullivan cites as a typical alcoholic family one in which "the first three children were healthy, the fourth was of defective intelligence, the fifth was an epileptic idiot, the sixth was dead-born, and finally the productive career ended with an abortion." Dr. Claye Shaw told the Interdepartmental Committee on Physical Deterioration, "we have inebriate mothers, and either abortions or degenerate children. The teleological [1] relationship between the two seems to be as certain as any other conditions of cause and effect." The general rule is that any narcotic substance affects highly developed tissues sooner and more markedly than simpler tissues, and so it is in the case of alcohol and the infant. It is the developing nervous system that is most markedly affected. This leads, of course, to an increased child mortality, especially by way of convulsions. This was the cause of sixty per cent. of all the deaths that occurred amongst the six hundred children in Dr. Sullivan's series. But it has especially to be remembered that a large number of children

[1] The use of this word thus is unusual, to say the least of it. Dr. Claye Shaw simply means *causal relation*.

whose nervous systems are injured for life by parental and more especially by maternal alcoholism do not die either as infants or children. Instead of dying of convulsions they live as epileptics. Of the children in Dr. Sullivan's series "219 lived beyond infancy, and of these 9, or 4.1 per cent., became epileptic, as compared with 0.1 per cent. of the whole population." Other observers have found epilepsy in 12 per cent. and even 15 per cent. of the children of alcoholic parents. It is, I submit, impossible any longer to question Dr. Sullivan's conclusion that "this action of alcoholism on the health and vitality of the stock is the most serious of the evils that intemperance brings on the community."

Dr. Sullivan's inquiries show a very high rate of still-births and abortions amongst the children of drunken mothers — quite sufficient to prove that "the detrimental effect of maternal alcoholism must be in a large measure due to a direct influence on the germ-cells and on the developing embryo, and cannot be explained as merely a result of the neglect and malnutrition from which the children of a drunken mother are naturally apt to suffer." The point is of some theoretical importance. Practically it matters little; *in either case the drunken woman must not become a mother.*

The same conclusion is reached even though we accord unlimited weight to the unquestionably valid argument that the drunkard is himself or herself usually degenerate from the first, and that the children are therefore degenerate, and would indeed be degenerate even if the parents had taken no alcohol. Let us, then, erroneously enough, but for the sake of the argument, assume that solely and always alcoholism is a symptom of degeneracy. It is, then, an indication of unfitness for parenthood no less, and the practical issue is the same: one radical cure for alcoholism, at any rate, is the prohibition of parenthood on the part of the alcoholic.[1]

THE MOST RECENT EVIDENCE.—The most thorough and comprehensive inquiry into this matter yet made is also the most recent. We owe it to Dr. W. A. Potts, of the University of Birmingham, who did valuable work as Medical Investigator to the Royal Commission on the Care and Control of the Feeble-minded. His paper, entitled "The Relation of Alcohol to Feeble-mindedness," is printed in the *British Journal of Inebriety* for January, 1909, together with communications from many authorities. It is quite impossible to summarize here the enormous mass of evidence which Dr. Potts has accumulated from the literature of the subject, and to which he has added his own work. I believe that nothing could be more moderate and assured than the following conclusions to which

[1] The subject of alcoholism and race-culture really demands a large volume. There is no space here to detail the fashion in which the drunken mother poisons her child after birth, when she nurses it, since, as has been chemically proved, alcohol is excreted in her milk. Says a most distinguished authority, Mrs. Scharlieb, "the child, then, absolutely receives alcohol as part of his diet, with the worst effect upon his organs, for alcohol has a greater effect upon cells in proportion to their immaturity" ("The Drink Problem," in the New Library of Medicine), and Dr. Sullivan refers to "numerous cases on record of convulsions and other disorders occurring in infants when the nurse has taken liquor, and ceasing when she has been put on a non-alcoholic diet." The reader may be referred to my brief paper, "Alcohol and Infancy," published in the form of a tract by the Church of England Temperance Society.

he commits himself after a study of the subject the quality and range of which can only be appreciated at first hand: —

> ". . . the evidence is not clear that alcoholism, by itself, in the father will procure amentia; but it is quite plain that in combination with other bad factors it is a most unfavorable element, while maternal drinking, and drinking continued through more than one generation, are potent influences in mental degeneracy."

It is impossible, within the scope of the present volume to analyze in detail the Report of the Royal Commission on the Care and Control of the Feeble-minded. In this present outline of eugenics, it is our business, however, to show main principles, and as the principle expressed in the phrase "racial poisons" is to my mind absolutely cardinal for eugenics, it is necessary here to comment, as I have already done in the *Journal* above quoted, upon the following most unfortunate deliverance of the Commissioners: "That both on the grounds of fact and of theory, there is the highest degree of probability that feeble-mindedness is usually spontaneous in origin — that is, not due to influences acting on the parent. . . ."

The word spontaneous has, of course, no meaning for science, or rather is a denial of the fundamental axiom of science that causation is universal. What the Commissioners mean when they say spontaneous is "sportaneous," like the occasional production of a nectarine by a peach tree. Apart from this highly suspicious phraseology, there is the still more unfortunate fact that the Commissioners have lent their authority to the view that feeble-mindedness is not due to influences acting on the parent. The modern student of syphilis will be astonished at this pronouncement, and also the student of lead-poisoning, as we shall see in the following chapter.

Every reader of Dr. Potts's admirable paper will realize that this conclusion of the Commissioners — "not due to influences acting on the parent"— is directly opposed to an extraordinary mass of evidence and to the opinion of, I suppose, every authority on the subject, British, Continental or American. The Commissioners' reference to "theory," coupled with portions of the evidence given before them by witnesses who suppose that the alleged influence of alcohol as a cause of feeble-mindedness controverts the doctrine of the non-transmission of "acquired characters," makes it necessary to point out for the hundredth time that, for lack of analysis and criticism of terms, the most prominent followers of Galton and Weismann persistently misunderstand their masters' teaching. The modern doctrine of the individual as the trustee of the germ-cells and of the non-transmission of acquired characters is Mr. Galton's. Mr. Galton himself does not question and never has questioned the possibility that alcohol may cause feeble-mindedness. There is no reason why he should. If we take the somewhat unusual course of consulting the words of the masters before we swear by them, we find — as has been shown — that Weismann, who subsequently stated and has so greatly supported Mr. Galton's view, has expressly repudiated the Commissioners' idea of his "theory." The Galton-Weismann doctrine is a doctrine of heredity proper,— the organic relation of living generations. It does not assert that there are two unconnected universes — the one made of germ-plasm and the other of the rest of nature. The "grounds of theory," or rather, our elementary physiological knowledge of the nutrition of the germ-plasm by the blood of its host, are in reality precisely the grounds which would lead us to expect those consequences of parental alcoholism which in fact we find.

ALCOHOLISM AS A SYMPTOM OF DEGENERACY.— We have seen that alcohol may be a cause of degeneracy: we now have to recognize the converse relation. For an authoritative and radical discussion of the problem, the reader may be referred to the second Norman Kerr Memorial Lecture, delivered by Dr. Welsh Branthwaite, H.M. Inspector under the Inebriates' Act, in 1907.[1] He speaks as "the only man in close touch with all inebriates under legal detention in England." He reaches most important conclusions which are generally accepted, as the discussion shows. He says, "the more I see of habitual drunkards, the more I am convinced that the real condition we have to study, the trouble we have to fight, and the source of all the mischief, is . . . defect[2] in mental mechanism, generally congenital, sometimes more or less acquired. . . . In the absence of alcohol, the same persons, instead of meriting the term inebriate would have proved unreliable in many ways; they would have been called ne'er-do-weels, profligates, persons of

[1] This is printed in the *British Journal of Inebriety*, January, 1908, under the title "Inebriety, its Causation and Control"— with comments by numerous authorities.

[2] The author says "inherent defect." I have omitted the adjective, as it is obviously misused. *Antecedent* would have been the better word, surely.

lax morality, excitably or abnormally passionate individuals, persons of melancholic tendency or eccentric. . . . It seems to me exceedingly doubtful whether habitual inebriety. . . . is ever really acquired in the strictest sense of the word — *i.e.* in the absence of some measure of pre-existing defect." Having studied 2,277 inebriates, committed under the Inebriates Acts, up to December 31st, 1906, Dr. Branthwaite *finds 62.6 per cent. of these mentally defective.* The remainder he regards as of average mental capacity, using, however, an exceedingly low standard of what that capacity is. He concludes that in a large majority of police-court cases, "mental disease was the condition for which they were repeatedly imprisoned — mental disease merely masked by alcoholic indulgence. . . . The majority of our insane inebriates have become alcoholic because of their tendency to insanity. . . . Certain peculiarities in cranial conformation, general physique, and conduct, have long been recognized as evidences of congenital defect. Nearly all the 1,375 cases included in the two defective sections of our table have given evidence of possessing some of these characteristic peculiarities, and *it is morally certain that the large majority of them started life handicapped by imperfect brain development.*"[1] The lecture is accompanied with many photographs clearly showing the physical marks of congenital defect, and Dr. Branthwaite remarks that "even the untrained eye should meet with no difficulty in recognizing 'something wrong' with all of them."

Of the proportion of mentally defective inebriates

[1] Italics mine.

(62.6 per cent. of the whole) mentioned by Dr. Branthwaite, *all* are "practically hopeless from a reformation standpoint." This is a sufficient comment, if any were needed, upon repeated imprisonment for habitual drunkenness—which, as Dr. Branthwaite says "is indefensible and inhumane." He adds in closing that, in his judgment, habitual drunkenness, so far as women are concerned, has materially increased, during the last twenty-five years, "which I have spent entirely amongst drunkards and drunkenness." The unfortunate people whom he studies "*are not in the least affected by orthodox temperance efforts; they continue to propagate drunkenness, and thereby nullify the good results of temperance energy. Their children, born of defective parents, and educated by their surroundings, grow up without a chance of decent life, and constitute the reserve from which the strength of our present army of habituals is maintained. Truly we have neglected in the past, and are still neglecting, the main source of drunkard supply—the drunkard himself; cripple that, and we should soon see some good result from our work.*"

A foremost authority, Dr. F. W. Mott, F.R.S., has independently reached the same conclusion as Dr. Branthwaite—that the chronic inebriate comes as a rule of an inherently tainted stock. (Dr. Mott, however, reminds us that "if alcohol is a weed killer, preventing the perpetuation of poor types, it is probably even more effective as a weed producer.") Professor David Ferrier, F.R.S., the great pioneer of brain localization, in reference to these people, speaks of "the risk of propagation of a race of drunkards and imbeciles." Dr. J. C. Dunlop, H.M. Inspector under the Inebriates Act, Scotland, states that his experience leads him to precisely the same conclusion as that of Dr. Branthwaite. Dr. A. R. Urquhart, an asylum authority, affirms that chronic inebriety "is largely an affair of heredity . . . is a symptom of mental defect, disorder, or disease." Dr. Fleck, another authority, says: "It is my strong conviction that a large percentage of our mentally defective children, including idiots, imbeciles and epileptics, are the descendants of drunkards." Mr. McAdam Eccles, the distinguished surgeon, agrees; so does Dr. Langdon Down, Physician to the National Association for the Welfare of the Feeble-minded; so does Mr. Thomas Holmes, the Secretary of the Howard Association, who remarks that "our habitual criminals, equally with our mental inebriates, are not responsible beings, but victims of mental disease." Finally Miss Kirby, Secretary of the National Association for the Feeble-minded, insists upon the obvious conclusion that these people must be detained permanently. She says, "when one case of a dissolute feeble-minded woman in America is quoted as the mother of nine feeble-minded children, we see the cause why inebriate homes, and also reformatories, penitentiaries, and workhouses are full to overflowing, and society taxed beyond bearing to keep them there. *Such institutions outnumber homes for the feeble-minded.*"[1] Speaking of the 62.6 per cent. noted by Dr. Branthwaite, she says "would it not have been the more logical course to

[1] Italics are mine. A thousand pounds for cure — which does not cure — and twopence for prevention is, of course, the rule with a half-educated nation always.

have dealt with them in earlier years?" Now what would that have accomplished? *It would have saved the future.*

THE INEBRIATE AS PARENT.— Is it a mere supposition that these women become mothers? Amongst those committed as criminal inebriates (under the London County Council) in 1905-6, three hundred and sixty-five of those admitted to reformatories had two thousand two hundred children. These are the official figures. As to the quality of these children there is unfortunately no possibility of question.

We may quote from Dr. Sullivan a notable inquiry: —

> "Even more striking results with regard to the several forms of degeneracy were obtained by Legrain, who investigated the question from a somewhat different point of view. Selecting from the material at his disposal all those cases in which ancestral intemperance had appeared to exercise a causal influence, and working out their family history, he collected 215 observations of heredo-alcoholism referring to one generation, 98 referring to two generations, and 7 referring to three generations. Of the children of the first generation, 508 in number, 196 were mentally degenerate, the affection of the brain being shown more particularly by moral and emotional abnormality, while intellectual defects were less pronounced; 106 were insane, 52 were epileptic, 16 suffered from hystero-epilepsy, and 3 from chorea; and 39 had convulsions in infancy. Amongst the children of the second generation, who numbered 294, the intellectual defects were more marked, idiocy, imbecility, or debility, being noted in the offspring of 54 out of the 98 families investigated. In 23 out of the 33 families in which the children of the second generation had reached adult age, one or more of them were insane. Epilepsy was found in 40 families, infantile convulsions in 42, and meningitis in 14. The third generation in 7 families was represented by 17 children, all of whom were weak-minded, imbecile, or idiotic; 2 suffered, moreover, from moral insanity, 2 from hysteria, and

2 from epilepsy; 3 were scrofulous, and 4 had convulsions in childhood. In the three generations taken together there were, in addition to the children referred to above, 174 infants who were dead-born or died shortly after birth."

Therefore, the chronic inebriate must not become a parent. Let it be said that these people are wicked or have no self-control, drink for fun or love of degradation, then become drunkards, and prejudicially affect their children. The conclusion is the same. Have any theory of heredity you please — Lamarckianism, Darwin's pangenesis, Weismannism, Mendelism; it matters not a straw. Look at the thing from the uncharitable religious point of view, or from the charitable scientific view which realizes, in the case of these women, that to know all is to pardon all — the conclusion is still the same.

THE PRESENT SCANDAL OF LONDON'S INEBRIATES.— This then, being so, abundance of official evidence having been gathered in addition to all the unofficial evidence, let us consider the shameful facts which are in process as I write, and are still so, on revision of these pages a year later. They are outlined in the reply of Mr. Herbert Gladstone, the Home Secretary, to a question in the House of Commons. The reply is printed in full in *The Times,* February 19th, 1908. There was a paltry squabble between the Government and the London County Council as to the exact number of shillings that each was to contribute per week for the maintenance of inebriates. The London County Council was plainly in the wrong, its ignorance being sufficiently indicated by the letter to *The Times,* which I will quote. The result of the squabble is that, as Mr. G. R. Sims said, "We shall have something like five hundred women, all habitual drunkards, passing in and out of the prisons, a peril to publicans, a pest to the police, an evil example to the women with whom they mix, and free to bring children into the world, their little lives poisoned at the source." We have therefore reverted to the shameful, brutal, and disastrous system sufficiently indicated by the history of Jane Cakebread, at whom, when one was a schoolboy as ignorant as those who now govern us, one used to laugh because she had been convicted so many hundreds of times.[1] As the present writer said in raising the matter at a meeting of the Eugenics Education Society, the future children of these women are not only doomed by the very nature of their germplasm, but they will actually be many times intoxicated not merely in their cradles but before their birth. There is no wealth but life, and this future wealth of England is to be fed on poisoned food and many times made drunken before it sees the light. The meeting of the Society passed a unanimous resolution—"that this society enters a protest against the present administration of the Inebriates Act, whereby through the closing of inebriate homes some hundreds of chronic inebriate women will be set adrift in London, with an inevitably deteriorating result to the race."[2]

For this particular scandal the London County Council was the more to blame. Let not the reader suppose that a Liberal government, however, was

[1] She died in a lunatic asylum. I have not heard that society ever offered her a public apology for its brutality to her.

[2] See *Times* Report, February 28, 1908.

likely to remedy the immoderate ignorance of a "Moderate" County Council on this matter. Mr. Gladstone's reply in Parliament was an exceptionally long one, but did not contain a syllable to suggest that any question of the future is involved, or that a woman may become a mother. Further, the Licensing Bill introduced just when we were drawing public attention to this scandal contained nowhere any hint of the principle that you must attack drunkenness by attacking "the main source of drunkard supply — the drunkard himself." These, the reader will remember, are the words of His Majesty's Inspector. There is no question of party-feeling, then, the reader will understand, in what has here been said. Whether labeled Liberal, Conservative, Progressive or Moderate, ignorance is still ignorance, and when in action is still what Goethe called it, the most dangerous thing in the world.

Pure ignorance, of course, is one of the things against which the advocate of race-culture must fight. The lack of imagination, however, is another. At present we have few homes for the feeble-minded, and many for what the feeble-minded become: few for prevention which is possible and cheap, many for cure, which is impossible and dear. The average county councillor or politician, of course, is rather more shortsighted than the average man, simply because you cannot be far-sighted and a partisan. What his defect of vision requires is impossible, but it would be effective. It is that the consequences of unworthy parenthood should be immediate, instead of taking months or years to develop. Any one, even a politician, can see cause and effect when they are close enough together. It is the little interval that the political eye cannot pierce. Nevertheless, we shall one day learn to think of the next generation and then there will be an end of the politician who thinks only of the next election.

Ignorance on its defense.— The state of what has no excuse for being uninformed opinion was only too well illustrated in a letter from the Chairman of the Public Control Committee of the London County Council which appeared in *The Times* for February 27th, 1908. In defending the London County Council the writer used the following words: "Reformation, not mere detention, was its object when it instituted its reformatory under the Inebriates Acts. . . . The case of the Public Control Committee is that the removal and detention of the hopeless habituals is a matter for the police." The explanation aggravates the offense. In the face of reiterated expert opinion, which has no dissentient, as to the practical impossibility of reformation — you cannot *re*form what has never been formed, viz., a normally developed brain — here we find a man in this responsible position, a man who has the power to put his ignorance into action, telling us that the London County Council aims at the impossible in this respect; whilst, in utter defiance of the future and of the useless brutality of the police court method, he tells us that these "hopeless habituals" are a matter for the police. Then, by way of making the thing complete, he speaks of "mere detention." What he calls "mere detention" is everything, for it saves the future by preventing parenthood on the part of members of the community who, more certainly than any others that can be named, are unworthy of it. The adjective "mere" is only too adequate a measure of the state of opinion which, by such retrograde courses as that under discussion, promises to destroy the British people ere long — and therefore, of course, the Empire of which that people is the living and necessary foundation.

It may be noted in passing that the word "reformatory," employed in the Inebriates Act of 1898, is a highly unfortunate one. It suggests a practically impossible hope, and it ignores what, I submit, must and will ere long be regarded as the essential purpose, function and value of the detention of inebriates — the prohibition of parenthood on their part. In the case of women beyond the child-bearing age, the whole is radically altered. If it amuses the legislature to cherish fantastic hopes, let it speak about the reformation of these women. If it prefers the futile and disgusting cruelty of the Jane Cakebread method for such women, when the plan for reformation is found to fail, that is no affair of ours in the present volume. Such women have been in effect sterilized by natural processes, and the advocate of race-culture can afford to ignore them, for they do not concern him. Let me note, however, that, of 294 female inebriates admitted to reformatories in the year 1906, 170 were under forty years of age, 92 of whom a considerable proportion would be possible mothers, were between forty and fifty, and only 32 of the total were over fifty years of age.[1] It may be said that the lives of these unhappy women tend to be terminated early. The only pity is that our present blindness and ignorance in dealing with them are not neutralized, so far as the future is concerned, by death at much earlier ages. If such a reflection strikes the reader as cruel, how much more cruel are those who are responsible for the present case of the women inebriates of London?

The *Pall Mall Gazette,* on March 4th, 1908, gave the utmost prominence to an article of mine on this subject, entitled "An Urgent Public Scandal, The Case of London's Inebriates." In this article I quoted *The Times* letter referred to above, and leveled the most vigorous indictment I could against the authors of the outrage under discussion. None of them ventured to reply. In the *Referee* for March 8th, 1908, however, a member of the Public Control Committee of the London County Council made an attempt to defend its action. The curious reader may refer to that letter as one more instance of that absolute blindness to the nature of the problem and to any question of the future which had already been indicated in *The Times* letter from the Chairman of the Committee. Taking these two letters together, we may say that never has a public outrage committed by men in authority been more lamely or ignorantly defended.

IGNORANCE IN ACTION — THE PRESENT FACTS.— Since the beginning of January, 1908, the brutal

[1] Report of the Inspector under the Inebriates Acts for the year 1906.

course decreed by the London County Council has been pursued. The wretched and deeply to be pitied women have been and are being discharged at the rate of some twenty to twenty-five per month as their terms expire. The wiser sort of Magistrates and the Police-court missionaries are at their wits' ends, and no wonder. This country offers these women at the moment no refuge whatever; nothing but the degrading and destructive round — police-court, prison, public-house, pavement; *da capo*. Writing to *The Times* in relation to the correspondence there published (April 18th, 1908) between the London County Council and the Eugenics Education Society, Sir Alfred Reynolds, Chairman of the State Inebriate Reformatory Visiting Board and a Visiting Justice of Holloway Prison, said (April 21st, 1908): —

"The correspondence published in *The Times* of April 18, between the London County Council and the President of the Eugenics Education Society convinces me more than ever that the dispute between the London County Council and the Treasury is a scandal and folly of the worst description. For the sake of 6d. per case per day, the London County Council (the same body which receives half a million sterling from the sale of intoxicating liquor) has made it impossible for the metropolitan magistrates to carry out the Act of 1898, and the result is that 500 of the worst female inebriates are alternately on the streets or in prison again, and the former scenes of horror and drunken violence reappear. Holloway Prison will soon fill up again, and all the good which has been done during the last few years will be lost. . . . I will not trouble you further, except by emphasizing what I have said by adding that since January last year 1,500 women have been notified to Scotland Yard as always in and out of prison from the County of London, are qualified for inebriate homes, and at the present moment there are over 50 of this number in

Holloway Prison serving absolutely useless short terms of imprisonment."

THE LONDON COUNTY COUNCIL PERFORMS A SERVICE FOR PHILOSOPHY.— As we have seen, there exists or seems to exist a radical antagonism in certain groups of cases between the interests of the individual and the interests of the race. You may preserve the quality of the race, as the Spartans did, by exposing defective infants; you may be kind to feeble-minded children, as we are, but you will injure the race in the long run. Darwin saw this more than a generation ago, but instead of suggesting the prohibition of parenthood to the unfit, he said that we must bear the ill effects of their multiplication rather than sacrifice the law of love. Huxley similarly said that moral evolution consisted in opposing natural evolution. Now it has for some time been evident that this antagonism need not be radical if, whilst devoting hospitals and charity and medical science to the care of the unfit, we deny them the privilege of parenthood. On the other hand, the London County Council by its present action has performed a service to biological philosophy by showing that *it is possible to combine the maximum of brutality to the individual and to the present with the maximum of injury to the race and to the future.* In his report for 1906 Dr. Branthwaite cites the history of a girl who, at the age of fifteen years and nine months, was convicted in 1881 for being drunk and disorderly. During the next quarter of a century she was sentenced 115 times, and in January 1906 was sent to a Reformatory.

She has twice attempted to commit suicide. Her case is, of course, now hopeless, and Dr. Branthwaite predicts that her life will end by suicide. Let any one read Dr. Branthwaite's Report or Dr. Robert Jones' account of Jane Cakebread, or let him acquaint himself with instances as they are to be daily seen, and he will agree that the maximum of brutality is no excessive phrase to describe the policy of shame at present pursued in London: if, indeed, seeing that we now have knowledge, it should not be described as a policy of blackguardism.

As for the injury to the future, we already know what the present policy effects. We may grant, then, to the London County Council that it has performed a service for philosophy in showing that it is possible to combine both kinds of evil in one harmonious policy. Nor let the reader suppose that any partisan feeling infects this protest. The Government is also to blame. Even had the L.C.C. declined to contribute anything at all to the cost of the proper policy, no really educated and honorable Government had any choice but to undertake all the cost itself — even at the cost of office! Better were — in Mr. Balfour's words, the wisest ones he ever uttered "the barren exchange of one set of tyrants, or jobbers, for another," than the horrible birth of thousands of feeble-minded babies.

The argument of economy.— It would be easy to show that the present policy is not economical even as regards the cost of these women themselves, and even if it be assumed that gold is wealth. But consider the remoter cost. During the period when the present writer was making public protests very nearly every day on this matter without any immediate effect, and only one month after the London County Council had attempted to defend itself on the ground of economy when challenged by the Eugenics Education Society, there was formally opened, with a flourish of trumpets, the eighty-seventh school for feeble-minded children established by the London County Council. It accommodates sixty such children (besides sixty physically defective). This school cost £6,000 to build alone. The sixty feeble-minded children whom it accommodates are not a very large proportion of the 7,000 admittedly feeble-minded school children in London — a number which is probably not more than a third or a fourth of the real number. It has been exhaustively proved that feeble-minded children are mainly, at any given time, the progeny of feeble-minded persons such as constitute the majority of chronic inebriates. Ignorance is again in action. On the one hand, the London County Council, quarreling over pence, effectively suspends the working of the Inebriates Acts, and thus ensures that the supply of feeble-minded children shall be kept up. On the other hand, it takes these children, cares for them until they are capable of becoming parents, and then turns them upon the world. The Chairman at the opening ceremony of the School referred to said that "at the special schools work was being done which would advance the intelligence of the pupils, and thus benefit the entire race." It would be difficult to concentrate more ignorance in fewer words or in ten times as many.

A Home Office Committee appointed.—The almost continuous protest of two months did, however, bear fruit, the Home Secretary appointing a Committee to consider the question of the amendment of the Inebriates Acts. But the legal brutalities described are still being perpetrated, and the future is being compromised. The London County Council may be advised to make arrangements for building a few score more schools for defective children in anticipation of the growing need which it is assuring.

Never again, when it is past, must we permit the present abominable policy. It is for public opinion to effect this, and public opinion has only to be directed to the case in order to realize its nature. If the reader pleases he may discount altogether the eugenic argument, though I believe that in the long run that is more important than any other. But if he confines his attention solely to the cruelties perpetrated upon these helpless women, infinitely more sinned against than sinning, and especially if he considers the testimony of Sir Alfred Reynolds above quoted, he will surely lend his aid to put an end to a state of affairs which is a disgrace to our civilization. We talk of progress, and we are indeed incalculably indebted to our ancestors, but let any one consider the case of the poor child, now a wrecked woman, quoted above, and let him consider what it may be to be an heir of all the ages in the greatest city of the world to-day.

It will be sufficiently evident that if any warrant were needed for the formation of the Eugenics Education Society or for the publication of the present volume, it would be found only too abundantly in the outrage upon decency and morality and science and the future which is at present in perpetration. Further, if any warrant were required for the incessant reiteration of the principle that there is no wealth but life, it would be found in the fact that this outrage is being committed in the name of economy. Yet even if the sane and sober London rate-payer were saved a few shillings now, as he will not be, his children will have to pay pounds in the future for the support of these women's children. Economy, forsooth, when the rates of London benefited to the extent of £559,000 out of the sale of intoxicating liquors in 1905, and spent £8,000 in the maintenance of committed inebriates! Need one apologize for declaring again, that we require a new political economy which teaches that gold is for the purchase of life, and not life for the purchase of gold. For the public outrage under discussion, whereby an untold measure of life, present and to come, "breathing and to be" is to be destroyed and defiled for a squabble over shillings, one can adequately quote only the words of Romeo to the apothecary: "There is thy gold; worse poison to men's souls, doing more murders in this loathsome world, than those poor compounds that thou may'st not sell."

THE LAST TOUCHES OF ART.—If this protest hurts any one's feelings, that cannot be helped. When the production of thousands of feeble-minded children is involved, the self-esteem of what Mr. George Meredith calls the "accepted imbecile" does not matter. The question is how soon do we propose to rectify our present course in this respect, a course which is a shame and a disgrace to our age and nation, and which shall in any case be placed on record in printed words, as well as in young children stamped with degeneracy — in order to point for future ages the question "*An nescis, mi fili, quantilla prudentia regitur orbis?*" "With how little wisdom"— and, whilst perpetrating this shame, ignoring the *one* indisputable means by which legislation can and must check drunkenness, nearly all other measures having failed since Babylon was an Empire, they were quarreling about a temperance measure, so-called, which regarded the question of transference of money from one pocket to another as vital, and ignored the one vital question, which is the question of life: a measure showing scarcely a sign, either in its text or in the words of its supporters or in the words of its opponents, that the question of the future race had ever entered into the head of a public man; a measure which left the protection of children from the public-house to the discretion of local magistrates; a measure which certainly, whatever else it might effect, could not have been more carefully drawn if its object were to promote that secret drinking amongst women[1] which means the poisoning of the racial life even before it sees the light. This then "*mi fili,*" was what was called practical statesmanship in the year 1908 of the Christian Era: and in order that no last touch might be wanted from the hand of ignorance and the

[1] This drinking by women, which means drinking by mothers present, expectant or possible, is rapidly increasing in Great Britain, though almost unknown in our Colonies. It is at the heart that Empires rot.

blasphemous idolatry which worships gold to the neglect of the only true god, which is life, they announced just at this time the issue of a Royal Commission to inquire and report upon the manufacture and variations in the compositions of whiskey. It has been a public joke for years past that no one can answer the question "what is whiskey?" Well, then, I will answer the question, and we may save the labor of such commissions hereafter. Whiskey is a *racial poison,* and there is nothing else to know about it worth knowing *for the future.* Those who will never become, or can no longer become, fathers or mothers, may do as they please about whiskey, so far as the ideal of eugenics or race-culture is concerned. They may say, if they like, that their personal habits are their affair and concern no one else. Under the influence of whiskey they may, perhaps, even believe this. But for those who are to be the fathers and mothers of the future, such a plea is idle. The question is not solely their affair; it is the affair of the unborn, and we who champion the unborn are bound to say so.

The time will come when it is recognized that there are two classes of active mind in society: those who worship and uphold the past, and will always sacrifice the living to the dead, nay more, the unborn to the dead. The ultimate fate of these is the fate of her who looked backwards to the shame and destruction from which she had escaped. She was turned into a pillar of salt. And there are those who worship and work for the future, who will, without hesitation, sacrifice the interests of the dead (who are no longer interested) to those of the living and the coming race — nay more, who will even sacrifice the interests of a few worthless living to those of many yet unborn, *that they may be worthy.* Let the dead bury their dead; let the worshipers of the dead and dying ask themselves whether the life that is and the life that is to be do not demand their homage and service. Not until some such principles as these are recognized shall we rightly deal with the drink problem, amongst many others, and bring to it the mental and moral enlightenment which makes for life on the higher plane, just as surely and just as indispensably as the light of the sun creates all life whatsoever.

MR. BALFOUR ON LEGISLATION.— Surely the moral of this argument is clear. The most important, the most radical, the most practicable of all temperance measures is that which attacks the main source of supply of the drunkard. When a Licensing Bill is brought before the House of Commons, Mr. Balfour repeats the ancient piece of nonsense that you cannot make people moral by Act of Parliament — an assertion that any child can see to be a muddle. We may let that pass for the moment, but Mr. Balfour is a thinker, a student of biology, and heredity in especial, and he has lately been lecturing on "Decadence." Might it not have been expected that such a man would take an opportunity to say what the humblest serious student of the subject would have said, and thereby to bring far more damaging criticism against the opposing party's bill than any he hinted at? He might have said, "Your bill, even if passed, will accomplish little, or relatively little, at great cost, because you have no grasp of the principles of the subject. You have no idea of what drunkenness really is. If your bill were worth a straw it would seek as a primary principle to safeguard the race by arresting the supply of potential drunkards. Your endless financial clauses deal merely with the re-distribution of money, but your bill has no clause that deals with the only business of governments, the creation and the economy of the only real wealth, which is human life." That is what the ex-Premier did not say. He had plenty of passion, plenty of party-feeling to give fire to his words, but so far as knowledge is concerned or any conception of what alone is the wealth of nations, there was nothing to choose between Mr. Balfour and Mr. Asquith. Passion you must have if you are to do anything, but not party-passion: whereas if you have passion for life and for children, not only will it be effective, but notwithstanding all that psychologists tell us as to the vitiation of judgment by emotion, it will actually teach you the supreme and eternal truths.

In this book hitherto little has been said as to formal eugenic legislation. I believe with Étienne that it is opinion which governs the world: legislation in front of public opinion brings all law into contempt. But in his first speech opposing the Licensing Bill of 1908, Mr. Balfour, the author of the Licensing Bill of 1904, decried legislation. "Intemperance," he said, "is a vice:" and legislation can do practically nothing in dealing with vice. Plainly Mr. Balfour is ignorant of the nature of intemperance, which largely depends upon transmitted and inherent brain defect. He therefore lost his opportunity of pointing out in what fashion you *can* actually, notwithstanding the parrots, make people sober by Act of Parliament — viz., by forbidding parenthood to those whose children would almost certainly become drunkards. We who are not politicians, much less ex-Premiers, must make our own proposals then. Last year's criticism of the London County Council began, I believe, to educate public opinion to the necessary point. In the name of race-culture and the New Patriotism, in the name of morality and charity and science, we must demand, obtain and carry into effect the most stringent and comprehensive legislation, such as effectively to forbid parenthood on the part of the chronic inebriate. Ere long, the person who would have become a chronic inebriate will be cared for and protected during childhood and thereafter — with the same result. This solution of the problem is denounced, says Dr. Archdall Reid,

". . . as horrible, as Malthusian, as immoral, as impracticable. . . . The alternative is more horrible and more immoral still. If by any means we save the inebriates of this generation, but permit them to have offspring, future generations must deal with an increased number of inebriates. . . . The experience of many centuries has rendered it sufficiently plain, that while there is drink, there will be drunkards till the race be purged of them. We have therefore no real choice between Temperance Reform by the abolition of drink, and Temperance Reform by the elimination of the drunkard. . . . Which is the worse; that miserable drunkards shall bear wretched children to a fate of starvation and neglect and early death, or of subsequent drunkenness and crime, or that, by our deliberate act, the procreation of children shall be forbidden them? We are on the horns of a dilemma from which there is no escape. . . . But our time has seen the labors of Darwin. We know now the great secret. Science has given us knowledge and with it power. We have learnt that if we labor for the individual alone, we shall surely fail; but that if we make our sacrifice greater, if we labor for the race as well, we must succeed. Let us then by all means seek to save the individual drunkard; with all our power let us endeavor to make and keep him sober; but let us strive also to eradicate the type; for, as I have said, if we do it not quickly and with mercy, Nature will do it slowly and with infinite cruelty."

WOMEN AND CHILDREN FIRST.— The noble cry on a sinking ship is "women and children first." This perhaps is a plea for the service of helplessness as such, though it might be equally warranted as a demand for the sacrifice of the present for the future. And assuredly the cry for a sinking society must also be "women and children first." It is well if the cry be raised when the ship of state is not yet sinking, but only water-logged or alcohol-logged. Temperance legislation and the agitation for temperance reform are themselves in need of reform. Their appalling record of failure — for it is such a record — should help even the fanatic, one thinks, to accept the introduction of the eugenic idea as a new principle of life for the temperance cause. In the present state of custom and opinion, the teetotaler cannot force his own wise habits upon the vast majority who do not agree with him. If he has an infinite amount of energy and resources, let him spend as much of both as he pleases upon the sort of propaganda with which we are familiar: he will, by the hypothesis, still have an infinite amount of both available for the cause to which the principle of race-culture would direct him. If, however, his energy and resources are finite — if, indeed, they are by no means excessive in proportion to the urgent task which the ideal of race-culture asks of him, then let him not fritter away a moment or a penny or a breath until he has achieved the process of salvage or salvation which is expressed in the phrase "women and children first." More accurately, perhaps, our cry must be "parents and possible parents first," and this for present practical purposes is equivalent to "women and children first." It would have been well if the temperance propaganda from the first, say two generations ago in Great Britain, had adopted this motto. But its adoption is far more urgent today in consequence of the fact, unfortunately no longer to be questioned, that drinking amongst women, the mothers of the future, is, and has been for some time, steadily increasing. Children yet unborn must be protected from the injury which may be inflicted upon them by those who will be their mothers. Yet though there is more need for action in this regard than ever before, and though Mr. G. R. Sims in his books *The Cry of the Children* and the *The Black Stain* has lately drawn wide attention to the subject, we have seen that the principle of women and children first, a principle derived from the ideal of race-culture, and directly serving that ideal, was almost wholly ignored in the Licensing Bill of 1908. The motto "money not motherhood" is a bad one for the framers of a temperance measure. If ever we have a temperance measure worthy the name the motto of its framers will be "motherhood not money." Such a measure will most certainly have to introduce the principle of indeterminate sentences — or rather indeterminate *care* — in the treatment of the chronic inebriate. There is no possibility of two opinions as to the urgent and indispensable necessity of such treatment, nor yet as to its scrupulous humanity both for the unfortunate victim himself or herself and for the unborn.

The word "reformatory" had better be abolished from official language, since it leads accredited people to write to *The Times* such foolishness as "reformation, not mere detention."

Further, the expense of dealing with the chronic inebriate in this, the only humane and economical way, had better fall entirely and directly upon the state. It must not be possible again for a local authority, even the London County Council, however ignorant or criminally careless, to commit a public indecency like that already recorded — but the full record of which none of us will live to see.

AN UNPUNISHED MAGISTRATE. — Yet again, in this measure there must be some means of compelling such magistrates as cannot be educated. At present, even when accommodation is provided, the unfortunate creature of the Jane Cakebread type, when she is only just beginning to enter into competition with that horrible record, and when she is therefore most dangerous as regards the possibility of motherhood, can be detained only by the magistrate's order. Now it is very much less trouble for all concerned to say "five shillings or a week" than to make the necessary inquiries in such cases. Further, in putting this measure of one's dreams upon the statute book, we shall have to remember that the idea of protective care and the eugenic idea are, to say the least, not native in the mind of every magistrate. In Dr. Welsh Branthwaite's report for 1906, there is quoted a case where a woman had been habitually drunken for at least thirteen years previous to her committal to a reformatory. Her known sentences included 27 fines, and 138 terms of imprisonment. She was feeble-minded. On the termination of her reformatory sentence the discharge certificate described her as "quite unfit to control her own actions," and "certain to succumb to the first temptation to drink." The woman was found drunk a few hours after discharge. Said the magistrate, "this case clearly proves that it is almost useless trying to reform such women as this. . . . I think, after all, the old way is best and therefore I sentence her to one month with hard labor." I refrain from suggesting a suitable sentence for the magistrate; doubtless he got off scot-free.

Surely we might agree, as regards this racial poison, that at least parenthood and the future must be kept out of its clutches. It may be, it assuredly is, a deplorable thing that the woman of fifty, to take an instance, should become alcoholic, but at the worst this is only the fate of an individual — in the main at any rate. Such principles as these will some day be the cardinal principles of legislation, and not only in regard to alcohol. The time will and must come when public opinion will urge, whether in the name of a New Imperialism or of common morality or of self-protection, that in our attempts to deal with alcohol, we shall begin by removing its fingers from the throat of the race: "Women and children first."

THE REPORT OF THE INEBRIATES COMMITTEE.— In

January, 1908, the Committee which was at last appointed to consider this matter made its Report.[1] I have not the literary capacity to comment adequately upon the political wisdom which brings in a Licensing Bill, devotes vast labor and much time to it and has it rejected by the House of Lords, while such a Committee as this is at work. The spirit of the Prime Minister who spoke of "those damned professors" still reigns over us, and will certainly ruin us unless speedily deposed. However, here is the Report, and its recommendations are earnestly to be commended to the study of all students. New legislation, as it shows, is urgently required, and it is pre-eminently the duty of every eugenist to hasten its coming. This is not a party question, but merely a national one, and will therefore be dealt with by politicians only under external pressure, such as produced the Committee itself. The finger of public opinion must apply that pressure forthwith.

The recommendations of the Committee are so admirable and thorough and eugenic in effect as to temper one's disappointment that the Report contains no definite, overt recognition of the eugenic idea. I had hoped that the evidence prepared and submitted to the Committee for the Eugenics Education Society would suffice to ensure the recognition of the eugenic idea in the Report, for the first time, we may suppose, in official history. For the present we may merely note that the suggestions made in preceding pages are confirmed by the Committee's Report, and that the next

[1] Cd. 4438. Price 4½d. Volume of evidence Cd. 4439. Price 2s.

legislation bearing on the question of temperance will undoubtedly have to attack the subject in this radical manner — by what will be in effect the sterilization of the habitual drinker of either sex and any social status. The Committee do not recognize that that is what their Report involves, much less that that gives it its real value; but so it is, as the year 1950 will be late enough to show.

Much time and trouble were spent in preparing for the Eugenics Education Society answers to many of the questions submitted to it by the Committee, and the Society may fairly claim, I think, that its original services to this matter were well-continued. The present writer also prepared for the Society a Memorandum (Minutes of Evidence, p. 189), which perhaps fairly sums up, in the briefest possible space, the indisputable relations between alcohol and parenthood, and which may therefore be reprinted here. The reader will notice an omission in that nothing is said as to the effects of alcohol in injuring the germ-cells of healthy stock of either sex. The omission was made in order that nothing possibly disputable might be included. It has already been argued that on grounds both of fact and of theory there is every reason to recognize in alcohol, as in syphilis and in lead, a racial poison, originating racial degeneration which, in accordance with generally recognized principles, shows itself in the latest, highest and therefore most delicate portions of the organism.

The Memorandum is as follows:—

It may be pointed out that the children of the

drunkard are on the average less capable of citizenship on account of

(a) The inheritance of nervous defect inherent in the parent.

(b) Intra-uterine alcoholic poisoning in cases where the mother is an inebriate.

(c) Neglect, ill-feeding, accidents, blows, etc., which are responsible on the one hand for much infant mortality, and combined with the possible causes before mentioned, for the ultimate production of adults defective both in body and mind.

It would appear, then, that the drunkard, if not effectively restrained, conduces to the production of a defective race, involving a grave financial burden upon the sober portion of the community, to say nothing of higher considerations. It therefore seems to the Eugenics Education Society of extreme importance that some substantial effort should be made for the reform of existing drunkards or the permanent control of the irreformable.

Scientific warrant for the foregoing propositions is now to be found in no small abundance. Reference may be made, for instance, to the chapter on "Alcoholism and Human Degeneration," in Dr. W. C. Sullivan's recent work *Alcoholism* (Nisbet, 1906). Dr. Sullivan quotes the results of more than a dozen observers in this and other countries, and special attention may be drawn to his own well-known study of the history of 600 children born of 120 drunken mothers. The works of Prof. Forel of Zurich are widely known in this connection, notably *Die Sexuel Frage,* and *The Hygiene of Nerves and Mind* (Translation, Murray, 1907). Parental alcoholism as a true cause of epilepsy in the offspring is now generally recognized. For numerous and detailed proofs from many sources reference may be made to page 210 of the last work named.

It is not necessary, however, to go over the ground which has doubtless been covered by the Royal Commission on the Care and Control of the Feeble-minded.

The existing laws comply to only a very small and almost negligible extent with the eugenic requirement. They only deal with (a) the very minute proportion of inebriates who can be induced to voluntarily sign away their liberty, and (b) those who are also criminal or all but hopeless and who have done harm already, either as individuals or in becoming parents. The third group of inebriates (c) not included in (a) or (b) constitute the overwhelming majority of the whole. They are absolutely untouched by the present law, and further powers are urgently required to deal with them.

Such legislation would be by no means without precedent, and may avail itself of the experience of several of our own colonies and various foreign countries. Such methods as compulsory control on petition, guardianship and so forth are in employment, for instance, in the Australian commonwealth and new Zealand, California, Connecticut, Massachusetts, various cantons in Switzerland, Nova Scotia, etc.

To sum up, the Society advocates the retention of the present law so far as classes (a) and (b) are concerned, but would most strongly urge the addition of powers to deal with that great majority of inebriates whom the present law does not touch.

THE FRIENDS OF ALCOHOL.— Those who defend the alcoholic poisoning of the race may be easily classified. Some few honestly stand for liberty. Like Archbishop Magee, they would rather see England free than England sober, not asking in what sense England drunken could be called free. Some are merely irritated by the temperance fanatic. Many fear that their personal comfort may be interfered with. But probably the overwhelming majority are concerned with their pockets. They live by this cannibal trade; by selling death and the slaughter of babies, feeble-mindedness and insanity, consumption and worse diseases, crime and pauperism, degradation of body and mind in a thousand forms, to the present generation and therefore to the future, the unconsulted party to the bargain. Their motto is "your money and your life." So powerful are they that most of them are frank. They form associations for their defense, and hold mass meetings at which they condemn any temperance measure that is before the country, "whilst ready to welcome any real temperance reform." They demand adequate compensation: though, if they disgorged every farthing they possess, and devoted themselves body and soul for the rest of their lives to the human cause, they could never compensate us who are alive, let alone the dead or the unborn, for the human ruin on which they build their success. They build their palaces before our eyes; but where most see only fine stone, the student of infant mortality, the lover of children, he who works and looks for the life of this world to come, sees the bodies of the children of men and is tempted to recall the curse of Joshua, "He shall lay the foundation thereof in his first born, and in his youngest son shall he set up the gates of it."

ALCOHOLIC IMPERIALISM.—At least let the alcoholic party refrain from calling themselves Imperialists. Amongst them, for instance, is the "Imperial bard," the "poet of empire," he who has appealed to the "god of our fathers," and who warns us lest it shall be said that "all our pomp of yesterday is one with Nineveh and Tyre": and appeals to deity—

> "Judge of the Nations, spare us yet,
> Lest we forget, lest we forget!"

This prophet of what some may think a blasphemous Imperialism gives his name to the association which frankly in this matter of alcohol stands for gold as against life. We are to beware lest "drunk with sight of power" we boast as do the "lesser breeds" to whom the "awful Hand" of God has not granted dominion: nor are we to put our trust in reeking tube and iron shard. We may freely call ourselves Imperialists, however, even though we should be numbered amongst those whom Ruskin, himself the son of a wine merchant, called the "vendors of death." One wonders whether the "Lord God" exists that he can withhold his "awful Hand" at such a spectacle as this. If some amongst us are to win gold by the sale of this racial poison, and if it must be so, let them at least be consistent, and label themselves *the very littlest of little*

Englanders, which they are. An alcoholic Imperialism is of the kind which no Empire can long survive.

Those of us whom such things as these make sick and who yet, with true poets like Wordsworth, are proud of "the tongue that Shakespeare spake," and who with him declare "It is not to be thought of that the Flood which, to the open sea of the world's praise from dark antiquity hath flowed — that this most famous stream in bogs and sands should perish; and to evil and to good be lost for ever,"— those of us who know that the foundations of any Empire are living men and women, and that, *to quote Mr. Kipling,* "when breeds are in the making everything is worth while," may wonder what process has been afoot that in three generations English poetry should pass from the sonnets of Wordsworth to "Duke's son, cook's son," etc.; and may even at times, especially those of us who know what alcohol costs in life, feel a momentary recession of our faith that Great Britain need not be writing the last page of her great history. Meanwhile, we read the controversy in Parliament and the press concerning alcohol. We see the cannibal cause of beer and spirits, which makes many widows and orphans every day,[1] represented, with an effrontery to which no parallel can ever be imagined, as the cause of widows and children, and we recall the lines which Wordsworth wrote rather more than a century ago: —

[1] A careful and detailed inquiry by the present writer, published in the *Westminster Gazette* (Nov. 21, 1908), *Daily Chronicle,* and *Manchester Guardian,* and hitherto unchallenged, showed that, on the most moderate reckoning, alcohol makes 124 widows and orphans in England and Wales every day, or more than 45,000 per annum.

"How piteous, then, that there should be such dearth
Of knowledge; that whole myriads should unite
To work against themselves such fell despite;
Should come in frenzy and in drunken mirth,
Impatient to put out the only light
Of liberty that yet remains on earth!"

CHAPTER XIV

THE RACIAL POISONS: LEAD, NARCOTICS, SYPHILIS

THE term racial poisons teaches us to distinguish, amongst substances known to be poisonous to the individual, those which injure the germ-plasm: and amongst substances poisonous to the expectant mother herself, we must distinguish those which may also poison her unborn child. Alcohol is pre-eminently *the* racial poison, thus defined, and I plead for its recognition as primarily a racial poison, this being immeasurably the most important aspect of the whole alcohol question. Readers of Professor Forel will not lightly question this assertion.

The total number of racial poisons is, of course, very large. Amongst them must theoretically be included all abortifacient drugs. There are also various poisons of disease to be included in this category. Later pages must be devoted to what is by far the most important of these. But we may observe in passing that such a disease as rheumatic fever or acute rheumatism has especial significance for the student of race-culture since, as he knows, its poisons circulating in the blood of an expectant mother may not only injure her own heart for life but may pass through the placenta and deform the valves of the child's heart with the subsequent result loosely described as "congenital heart disease." The conditions giving rise to rheumatic fever, then, are conditions from which the expectant mother, even more than the ordinary individual, is entitled to be protected. But this is of minor importance. We may here refer, however, to one or two striking cases, especially since they bear in some degree upon social and individual duty.

THE RACIAL INFLUENCE OF LEAD.—In the first place, it is necessary to draw attention to a really notable racial poison, viz., lead.

Says Sir Thomas Oliver,[1] "Lead destroys the reproductive powers of both men and women, but its special influence upon women during pregnancy is the cause of a great destruction of human life." It may be said that in a sense the production of miscarriages and still-births, and also of infant mortality by lead, does not concern the student of race-culture. Nevertheless some of these children survive. Says Sir Thomas Oliver: "I have seen both cretinism and imbecility in infants in whom, as there could have been no possible influence of alcohol, and presumably none of syphilis, the occupation of one or other parent as a lead worker must have determined the imperfectly developed nervous system of the child." Later he says (page 202): "Salpêtrière and Bicêtre are large hospitals in Paris set aside for the reception and treatment of nervous diseases. The experience of the physicians of these institutions is unrivaled. One of the physicians, M. Roques, speaking of the degenerates found in these hospitals, says that slowly induced lead

[1] *Diseases of Occupation* by Sir Thomas Oliver. (The New Library of Medicine, 1908.)

poisoning on the part of both parents or in one or other of them is not only a cause of repeated abortions, high percentage of still-birth and high death-rate of infants, but is the cause of convulsions, imbecility, and idiocy in many of the children who survive the first year of existence. Of nineteen children born to parents who were lead workers, Rennert found that one child was still-born and that seventeen were macrocephalic. In his studies upon hereditary degeneration and idiocy, Bourneville places house-painters in the unenviable first rank of the occupations followed by parents of mentally weak children. Out of eighty-seven cases relating to unhealthy trades, fifty-one were connected with white lead in some form or another, while syphilis was only responsible for nineteen."

This racial influence of lead is by no means generally recognized — even by Royal Commissioners. Its parallelism with the case of alcohol is striking. We may note, for instance, that paternal lead-poisoning, like paternal alcoholism, can cause degeneration in the offspring, if not indeed death before or shortly after birth. To quote Oliver again: "taking seven healthy women who were married to lead workers, and in whom there was a total of thirty-two pregnancies Lewin tells us that the results were as follows: eleven miscarriages, one still-birth, eight children died within the first year after birth, four in the second year, five in the third, and one subsequent to this, leaving only two children out of thirty-two pregnancies, as likely to live to manhood. In cases where women have a series of miscarriages so long as their husbands worked in lead, a change of industrial occupation on the part of the husband restores to the wives normal child-bearing powers." According to the statistical inquiry of Rennert, the malign influence of lead is exerted upon the next generation, ninety-four times out of one hundred when both parents have been working in lead, ninety-two times when the mother alone is affected, and sixty-three times when it is the father alone who has worked in lead. Here, then, as in the case of alcohol, the racial poison may act either through the father or through the mother, but especially through the mother. The importance of the demonstration as regards the father in the case of both poisons is that it means a poisoning of the paternal germ-cell. The facts may be commended to those extremists, so much more Weismannian than Weismann, who regard the germ-cells as existing in a universe of their own, wholly unrelated to the rest of existence.

Another extremely interesting parallel between these two racial poisons may be noted. It is found, according to Professor Oliver, that "While following a healthy occupation these women, after having frequently miscarried when working in lead factories, would have two or three living healthy children, but circumstances necessitating the return of these women to town, and resumption of work in the lead factory, they in each successive pregnancy again miscarried." He then quotes the following most remarkable case: — "Mrs. K., aged thirty-four, had four children before going into the factory and two children after. She then had six miscarriages in succession, when she came under my care in the Royal Infirmary, having become the victim of plumbism and having lost the power in her arms and legs. She made a slow but good recovery and did not return to the lead works. In her next pregnancy she went to full term and gave birth to a living child."

We see here that, as is also true in the case of alcoholism, the germinal tissue itself may escape or at any rate may recover from the effects of chronic poisoning of the individual who is its host. The race is more resistant than the individual. If, however, the poisoning continues whilst a new individual is being formed — that is to say, during pregnancy — that new individual succumbs, and indeed is far more gravely affected than its mother. Such a pregnant woman presents three distinct living objects for our study. Her own body is one: and this is already developed. It has some measure of resistance to the poison but is gravely affected. The embryo is the second; it is developing and because developing is susceptible. It is usually killed before birth. The third is the germ-plasm or the race, and this, as we have seen, may withstand the poison so well that when the poisoning is discontinued healthy children may be produced from it. Undoubtedly the case is the same as regards alcohol. The race or germ-plasm is most resistant, the developing individual is least resistant, and the adult individual — that is to say, the mother — occupies an intermediate position in this respect.

This parallelism, which has escaped previous observers, may be pointed out and its remarkable interest and significance suggested as a definite advance upon the absurd view that the germ-plasm is incapable of being poisoned. On the contrary, we know that many poisons will kill it outright so that sterility results. But its high degree of resistance is a fact of great interest. Doubtless Dr. Archdall Reid's acute explanation of it is correct: namely, that natural selection would tend to evolve a resistless germ-plasm. Dr. Reid will, I think, be interested to notice in these remarkable observations on lead-poisoning a conspicuous illustration of this resistance.

Our business here, however, is with the practical issue. This fortunately is plain, nor are there the same difficulties of vested interests which arise in the case of alcohol. Lead-poisoning must be ended in the interests of race-culture and the essential wealth of the nation or, if it is to be continued, it must at least have its clutches kept clear of parenthood.

THE POSSIBLE RACIAL INFLUENCE OF NARCOTICS.— Alcohol is of course a narcotic poison, or more precisely still, a narcotic-irritant poison, but here we may briefly refer to the possible racial influence of certain other poisons. There is, for instance, the case, noted on p. 245, of the disastrous racial consequences of the cocaine habit. The matter demands only a paragraph, since for the present, at least, it is of small general importance, and since we must beware of going beyond the facts; but when once the idea of race-culture has reached the popular and professional mind — the latter at present frequently feeding the pregnant woman with alcohol, as we all know — the whole question of narcomania will have to be looked at from this aspect, and the measure of danger in particular cases will then be ascertained. It is probably safe to assume, however, that, on the whole, alcohol will be found to stand somewhat apart from other narcotics, and for the reason that it is not a pure narcotic but also an irritant. Thus, to take the case of opium, it will probably be very difficult and, one may hope, impossible to show that, shall we say, opium smoking or eating has an injurious racial influence where it is practiced. Here we have a narcotic which is not an irritant. The individual may recover perfectly from its abuse, as he may often fail to recover from the abuse of alcohol, since this poison leaves permanent changes in the brain, and elsewhere, dependent upon the fact that it is not merely a narcotic but also a local irritant. The action of a pure narcotic on the germ-plasm as compared with the action of a narcotic which is also an irritant may afford a parallel. The abuse of opium by an expectant mother (see p. 245) is not of the same order: it means simply dosing a very small baby with opium.

TOBACCO AND THE RACE.—The poisonous compounds absorbed from tobacco smoke are of interest in this connection. The question as to the proportion of nicotine included amongst them is immaterial here. It suffices to know, as we do, that certain substances, doubtless including some proportion of nicotine, rapidly absorbed into the blood by the smoker, are poisons to the individual body. The familiar fact of the acquirement of immunity affects in no degree the statement as to the toxic character of these substances.

No one but the fanatic would venture to say that any racial degeneration can be traced to tobacco-smoking. It would be hard to prove the existence of any injury thus inflicted upon the children of the father who is a smoker, though the question of the acquirement of immunity is not without relevance here. The immunizing substances or anti-toxins which are doubtless produced in the smoker's blood may protect the germ-plasm which he bears as well as his own body.

But in the case of the expectant mother there is more warrant for offering an opinion even in the absence hitherto of definite evidence. Apart from any opinion as to the propriety of smoking by women in general, there is a definite issue in the case of the expectant mother. A very young child is now being exposed to the poisons of tobacco smoke, and if we are right in passing laws to prevent this poisoning in the case of the urchin of eight years (who is really, of course, eight years and nine months old) what shall we say regarding the unborn child who is only eight months old? I have observed that the expectant mother may have her liking for tobacco replaced by violent dislike during pregnancy.

THE POISON OF SYPHILIS.—Brief mention must here be made of syphilis as a racial poison. Sooner or later the eugenic campaign must and will face this question, about which a murderous silence is now maintained. No other disease can rival syphilis in its hideous influence upon parenthood and the future. But it is no crime for a man to marry, infect his innocent bride and their children: no crime against the laws of our little lawgivers, but a heinous outrage against Nature's decrees. When, at last, our laws are based on Nature's laws, criminal marriages of this kind may be put an end to.

The lay reader should acquaint himself with the play

of Brieux, *Les Avariés.* The student may be referred to Forel's *Sexual Question,* Dr. C. F. Marshall's *Syphilology and Venereal Diseases,* and his article, "Alcohol and Syphilis" in the *British Journal of Inebriety,* January, 1908.

This chapter and the last do not profess to do more than indicate the field of eugenics which the term racial poisons suggests. Our business in the present volume is, if possible, to see eugenics whole: to treat of this new science adequately is not for one author or one generation. It is earnestly to be hoped that the medical profession will speedily take up this question of the racial poisons. Already the profession is beginning to become the great instrument of *individual hygiene:* and every year will enhance the importance of this work as compared with the cure of disease. Now negative engenics is substantially *racial hygiene:* and the next great epoch in the evolution of medicine and the medical profession will be the enrolment of its knowledge and influence in the cause of racial hygiene. May this book do a little to hasten that day.

The two next chapters are destined to introduce that aspect of our subject which may be called National Eugenics, and especially with reference to decadence. Here is a matter which appeals to minds of type and training often very different from the typical medical mind. But it is part of one's purpose to show, if possible, that the historian must become a eugenist, just as the physician must, for eugenics needs and claims the work and help of both.

CHAPTER XV

NATIONAL EUGENICS: RACE-CULTURE AND HISTORY[1]

THE reader will not expect to be insulted here with any discussion of the garbage and gossip, records of scoundrels, courts and courtesans, battles, murder and theft, which we were taught at school, under the great name of history.[2] If history be, as nearly all historians have conceived it, and as Gibbon defined it, "little more than the register of the crimes, follies, and misfortunes of mankind," it is an empty and contemptible

[1] This chapter contains the substance of the author's Friday evening discourse, entitled "Biology and History," delivered before the Royal Institution of Great Britain and Ireland, February 14, 1908. The substance of two lectures to the Royal Institution, entitled "Biology and Progress," and delivered in February, 1907, is also included in the present volume.

[2] It is thus everywhere that foolish Rumor babbles not of what was done, but of what was misdone or undone; and foolish History (ever, more or less, the written epitomized synopsis of Rumor) knows so little that were not as well unknown. Attila invasions, Walter-the-Penniless Crusades, Sicilian Vespers, Thirty-Years' Wars: mere sin and misery; not work, but hindrance of work! For the Earth, all this while, was yearly green and yellow with her kind harvests; the hand of the craftsman, the mind of the thinker rested not: and so, after all, and in spite of all, we have this so glorious high-domed blossoming World; concerning which, poor History may well ask, with wonder, Whence *it* came? She knows so little of it, knows so much of what obstructed it, what would have rendered it impossible. Such, nevertheless, by necessity or foolish choice, is her rule and practice; whereby that paradox, 'Happy the people whose annals are vacant,' is not without its true side."—CARLYLE, *French Revolution.*

"In a little while it would come to be felt that the true history of a nation was indeed not of its wars but of its households."—RUSKIN, *Time and Tide.*

study, save for the social pathologist. But if history without by any means ignoring great men or underrating their influence, is, or should be, the record of the past life of mankind, of progress and decadence, the rise and fall of Empires and civilizations, and their mutual reactions; if it be the record of the intermittent ascent of man, "sagging but pertinacious"; if this record be subject to the law of causation, and therefore susceptible, in theory, at least, of explanation as well as description; if its factors are at work to-day and will shape the destiny of all the to-morrows; if it be neither phantasmagoria nor panorama nor pageant nor procession but *process,* in short, an organic drama,—then, indeed, it is more than worthy of all the study and thought of all who ever study or ever think. Especially must it appeal to us, who boast a tradition greater than the world has ever yet seen, and kinship with men who represent the utmost of which the human spirit has yet shown itself capable,— to us who speak the tongue that Shakespeare spake, but to whom the names of all our Imperial predecessors, from Babylon to Spain, serve as a perpetual *memento mori.* Our special question here is whether there are inherent and necessary reasons why our predecessors' fate must sooner or later be ours. Must races die? — or, if we are sceptical about races and more especially about the so-called Anglo-Saxon race, must civilizations, states, or nations die? What comment does modern biology, or the theory of organic evolution, make upon the familiar words of Byron in his address to the ocean:

> "Thy shores are empires, changed in all save thee—
> Assyria, Greece, Rome, Carthage, what are they?

> Thy waters wasted them while they were free
> And many a tyrant since: their shores obey
> The stranger, slave, or savage."

And these, a few pages earlier in the same poem: —

> "There is the moral of all human tales;
> 'Tis but the same rehearsal of the past,
> First Freedom and then Glory — when that fails,
> Wealth, vice, corruption — barbarism at last.
> And History, with all her volumes vast,
> Hath but *one* page" . . .

Nations, races, civilizations rise, we shall all agree, because to inherent virtue of breed they add sound customs and laws, acquirements of discipline and knowledge. But, these acquirements made, power established, and crescent from year to year — why do they *then* fall? If they can *make* a place for themselves, how much easier should it not be to *maintain* it?

Two explanations, each falsely asserting itself to be rooted in biological fact, have long been cited and are still cited in order to account for these supreme tragedies of history.

THE FALLACY OF RACIAL SENILITY.— The first may claim Plato and Aristotle as its founders, and consists of an argument from analogy. Races may be conceived in similar terms to individuals. There are many resemblances between a society — a "social organism," to use Herbert Spencer's phrase — and an individual organism. Just then, as the individual is mortal, so is the race. Each has its birth, its period of youth and growth, its maturity, and, finally, its decadence, senility and death. So runs the common argument.

We must reply, however, that biology, so far from confirming it, declares as the capital fact which contrasts the individual and the race that, whilst the individual is doomed to die from inherent causes, the race is naturally immortal. The tendency of life is not to die but to live. If individuals die, that is doubtless because, as I believe, more life and fuller is thus attained than if life bodied itself in immortal forms: but the germ-plasm *is* immortal; it has no inherent tendency either to degenerate or to die. Species exist and flourish now which are millions of years older than mankind. "The individual withers, the race is more and more."

It may be added that, in historical instances, civilizations have, on the one hand, persisted, and, on the other, fallen, despite change, and even substitution, in the races which created them: and, on the other hand, the most conspicuously persistent of all races in the historic epoch, the Jews, have survived one Empire after another of their oppressors, but have never had an Empire of their own. Thus, so far as the historian is concerned, it is not races at all that die, but civilizations and Empires. Plato's argument from the individual to the race is therefore irrelevant, as well as untrue. The fatalistic conception to which it tempts us, saying that races must die, just as individuals must, and that therefore it is idle to repine or oppose, is utterly unwarrantable and extremely unhealthy. To take our own case, despite the talk about our own racial decadence, nearly all our babies still come into the world fit and strong and healthy — the racial poisons apart. We kill them in scores of thousands every year, but this infant mortality is not a sign that the race is dying, but a sign that even the most splendid living material can be killed or damaged if you try hard enough. The babies do not die because races are mortal, but because individuals are and we kill them. The babies drink poison, eat poison, and breathe poison, and in due course die. The theory of racial senility, inapplicable everywhere because untrue, is most of all inapplicable here. If a race became sterile, Plato and Aristotle would be right. There is no such instance in history, apart from well-defined external, ***not inherent,*** causes, as in the case of the Tasmanians. Dismissing this analogy, we may also dismiss, as based upon nothing better, the idea that the great tragedies of history were necessary events at all. We must look elsewhere than amongst the inherent and necessary factors of racial life for the causes which determine these tragedies; and we shall be entitled to assume as conceivable the proposition that, notwithstanding the consistent fall of all our predecessors, the causes are not inevitable, but, being external and environmental, may possibly be controlled: men being not only creature but creator also.

The Lamarckian explanation of decadence.—The second of the two false interpretations of history in terms of biology is still, and always has been, widely credited. When historians have paid any attention to the breed of a people as determining its destiny, they have invariably added to the fallacy of racial senility this no less fecund error. It is that, in consequence of success, a people become idle, thoughtless, unenterprising, luxurious, and that these *acquired characters are transmitted* to succeeding generations so that, finally, there is produced a degenerate people unable to bear the burden of Empire — and then the crash comes. The historian usually introduces the idea already dismissed by saying that a "young and vigorous race" invaded the Imperial territories — and so forth. The terms "young" and "old" applied to human races, usually mean nothing at all.

The reader will recognize, of course, in this doctrine of the transmission to children of characters acquired by their parents, the explanation of organic evolution advanced by Lamarck rather more than a century ago. It is employed by historians for the explanation of both the processes they record, progress and retrogression. Thus they suppose that for many generations a race is disciplined, and so at last there is produced a race with discipline in its very bone; or for many generations a nation finds it necessary to make adventure upon the sea, and so at last there is produced a generation of predestined sailors with blue water in its blood. And in similar terms moral and physical retrogression or degeneration are explained.

Let us consider the contrast between the interpretation which accepts the Lamarckian theory of the transmission of acquired characters and that which does not. Consider the babies of a new generation. According to Lamarck, these have in their blood and brain the consequences of the habits of their ancestors. If these have been idle and luxurious, the new babies are predestined to be idle and luxurious too. This, in short, is a "dying nation." But, if acquired characters are not transmitted, the new generation is, on the whole, not much better, not much worse, than its predecessors — so far as this supposed factor of change is concerned. Each generation makes a fresh start, as we see in the babies of our slums to-day. It does not begin where the last left off — whether that means beginning at a higher or at a lower level than that at which the last started: but it makes a fresh start where the last did.

Now, in general, we have seen that Lamarck's theory is discredited. The view of Mr. Galton is accepted, that acquired characters are not transmitted, either for good or for evil. If there are no other factors of racial degeneration or racial advance, then races do not degenerate or advance, but make a fresh start every generation: and Empires rise and fall without any relation to the breed of the Imperial people — an incredible proposition.

THE RACIAL POISONS AND DECADENCE.— Certain apparent, though not real, exceptions exist to the denial of the Lamarckian theory of the transmission of acquired characters. These exceptions are furnished by what I here call the *racial poisons*. Alcohol, for instance is a substance, certainly poisonous in all but very small doses, if not in them, which is carried by the blood to every part of the body and may and does injure *its racial* elements. Thus a true racial degeneration may be caused by its means: and the possibility of this is not to be ignored. Other poisons, such as those of certain diseases, act similarly.

We must therefore note in passing a biological factor of historical importance, though hitherto entirely unrecognized by historians, and that is disease. Certain of our diseases, and especially consumption or tuberculosis, are at present making history by their extermination of aboriginal races. Minute living creatures, which we call microbes, are introduced into the new and favorable environment constituted by the blood and tissues of human races hitherto unacquainted with them: and the consequences are known to all. But further, it has lately been suggested as highly probable, by Professor Ronald Ross, that the fall of Greece, that incalculable disaster for mankind, was due to the invasion not of human foes but of the humble living species which are responsible for the disease miscalled malaria. The evidence for this view is by no means slight, and the most recent explanation of an event so abrupt and so disastrous is in all likelihood the correct one. Malaria, like alcohol, produces true racial degeneration, its poisons affecting *those racial elements* of which the individual body, biologically conceived, is merely the ephemeral host: recalling the great line of Lucretius, "*et quasi cursores, vitai lampada tradunt.*" To lame the runner is not to injure the torch he bears — acquired characters are not transmitted; but the racial poison makes dim the lamp ere he passes it on.

SELECTION AND RACIAL CHANGE.— But, leaving poisons out of the question, races of men and animals *do* undergo change, progressive and retrogressive, in consequence of the action of another factor than that advanced by Lamarck: and this is the factor of "natural selection," so termed by Charles Darwin in 1858, or "survival of the fittest," to use Herbert Spencer's phrase. If, of any generation, individuals of a certain kind are chosen by the environment for survival and parenthood, the character of the species will change accordingly. If what we call the best are chosen, their goodness will be transmitted in some degree, and the race will advance: if what we call the worst are chosen, their badness will be transmitted in some degree, and the race will degenerate

THE TWO KINDS OF PROGRESS.— Now in the case of all species other than man, the only possible progress is this racial or inherent progress, dependent upon a choice or selection of parents, and comparable in some measure, as Darwin showed, with the change similarly produced in the selective breeding or "artificial selection" of the lower animals by man. But in the case of man himself, there is a wholly different kind of progress also attainable, which is not inherent or racial progress at all, but yet is real progress: and which has the most important relations to the inherent or racial progress that might be achieved by the process of natural selection, or the choice of parents.

It has been laid down that acquired characters are not transmissible by heredity: but man has learnt — and it is well for him — to circumvent the laws of heredity by transmitting his spiritual acquirements through language and art. Even before writing there was tradition, passed on from mouth to mouth. As long as man was without writing he advanced little faster than other creatures, we may surmise: we know that he has an undistinguished past of probably at least six million years: but with speech *and writing* came the transmission of acquirements in this special sense; not that the past education of a mother will enlarge her baby's brain, but that she can teach her daughter what she has learnt, and so the child can begin where the parent left off, just as Lamarck wrongly imagined to be the case with the young giraffe, that he supposed to profit by the stretching of the parental necks. It is this transmission of spiritual acquirements — outside the germ-plasm and in defiance of its laws — that explains the amazing advance of man in the last ten or twenty thousand years as compared with the almost speechless ages before them.

This kind of progress is peculiar to man,[1] it is the gift of intelligence, and we may call it traditional or acquired progress. It is an utterly different thing from inherent or racial progress, an improvement in the breed dependent upon the happy choice of parents. And it is surely evident, on a moment's consideration, that acquired progress is compatible with inherent decadence. To use Coleridge's image, a dwarf may see further than a giant if he sits on the giant's shoulders: yet he is a dwarf and the other a giant. Any schoolboy now knows more than Aristotle, and that is true progress of a kind, but the schoolboy may well be a dwarf compared with Aristotle, and may belong to a race degenerate when compared with his; *and that is inherent or racial decadence subsisting with acquired or traditional progress.*

Now whilst the accumulation of knowledge and art and power from age to age is real progress, it evidently

[1] "Literature, taken in all its bearings, forms the grand line of demarcation between the human and the animal kingdoms." — Wm. Godwin.

depends for its stability and persistence upon the quality of the race.[1] If the race degenerates — through, say, the selection of the worst for parenthood — the time will come when its heritage is too much for it. The pearls of the ancestral art are now cast before swine, and are trampled on: statues, temples, books are destroyed or burnt or lost. If an Empire has been built, the degenerate race cannot sustain it. *There is no wealth but life: and if the quality of the life fails, neither battleships nor libraries nor symphonies nor anything else will save a nation.* This we all know, though no one who observed our legislation or read our Parliamentary debates would suspect that it had ever entered into our minds. Empires and civilizations, then, have fallen, despite the strength and magnitude of the superstructure, because the foundations decayed: and the bigger and heavier the superstructure the less could it survive their failure. If the Fiji islanders degenerate, there is little consequence: if the breed of Romans degenerate, all their vast mass of acquired progress and power crushes them into dramatic ruin. This image, I believe, truly expresses the relation between the two wholly distinct kinds of progress, which we have yet to learn to distinguish. Acquired progress will not compensate for racial or inherent decadence. If the race is going down, it will not compensate to add another colony to your Empire: on the contrary, the bigger the Empire the stronger must be the race: the bigger the superstructure the stronger the foundations. Acquired progress is real

[1] See the author's paper, "The Essential Factor of Progress," published in the *Monthly Review*, April, 1906.

progress but it is always dependent for its maintenance upon racial or inherent progress — or, at least, upon racial maintenance.

NOTHING FAILS LIKE SUCCESS.— I believe, then, that civilizations and Empires have succumbed because they represented only acquired or traditional educational progress and this availed not at all when the races that built them up began to degenerate. Now the only explanation of racial degeneration yet offered by the historians — apart from the foolish one of racial senility — is the Lamarckian one of the transmission of habits of luxury and idleness from parent to child: an explanation which the modern study of heredity empowers us to repudiate. What theory of this alleged degeneration is there to offer in its place: and especially what theory which explains racial degeneration amongst not the conquered but the conquerors: amongst the successful, the Imperial, the cultured, the leisured, the well-catered for in all respects, bodily and mental. Why is it that not enslaved but Imperial peoples degenerate? Why is it that nothing fails like success?

What I believe to be the true and sufficient answer has been given by no historian: but the key to it is only fifty years old. The reason is that no race or species, vegetable or animal or human, can maintain — much less raise — its organic level unless its best be selected for parenthood. It is true of a race as of an individual that it must work for its living — so to speak — if it is not to degenerate. When the terms are too easy, down you go. The tape-worm has given up even digesting for its living, and we know its degeneracy — all hooks and mouth. Society works and hands over its predigested food to such social parasites amongst ourselves. You must struggle or you will degenerate — even if only with rhyme or counterpoint, not necessarily for bread. "Work is the law," as Ruskin said: whether for a livelihood or for enjoyment. Living things are the product of the struggle for existence: we are thus evolved strugglers by constitution: and directly we cease to struggle we forfeit the possibilities of our birthright. "Thou, O God," said Leonardo, "hast given all good things to man at the price of labor."

The case is the same with races. Directly the conditions become too easy, selection ceases, and it is as successful to be incompetent or lazy or vicious as to be worthy. The hard conditions that kept weeding out the unworthy are now related and the fine race they made goes back again. Finally there occurs the phenomenon of *reversed selection,* when it is fitter to be bad than good, cowardly than brave — as when religious persecution murders all who are true to themselves and spares hypocrites and apostates: or when healthy children are killed in factories whilst feeble-minded children or deaf-mutes are carefully tended until maturity and then sent into the world to reproduce their maladies. Under reversed selection such results are obtained as a breeder of race-horses or plants would obtain if he went to work on similar lines: the race degenerates rapidly: and if it be an Imperial race its Empire comes crashing down about its ears. All Empires and civilizations hitherto have involved the partial or complete arrest or reversal of the process of natural selection: and the racial degeneration which necessarily ensued has been the cause of their invariable doom.

When a primitive race is making its way by force, selection is stringent. The weak, cowardly, diseased, stupid are expunged from generation to generation. As civilization advances, a higher ethical level is reached: all true civilization tending to abrogate and ameliorate the struggle for existence. The diseased and weakly and feeble-minded are no longer left to pay the penalty sternly exacted by Nature for unfitness: they are allowed to survive and multiply. A successful race can apparently afford to permit this, as a race that is fighting for its existence cannot. But in reality no race can afford this absolutely fatal process.

There is thus a real risk involved in the accumulation of acquired, traditional or educational progress. Not only does it tend to abrogate or even to reverse selection, but it serves to disguise the consequences of this abrogation. If a subhuman race degenerates the fact is evident: but such a nation as our own may quite well degenerate whilst the accumulation of acquired progress, transmitted by education, almost completely cloaks the fact for a time. We may be congratulating ourselves upon our progress, upon our knowledge, our science and art, our institutions, legal and charitable, whilst all the time the breed is undergoing retrogression.

We see now, I think, the explanation of the truth expressed by Gibbon,—"all that is human must retrograde if it do not advance." Why should this be so? Why should it not be possible merely to maintain a position gained? The answer is that the civilization which merely maintains its position is one in which selection has ceased: if selection had not ceased, the position would be more than maintained, there would be advance. But without selection the breed will certainly degenerate, the lower individuals multiplying more rapidly than higher ones, in accordance with Spencer's law that the higher type of the individual the less rapidly does he multiply; and thus the race which is not advancing is retrograding, as Gibbon declared.

Natural selection is the sole factor of efficient and permanent progress, but the traditional or acquired progress which we call civilization tends to thwart or abrogate or even invert this process. I thus believe that the conditions necessary for the *secure* ascent of any race, an ascent secured in its very blood, made stable in its very bone, have not yet been achieved in history; *and I advance this as the reason why history records no enduring Empire.*

Some historical instances.— In the face of certain facts of contemporary history I do not for a moment assert that there are no other causes of Imperial failure than the arrest or reversal of selection. But I do assert that if this is not the cause, then, in the absence of the transmission of acquired characters, the race has not degenerated, and is capable of reasserting itself. Only by the arrest or reversal of selection can a race degenerate — apart from the racial poisons. If, then, a civilization or Empire has fallen through causes altogether non-biological — through carelessness, or neglect of motherhood or alteration of ideals

— the changes in character so produced are not transmitted to the children, and the race is not degenerate but merely deteriorated in each generation.

For instance, we have been brought up to believe that there is no possible future for Spain; it is a dying nation, a senile individual, a people of degenerates; it has had its day, which can never return. The historian explains this by the false analogy between a race and an individual, and by the false Lamarckian theory of heredity. To these the biologist retorts with comments upon their falsity, and with the conviction that since Spain, even allowing for the anti-eugenic labors of the Inquisition, has not been subjected to the only process which can ensure real degeneration — viz., the consistent and stringent selection of the worst — she is yet capable of regeneration. Regeneration is not really the word, because there has been little real degeneration, but only the successive deterioration of successive and undegenerate generations.

If we took an animal species that *has* degenerated, such as the intestinal parasites, and endeavored to regenerate them, we should begin to realize the magnitude of our task. That is not the task for Spain, the biologist asserts. Merely the environment must be altered,— not the mountain ranges and the rivers, Buckle notwithstanding, but the really potent factors in the environment, the spiritual and psychical and social factors, and the deterioration of each new generation, inherently undegenerate, will cease. I am using these opposed terms with great care and of set purpose.

And the biologist is right. The facts concerning

which so many historians have shaken their heads, and upon which they have based so many moralizings and theories of history, the facts which they have cited in support of their false analogies and misconceptions of heredity — due, of course, to the errors of former biology — turn out to be not facts at all, or, at any rate, only facts of the moment. The "dying nation," as Lord Salisbury called it, has occasion to alter its psychical environment. It introduces the practice of education; it begins to shake off the yoke of ecclesiasticism; and what are the consequences?

The new generation is found to be potentially little worse and little better than its predecessors of the sixteenth century. There has been no national or racial degeneration. The environment is modified for the better, *i.e.,* so as to choose the better, and Spain, as they say in misleading phrase, "takes on a new lease of life." The historian of the present day, knowing as a historian what qualities of blood have been in the Spanish people, and basing his theories upon sound biology, must confidently assert that that blood, incapable, as he knows, of degeneration by any Lamarckian process, may still retain its ancient quality and will yet make history.

But the historian might well write a volume upon the same thesis as applied to China and Japan. We know historically what were the immediate effects in one generation of a total change of environment in Japan. That change has not yet occurred in China, but must inevitably occur. Consider for a moment how the historian, made far-sighted and clear-sighted by biology, must contemplate the history of this astounding people. The popular belief used to be that China illustrated the so-called law of nations. It was the decadent, though monstrous, relic of an ancient civilization; it had had its day. Inevitable degeneration, which must befall all peoples, had come upon it. Behold it in the paralysis which precedes death!

But in the light of the facts of Japan, the man in the street and the historian alike have in this case found modern biology superfluous in enabling them to arrive at sound conclusions. They now believe what the Darwinian has been compelled to believe for half a century, and more strongly than ever during the latter part of that period, when the doctrine of the transmission of modifications was finally discredited. A clever writer invents the phrase "the yellow peril," and people discard their old theories. The metaphor must be changed. This is not paralysis, but merely slumber. Doubtless, it is an unnatural slumber; doubtless, it is not the slumber which brings renewed strength. It is suspense or stupor, not recuperation; but assuredly it is not paralysis. Who now would dare to say that China has had its day, even if he still clings to the old fictions about Spain?

MOTHERHOOD AND HISTORY.— Here, also, reference must again be made to another factor of history to which, as I think, the biologist must attach enormous importance, but which no historian yet has adequately reckoned with. Our prime assumption from beginning to end is that "there is no wealth but life," or, if one may venture to improve upon Ruskin, *there is no wealth but mind;* and in the attempt to suggest interpretations of history based upon this truth, so little recked of by the historian, we have considered the life in question from the point of view of its determination by heredity, and its varying value according to the inherent and transmissible characters selected in each generation. But a word must be said as to the other factor which, with heredity, determines the character of the individual — and that factor is the environment. I wish merely to note the most important aspect of the environment of human beings, and to observe that historians hitherto have wholly ignored it; yet its influence is incalculable. I refer to motherhood.

One might have the most perfect system of selection of the finest and highest individuals for parenthood; but the babies whose potentialities — heredity gives no more — are so splendid, are always, will be always, dependent upon motherhood. What was the state of motherhood during the decline and fall of the Roman Empire? This factor counts in history; and always will count so long as, three times in every century, the only wealth of nations is reduced to dust, and is raised again from helpless infancy. As to Rome we know little, whatever may be suspected: but we know that here in the heart of the greatest Empire in history — and it is at the heart that Empires rot — thousands of mothers go out every day to tend dead machines, whilst their own flesh and blood, with whom lies the Imperial destiny, are tended anyhow or not at all. It may be said by some enlightened historian of the future that the living wealth of this people, in the twentieth century, began to be eaten away by the cancer which we call "married women's labor," and that, as will be evident to that historian's readers, its damnation was sure. To-day our historians think in terms of regiments and tariffs and "Dreadnoughts": the time will come when historians think in terms of babies and motherhood. We must think in such terms too if we wish Great Britain to be much longer great. Meanwhile some of us see the perennial slaughter of babies in this land, and the deterioration of many for every one killed outright, the waste of mothers' travail and tears: and we recall Ruskin's words:—

"Nevertheless, it is open, I repeat, to serious question, which I leave to the reader's pondering, whether, among national manufactures, that of Souls of a good quality may not at last turn out a quite leadingly lucrative one? Nay, in some far-away and yet undreamt-of hour, I can even imagine that England may cast all thoughts of possessive wealth back to the barbaric nations among whom they first arose; and that, while the sands of the Indus and adamant of Golconda may yet stiffen the housings of the charger, and flash from the turban of the slave, she, as a Christian mother, may at last attain to the virtues and the treasures of a Heathen one, and be able to lead forth her Sons, saying:—These are MY Jewels."

Had all Roman mothers been Cornelias, would Rome have fallen?[1] Consider the imitation mothers — no

[1] Gibbon does not enlighten us much on such vital matters: but my attention has been called to the following passage, not irrelevant here. It is from the *Attic Nights* of Aulus Gellius, Book xii., chap. i., written about A.D. 150 — a point worth noting. I use the free translation of Mr. Quintin Waddington:—

"Once when I was with the philosopher Favorinus, word was brought to him that the wife of one of his disciples had just given birth to a son.

"'Let us go,' said he, 'To inquire after the mother, and to congratulate the father.' The latter was a noble of Senatorial rank.

"All of us who were present accompanied him to the house and went in with him. Meeting the father in the hall, he embraced and congratulated him, and, sitting down, inquired how his wife had come through the ordeal. And when he longer mammalia — to be found in certain classes to-day — mothers who should be ashamed to look any tabby-cat in the face; consider the ignorant and down-

heard that the young mother, overcome with fatigue, was now sleeping, he began to speak more freely.

"'Of course,' said he, 'she will suckle the child herself.' And when the girl's mother said that her daughter must be spared, and nurses obtained in order that the heavy strain of nursing the child should not be added to what she had already gone through, 'I beg of you, dear lady,' said he, 'to allow her to be a whole mother to her child. Is it not against nature, and being only half a mother, to give birth to a child, and then at once to send him away? To have nourished with her own blood and in her own body a something that she had never seen, and then to refuse it her own milk, now that she sees it living, a human being, demanding a mother's care? Or are you one of those who think that nature gave a woman breasts, not that she might feed her children, but as pretty little hillocks to give her bust a pleasing contour? Many indeed of our present-day ladies — whom you are far from resembling — do try to dry up and repress that sacred fount of the body, the nourisher of the human race, even at the risk they run from turning back and corrupting their milk, lest it should take off from the charm of their beauty. In doing this they act with the same folly as those, who, by the use of drugs and so forth, endeavor to destroy the very embryo in their bodies, lest a furrow should mar the smoothness of their skin, and they should spoil their figures in becoming mothers. If the destruction of a human being in its first inception, whilst it is being formed, whilst it is yet coming to life, and is still in the hands of its artificer, Nature, be deserving of public detestation and horror, is it not nearly as bad to deprive the child of his proper and congenial nutriment to which he is accustomed, now that he is perfected, is born into the world, is a child.

"But it makes no difference — for as they say — so long as the child is nourished and lives, with whose milk it is done.

"Why does he who says this, since he is so dull in understanding nature, think it also of no consequence in whose womb, and from whose blood the child is formed and fashioned? For is there not now in the breasts the same blood — whitened, it is true by agration and heat — which was before in the womb? And is not the wisdom of Nature to be seen in this, that as soon as the blood has done its work of forming the body down below, and the time of birth has come, it betakes itself to the upper parts of the body, and is ready to cherish the spark of life and light by furnishing to the new-born babe his known and accustomed food? And so it is not an idle belief, that, just as the strength and character of the seed have their influence in determining the likeness of the body and mind, so trodden mothers amongst our lower classes; and ask whether these things are not making history.

THE SURVIVAL OF THE JEWS.— The principles the discussion of which has here been attempted had all been set down before it suddenly seemed clear that

do the nature and properties of the milk do their part in effecting the same results. And this has been noticed, not in man alone, but in cattle as well. For if kids are brought up on the milk of ewes, or lambs on that of goats, it is agreed that the latter have stiffer wool, the former softer hair. In the case of timber and fruit trees, too, the qualities of the water and soil from which they draw their nourishment have more influence in stunting or augmenting their growth than those of the seed which is sewn, and often you may see a vigorous and healthy tree when transplanted into another place perish owing to the poverty of the soil.

"Is it then a reasonable thing to corrupt the fine qualities of the new-born man, well endowed as to both body and mind so far as parentage is concerned, with the unsuitable nourishment of degenerate and foreign milk? Especially is this the case, if she whom you get to supply the milk is a slave or of servile estate, and—as is very often the case—of a foreign and barbarous race, if she is dishonest, ugly, unchaste, or *addicted to drink*. For generally any woman who happens to have milk is called in, without further inquiry as to her suitability in other respects. Shall we allow this babe of ours to be tainted by pernicious contagion, and to draw life into his body and mind from a body and mind debased?

"This is the reason why we are so often surprised that the children of chaste mothers resemble their parents neither in body nor character.

". . . And besides these considerations, who can afford to ignore or belittle the fact that those who desert their offspring and send them away from themselves, and make them over to others to nurse, cut, or at least loosen and weaken that chain and connection of mind and affection by which Nature attaches children to their parents. For when the child, sent elsewhere, is away from sight, the vigor of maternal solicitude, little by little dies away, and the call of motherly instinct grows silent, and forgetfulness of a child sent away to nurse is not much less complete than that of one lost by death.

"A child's thoughts and the love he is ever ready to give, are occupied, moreover, with her alone from whom he derives his food, and soon he has neither feeling nor affection for the mother who bore him. The foundations of the filial feelings with which we are born being thus sapped and undermined, whatever affection children thus brought up may seem to have for father and mother, for the most part is not natural love, but the result of social convention."

they found their warrant and application in the unexampled riddle of the persistence and success, throughout more than two thousand years and a thousand vicissitudes, of the Jewish people. It is true that we have here no exception to the apparent law that Empires are mortal, for within this period there never was a Jewish Empire: the Jews were never subject to the risk involved for racial or inherent progress by the possession of great acquired powers. But just as the fall of Empires has often *not* been the fall of races — various races having at various times carried on the same Imperial tradition — so the persistence of the Jews, as contrasted with the impermanence of Empires, *has* been the persistence of a race. I believe that the principles already laid down offer us an adequate explanation of this unique case: and further, that if we had begun with the case of the Jews, endeavoring, by the investigation of their case, to explain the contrasted case of other races and of all Empires hitherto, we should have arrived at the same principles.

It has been asserted that that race or people decays in which selection ceases or is reversed; that in the absence of selection of the worthy for parenthood, no species, vegetable, animal or human, can prosper — much less progress. Now the Jews, the one human race of which we know assuredly that it has persisted unimpaired, have been the most continuously and stringently selected of any race, I suppose, that can be named. Every measure of persecution and repression practiced against them by the people amongst whom they have lived, has directly tended towards the very end which those people least desired to compass.

Other peoples found themselves prosperous through the efforts of their fathers; the struggle for existence abated; it was, so to say, as fit to be unfit as to fit — with the inevitable result. But this has never been the case of the Jews. They have always had to struggle for life intensely: and their unexampled struggle has been a great source of their unexampled strength. The Jew who was a weakling or a fool had no chance at all; the weaklings and the fools being weeded out, intensity and strength of mind became the common heritage of this amazing people.

Secondly, there was everything to favor motherhood. Here religious precept and ethical tradition joined with stern necessity to the same end — the end which always meant a new and strong beginning for the next generation. Even to-day all observers are agreed that infant mortality is at a minimum amongst the Jews; their children are superior in height and weight and chest measurement to Gentile children brought up amidst poverty far less intense in our own great cities; *in a better material environment, but a far inferior maternal environment.* The Jewish mother is the mother of children innately superior, on the average, since they are the fruit of such long ages of stringent parental selection, and she makes more of them because she fails to nurse them only in the rarest cases, when she has no choice, and because in every detail her maternal care is incomparably superior to that of her Gentile sister. Given a high standard of motherhood in a highly selected race, what other result than that we daily witness and envy can we expect?

Thirdly, the Jews do not abuse alcohol, and thus avoid one of the few causes of true racial degeneration apart from the selection of the worst for parenthood.

If these principles are valid, it is evident that our redemption from the fate of all our predecessors is to be found only in eugenics — the selection of the best for parenthood. In his address to the Sociological Society in 1904, in which he defined this term, Mr. Galton named as one of the duties before the Society, "Historical inquiry into the rates with which the various classes of society (classified according to civic usefulness) have contributed to the population at various times, in ancient and modern nations." "There is strong reason for believing," he continued, "that national rise and decline is closely connected with this influence."[1]

WHAT IS A GOOD ENVIRONMENT? — Using the word environment in its widest sense, including, for instance, public opinion — and its use in any sense less wide is always erroneous and misleading — we may say that it is our business to provide the environment which selects the best for parenthood and discourages the parenthood of the worst — say the deaf and dumb, the feeble-minded, the insane, the epileptic, the inebriate, those afflicted with hereditary disease of other kinds, and so forth. Our principles should enable us, also, I think to define what we mean by a good environment. Comprehensive and indiscriminate charity means a good environment for many in a sense, but it may also mean the selection of the worst for parent-

[1] Cf. the similar dicta of Darwin and Pearson.

hood — *e.g.,* the feeble-minded. This "good" environment *then* means the degeneration of the race. We must therefore *appraise environment in terms of its selective action.* A good environment is that which selects the good, and the best environment is that which selects the best; discovers them, makes the utmost of them, and confers upon them the supreme privilege and duty of parenthood. That and that alone is the best environment, and all other moral judgments upon environment are fallacious and will be disastrous.

THE NECESSARY CONCLUSION.— National Eugenics teaches that the first duty of all governments, and patriots and good citizens is, to quote Ruskin again, "The production and recognition of human worth, the detection and extinction of human unworthiness." The idea is not new-fangled, but was clearly laid down by Plato, and by Theognis two centuries before him.

Eugenics is a project of the most elevated and provident morality, aiming at no object less sublime than the ennoblement of mankind; and if one may suggest its motto it would be, *The products of progress are not mechanisms but men.* It is based upon the principle of the selection or choice of the superior for parenthood, which has been the essential factor of all progress in the world of life, but which all civilizations have tended, in some degree to abrogate — or even to reverse, as when the feeble-minded child is cared for till maturity and sent out into the world to produce its like, whilst healthy children are daily destroyed by ignorance and neglect.

"Through Nature only can we ascend"— and the

merit of the eugenic proposal is that it is built upon "the solid ground of nature."

To the economist, it declares that *the culture of the racial life is the vital industry of any people.*

It is to work through marriage, an institution more ancient than mankind, and supremely valuable in its services to childhood — with which lies all human destiny.

Eugenics appeals to the individual, asking for a little imagination which will make us realize that the future will one day be the present and that to serve it is to serve no fiction or phantom, but a reality as real as the present generation.

It teaches the responsibility of the noblest and most sacred of all professions, which is parenthood, and it makes a sober and dignified claim to be regarded as a constituent of the religion of the future.

It goes to the root of the matter; where the well-meaning, but short-sighted, pin their faith on the hospitals, the eugenist seeks to brand the transmission of hereditary disease as a crime, and thus literally to extirpate it altogether.

That its methods are practicable is proven by the fact that it is practiced — as by the northern society for the "*Permanent* care of the feeble-minded," which serves the present and the future simultaneously and reconciles the law of love with the earlier law of nature — which asserts that parenthood must be denied to the unworthy — without blame or malice, but without exception. It suggests the principles of a New Imperialism, and offers, I submit, our sole chance of escape from the fate which has overtaken all previous civilizations. It honors men and women by declaring that human parenthood is crowned with responsibility to the unborn, and to all time coming, and that man, the animal in body, is also a self-conscious being, "looking before and after," who is human because he is responsible, and to whom the laws of nature have been revealed, not to satisfy an intellectual curiosity, but for the highest end conceivable — the elevation of his race.

Let me quote a fine passage from Wordsworth's "Prelude": —

"With settling judgments now of what would last
And what would disappear; prepared to find
Presumption, folly, madness, in the men
Who thrust themselves upon the passive world
As Rulers of the world; to see in these,
Even when the public welfare is their aim,
Plans without thought, or built on theories
Vague and unsound; and having brought the books
Of modern statists to their proper test,
Life, human life, with all its sacred claims
Of sex and age, and heaven-descended rights,
Mortal, or those beyond the reach of death;
And having thus discerned how dire a thing
Is worshipped in that idol proudly named
'The Wealth of Nations;' where alone that wealth
Is lodged, and how increased; and having gained
A more judicious knowledge of the worth
And dignity of individual man,
No composition of the brain, but man
Of whom we read, the man whom we behold
With our own eyes — I could not but enquire —
Not with less interest than heretofore,
But greater, though in spirit more subdued —
Why is this glorious creature to be found
One only in ten thousand? What one is,
Why may not millions be? What bars are thrown
By Nature in the way of such a hope?"

Consider how far we have come, the base degrees by which we did ascend, and answer with Shakespeare, "There are many events in the womb of time which will be delivered."

CHAPTER XVI

NATIONAL EUGENICS — MR. BALFOUR ON DECADENCE

(1) "If the various checks specified in the two last paragraphs, and perhaps others as yet unknown, do not prevent the reckless, the vicious, and otherwise inferior members of society from increasing at a quicker rate than the better class of men, the nation will retrograde, as has too often occurred in the history of the world. We must remember that progress is no invariable rule. It is very difficult to say why one civilized nation rises, becomes more powerful, and spreads more widely, than another; or why the same nation progresses more quickly at one time than at another. We can only say that it depends on an increase in the actual number of the population, on the number of the men endowed with high intellectual and moral faculties, as well as on their standard of excellence. Corporeal structure appears to have little influence, except so far as vigor of body leads to vigor of mind."—DARWIN, *The Descent of Man,* 1871.

(2) Referring to "the rates with which the various classes of society (classified according to civic usefulness) have contributed to the population at various times, in ancient and modern nations," Mr. Francis Galton said "there is strong reason for believing that national rise and decline is closely connected with this influence."—GALTON, *Sociological Papers,* 1904, p. 47.

(3) "The inexplicable decline and fall of nations following from no apparent external cause receives instant light from the relative fertility of the fitter and unfitter elements combined with what we now know of the laws of inheritance."[1]—PEARSON, 1904.

(4) To the question, what were the causes of the fall of Rome, Mr. Balfour replies "I feel disposed to answer Decadence."[2]— BALFOUR, 1908.

[1] *National Life from the Standpoint of Science,* p. 99.
[2] "Decadence," Henry Sidgwick Memorial Lecture, by the

THE lecture of which the previous chapter is the written form was prepared and delivered before I had an opportunity of seeing Mr. A. J. Balfour's lecture on "Decadence" delivered a few days before. That has since been printed, and is well worthy of our attention. In Mr. Balfour we have a representative political thinker, an experimental statesman and, furthermore, a former President of the British Association, deeply interested in, and favorably disposed towards, scientific inquiry and scientific method. Further, this lecture has been widely noticed, though all the criticisms I have seen seem to me to miss the point. No apology, then, is necessary for a special discussion of this most suggestive lecture in direct relation with the foregoing theory of its subject.

Political and national decadence is Mr. Balfour's theme, and we note first that here is a contemporary thinker, not unread in recent biology, including the work of Weismann, who is prepared to make use of the idea that societies are inherently mortal, as individuals are. One wonders when we shall be rid of this pernicious instance of the argument from analogy, which is already much more than two thousand years old.

Next it may be noticed that, though Mr. Balfour has deliberately discussed the idea of natural selection, he has been led wholly astray from its true relation to the question under discussion by reason of falling into the common error which Sir E. Ray Lankester has recently exposed, as Huxley did many decades ago.

Rt. Hon. A. J. Balfour, M.P., delivered at Newnham College, January 25, 1908. (Cambridge University Press.)

Mr. Balfour conceives natural selection to issue from the struggle for existence between species or societies. It has already been pointed out that the all-important natural selection is not between species or societies but within them. The struggle for existence is fought out mainly between the immature individuals of any species or society. Its issue determines the survivors for parenthood and the future. Mr. Balfour must have read Professor Ray Lankester's recent Romanes Lecture in which all this is so clearly shown, but he has unfortunately retained the popular conception of natural selection as acting between species or societies, and has in consequence failed, I will not say to find, but even to discuss in any adequate measure, the theory of racial and national decadence, advanced in the preceding chapter. He merely discusses "competition between groups of communities," and rightly finds it inadequate to account for the great tragedies of history.

There follows a passage which may be heartily assented to, on the very grounds on which the entire lecture may be welcomed, namely, that it suggests the inadequacy of the common explanations of racial decadence advanced by historians. Says Mr. Balfour: —

"It is in vain that historians enumerate the public calamities which preceded, and no doubt contributed to, the final catastrophe. Civil dissensions, military disasters, pestilences, famines, tyrants, tax-gatherers, growing burdens, and waning wealth — the gloomy catalogue is unrolled before our eyes, yet somehow it does not in all cases wholly satisfy us: we feel that some of these diseases are of a kind which a vigorous body politic should easily be able to survive, that others are secondary symptoms of some obscurer malady, and that in neither case do they supply us with the full explanation of which we are in search."

One must heartily thank the author for the abundant demonstration which follows, well-warranting our feeling that these explanations do not suffice — nor yet, in the case of Rome, diminution of population, nor the "brutalities of the gladiatorial shows," nor "the gratuitous distribution of bread to the urban mobs," nor yet slavery, lately declared, by Mr. W. R. Paterson, in his *Nemesis of Nations,* to be *the* cause of the fall of empires. As Mr. Balfour says, "Who can believe that this immemorial custom could, in its decline, destroy the civilization, which, in its vigor, it had helped to create?" It would have been more important, perhaps, to consider, as Mr. Balfour does not, the latest view, advanced by Professor Ronald Ross, that the incursion of malaria may have had something to do with the fall of Rome.

Mr. Balfour's theory — decadence the cause of decadence.— Mr. Balfour then falls back upon "decadence" as the explanation, and if it be answered that it helps us not to say that decadence is due to decadence, replies that it is something to recognize the possibility of "subtle changes in the social tissues of old communities." One regrets all the more that he should not have considered anti-eugenic practices as possibly accounting for these subtle changes. One must however quote the excellent passage in which Mr. Balfour supports his use of the word decadence, though one utterly disagrees with the suggestion that the term "old age" might be its equivalent. He says: "The facile generalizations with which we so often season the study of dry historic fact; the habits of political discussion which induce us to catalogue for purposes of debate the outward signs that distinguish (as we are prone to think) the standing from the falling state, hide the obscurer, the more potent, forces which silently prepare the fate of empires."

We may note with interest (and surely with surprise when we consider Japan and Spain and the China of to-morrow), Mr. Balfour's rejection of the doctrine that "arrested progress, and even decadence, may be but the prelude to a new period of vigorous growth. So that even those races or nations which seem frozen into eternal immobility may base upon experience their hopes of an awakening spring." It is, I fancy, Mr. Balfour's fondness for the Platonic idea of senility in the race as in the individual, that leads him to question what can surely be no longer denied. Thus a little later we find him saying, "*if civilization wear out, and races become effete,* why should we expect to progress indefinitely, why for us alone is the doom of man to be reversed?"

Nowhere in this lecture is there any recognition of what, I confess, seems to me to be an obvious and necessary truth, the distinction between the two kinds of progress — racial progress due to the choice of the best for parenthood, and acquired or traditional progress. It may be suggested that no one can usefully discuss decadence or progress until he has seen and perceived this absolutely cardinal distinction, suggested in my Royal Institution lectures in February, 1907, as one of the great lessons taught by the study of biology to the student of progress.

Mr. Balfour does indeed avoid all those false solutions which depend upon a Lamarckian belief in the transmission of acquired characters. This, however, instead of leading him to insist upon the Darwinian contribution to the study of decadence — the idea of *selection* — causes him to regard the racial question as unimportant. He notes one or two of the fashions in which the quality of a race may be modified, thus influencing national character, and then dismisses this question (wherein, as I cannot doubt, everything material lies) with the remark, "but such changes are not likely, I suppose, to be considerable, except perhaps those due to the mixture of races — and that only in new countries." — Reaching page 45, the reader finds himself confident that now at length the writer has put his finger on the crux of the problem. Yet that is how he dismisses it; adding, indeed, to make it quite clear, the following words: "The flexible element in any society, that which is susceptible of progress or decadence, must therefore be looked for rather in the physical and psychical conditions affecting the life of its component units, than in their inherited constitution."

Not a word as to the cessation of selection! This omission, which I regard as the omission of *the* fact of decadence, mainly depends, one fancies, upon that erroneous conception of natural selection as acting between species and societies rather than within them, which for so many decades the biologist has been at pains to correct. One would indeed have thought that, for a scholar and student like Mr. Balfour, Wordsworth's great sonnet would have sufficed to set up a train of thought, which, fusing with ordinary biological principles, would have led him to what I believe to be the truth. Let us for a moment turn to its consideration: —

> "When I have borne in memory what has tamed
> Great Nations, how ennobling thoughts depart
> When men change swords for ledgers. . . ."

Should not this be enough to suggest to us the real meaning of the consequence which has followed when men changed swords for ledgers, and which even those who hate war as a vile blasphemy against life, must recognize? It is that, as we have seen, when a nation is making its way there is selection of the fittest by the stern arbitrament of war, in which the battle is to the individually strong and fleet and brave and quick-witted. Later, "when men change swords for ledgers," selection ceases; and that is why nothing fails like success. Yet later still, as France should know, selection by war must take the form of reverse selection, the flower of a nation's youth being immolated on the battle-field, whilst its future is determined by the weak and small and diseased, whom the recruiting sergeant rejects. "You are not good enough to be a soldier," he says; "stay at home and be a father." That was what Napoleon did for France.

But to return — for the relations of war to eugenics would really demand a volume — it may be noted that, though rejecting the Lamarckian theory — the theory on which nothing should succeed like success — Mr. Balfour nowhere emphasizes the amazing paradox of history that nothing fails like success. If we consider this fact with the idea of natural selection in our minds (not between societies but within them), we cannot fail to perceive that success involves failure, because it involves failure of selection, and therefore indiscriminate survival; or indeed, survival of the worst.

POLITICS AND DOMESTICS.— It is, perhaps, a noteworthy comment upon what may be called the political state of mind, that even when the idea of natural selection has entered it, the bias is towards associating it with international and not with intra-national or domestic politics. The time will come, however, when the politician — or shall we say the statesman? — realizes that it is the domestic policy, it is the internal struggle for survival within a society, that conditions and fore-ordains all international politics. The history of nations is determined not on the battlefield but in the nursery, and the battalions which give lasting victory are battalions of babies. *The politics of the future will be domestics.*

Having rejected so many solutions of his problem, and having ignored the solution which is advanced in this volume, Mr. Balfour is reduced to such desperate resorts as phrases like this: "the point at which the energy of advance is exhausted"— a mere meaningless phrase; and even such an explanation as that through "mere weariness of spirit the community resigns itself to . . . stagnation." One is inclined to throw up one's hands and ask — Do you, then, who deny the Lamarckian theory, suppose that the fresh children come into the world with this "mere weariness of spirit"? Has this been observed in children? Is there anything conceivable that has been less observed in children, in all times and all places? And if that be so what kind of explanation of decadence is this?

SCIENCE AND INDUSTRY.— Lastly, in a series of fine passages, Mr. Balfour offers us some hope in the help of science. Politics, says our ex-Premier, too often means "the barren exchange of one set of tyrants or jobbers, for another"; a Daniel come to judgment. We owe the modern spirit and modern progress, he tells us, neither to politicians nor to political institutions, nor to theologians nor to philosophers, but to science, which, he well says, "is the great instrument of social change, all the greater because its object is not change but knowledge; and its silent appropriation of this dominant function, amid the din of political and religious strife, is the most vital of all the revolutions which have marked the development of modern civilization."

And our cause of hope is "a social force, new in magnitude if not in kind . . . the modern alliance between pure science and industry." To this I answer a thousand times yes, but I must define the kind of industry. It is the culture of the racial life which is the vital industry of any nation, and which Mr. Balfour has not even distantly alluded to. I agree that our hope for the future is to be found in science: that, as has been said already, perchance our acquired or traditional progress in knowledge has now reached the point at which we have sufficient to reveal to us the necessity of racial progress and the means by which it may be effected.

"Science and industry,"— yes, indeed! But the industry is to be the making not of machines, but men. *The products of progress are not mechanisms but men,* and one may now ask, what is the industry whose products can be named in the same breath with the men and women who shall yet be produced by the supreme industry of race-culture?

CHAPTER XVII

THE PROMISE OF RACE CULTURE

"The best is yet to be"

In its form of what we have called negative eugenics, the practice of our principle would assuredly reduce to an incalculable extent the amount of human defect, mental and physical, which each generation now exhibits. This alone, as has been said, would be far more than sufficient to justify us. A world without hereditary disease of mind and body would alone warrant the hint of Ruskin that posterity may some day look back upon us with "incredulous disdain." Yet, assuming that this could be accomplished, as it will be accomplished, what more is to be hoped for? Must race-culture cease merely when it has raised the average of the community by reducing to a minimum the proportion of those who are thus grossly defective in mind or body? Such disease apart, are we to be content, must we be content, with the present level of mediocrity in respect of intelligence and temper and moral sentiment? Can we anticipate a London in which the present ratio of musical comedy to great opera will be reversed, in which the works of Mr. George Meredith will sell in hundreds of thousands, whilst some of our popular novelists will have to find other means of earning a living? Can we make for a critical democracy which no political party can fool, and which will choose its best to govern it? Yet more, can we undertake, now or hereafter, to provide every generation with its own Shakespeare and Beethoven and Tintoretto and Newton? What, in a word, is the promise of positive eugenics? It is to this aspect of the question that Mr. Galton has mainly directed himself. Indeed he was led to formulate the principles and ideals of the new science by his study of hereditary genius some four decades ago. Let us now attempt to answer some of these questions.

The production of genius.— And first as to the production of genius. It is this, perhaps, that has been the main butt of the jesters who pass for philosophers with some of us to-day. It may be said at once that neither Mr. Galton nor any other responsible person has ever asserted that we can produce genius at will. The difficulties in the way of such a project — at present — are almost innumerable. One or two may be cited.

In the first place, there is the cardinal — but by no means universal — difficulty that the genius is too commonly so occupied with the development and expansion of his own individuality that he has little time or energy for the purposes of the race. This, of course, is an example of Spencer's great generalization as to the antagonism or inverse ratio between individuation and genesis.

Again, there is the generalization of heredity formulated by Mr. Galton, and named by him the *law of regression towards mediocrity.* It asserts that the children of those who are above or below the mean of a race, tend to return towards that mean. The children of the born criminal will be probably somewhat less criminal in tendency than he, though more criminal than the average citizen. The children of the man of genius, if he has any, will probably be nearer mediocrity than he, though on the average possessing greater talent than the average citizen. It is thus not in the nature of sheer genius to reproduce on its own level. It is only the critics who are totally ignorant of the elementary facts of heredity that attribute to the eugenist an expectation of which no one knows the absurdities so well as he does.

On the other hand, it is impossible to question that the hereditary transmission of genius or great talent does occur. One may cite at random such cases as that of the Bach family, Thomas and Matthew Arnold, James and John Stuart Mill: and the reader who is inclined to believe that there is no law or likelihood in this matter, must certainly make himself acquainted with Mr. Galton's *Hereditary Genius,* and with such a paper as that which he printed in *Sociological papers,* 1904, furnishing an "index to achievements of near kinsfolk of some of the Fellows of the Royal Society." There is, of course, the obvious fallacy involved in the possibility that not heredity but environment was really responsible for many of these cases. It must have been a great thing to have such a father as James Mill. But it would be equally idle to imagine that the evidence can be dismissed with this criticism. A Matthew Arnold, a John Stuart Mill, could not be manufactured out of any chance material by an ideal education continued for a thousand years.

THE TRANSMISSION OF GENIUS.— One single instance of the transmission of genius or great talent in a family may be cited. We shall take the family which produced Charles Darwin, the discoverer of the fundamental principle of eugenics, and his first cousin, Francis Galton. Darwin's grandfather was Erasmus Darwin, physician, poet and philosopher, and independent expounder of the doctrine of organic evolution. Darwin's father was a distinguished physician, described by his son as "the wisest man I ever knew." Darwin's maternal grandfather was Josiah Wedgwood, the famous founder of the pottery works. Amongst his first cousins is Mr. Francis Galton. He has four living sons, each a man of great distinction, including Mr. Francis Darwin and Sir George Darwin, both of them original thinkers, honored by the presidency of the British Association. No one will put such a case as this down to pure chance or to the influence of environment alone. This is evidently, like many others, a greatly distinguished stock. The worth of such families to a nation is wholly beyond any one's powers of estimation. What if Erasmus Darwin had never married!

No student of human heredity can doubt that, however limited our immediate hopes, facts such as those alluded to furnish promise of great things for the future. But let us turn now from genius to what we usually call talent.

THE PRODUCTION OF TALENT.— There can be no question that amongst the promises of race-culture is the possibility of breeding such things as talent and the mental energy upon which talent so largely depends. In his *Inquiries into Human Faculty,* Mr.

Galton shows the remarkable extent to which energy or the capacity for labor underlies intellectual achievement. He says, of energy: —

> "It is consistent with all the robust virtues, and makes a large practice of them possible. It is the measure of fullness of life; the more energy the more abundance of it; no energy at all is death; idiots are feeble and listless. In the enquiries I made on the antecedents of men of science no points came out more strongly than that the leaders of scientific thought were generally gifted with remarkable energy, and that they had inherited the gift of it from their parents and grandparents. I have since found the same to be the case in other careers. . . . It may be objected that if the race were too healthy and energetic there would be insufficient call for the exercise of the pitying and self-denying virtues, and the character of men would grow harder in consequence. But it does not seem reasonable to preserve sickly breeds for the sole purpose of tending them, as the breed of foxes is preserved solely for sport and its attendant advantages. There is little fear that misery will ever cease from the land, or that the compassionate will fail to find objects for their compassion; but at present the supply vastly exceeds the demand: the land is over-stocked and over-burdened with the listless and the incapable. In any scheme of eugenics, energy is the most important quality to favor; it is, as we have seen, the basis of living action, and it is eminently transmissible by descent."

Need it be pointed out that any political system which ceases to favor or actively disfavors energy, making it as profitable to be lazy as to be active, is anti-eugenic, and must inevitably lead to disaster? That, however, by the way. Our present point is that eugenics can reasonably promise, when its principles are recognized, to multiply the human [1] and diminish the vegetable type in the community. In so doing, it will greatly further the production of talent, and there-

[1] "Restless activity proves the man," as Goethe says.

fore of that traditional or acquired progress which men of talent and genius create. Such a result will also further, though indirectly, the production of genius itself. For, as Mr. Galton points out, " men of an order of ability which is now very rare, would become more frequent, because the level out of which they rose would itself have risen."

This is by no means the only fashion in which an effective and practicable race-culture would serve genius, and I shall not be blamed for considering this matter further by any reader who realizes, however faintly, what the man of genius is worth to the world. If it were shown possible to establish such social conditions that genius could never flower in them, we should realize that their establishment would mean the putting of an end to progress and the blasting of all the highest hopes of the highest of all ages.

The immediate need of this age, as of all ages, is perhaps not so much the birth of babies capable of developing into men and women of genius, as the full exploitation of the possibilities of genius with which, as I fancy, every generation on the average is about as well endowed as any other. There is, of course, the popular doctrine that there are no mute inglorious Miltons, that " genius will out," and that therefore if it does not appear, it is not there to appear. In expressing the compelling power of genius in many cases, this doctrine is not without truth. Yet history abounds in instances where genius has been destroyed by environment — and we can only guess how many more instances there are of which history has no record. To take the single case of musical genius, it is a lamentable thought that there may be those now living whose natural endowments, in a favorable environment, would have enabled them to write symphonies fit to place beside Beethoven's, but whom some environmental factors — conventional, economic, educational, or what not — have silenced; or worse, have persuaded to write such sterile nullities as need not here be instanced. There is surely no waste in all this wasteful world so lamentable as this waste of genius.

If, then, any one could devise for us a means by which the genius, potentially existing at any time, were realized, he would have performed in effect a service equivalent to that of which eugenics repudiates the present possibility — the actual creation of genius. But if we consider what the conditions are which cause the waste of genius, we realize at once that they mainly inhere in the level of the human environment of the priceless potentiality in question. As we noted elsewhere, in an age like that of Pericles genius springs up on all hands. It is encouraged and welcomed because the average level of the human environment in which it finds itself is so high. But if eugenics can raise the average level of intelligence, in so doing not merely does it render more likely, as Mr. Galton points out, the production of men of the highest ability, but it provides those conditions in which men of genius, now swamped, can swim. We could not undertake to produce a Shakespeare, but we might reasonably hope to produce a generation which would not destroy its Shakespeares. And even if men of genius still found it necessary, as men of genius have found it necessary, to "play to the gallery," they would play, as Mr. Galton says of the demagogue in a eugenic age, "to a more sensible gallery than at present."

Darwin somewhere points out that it is not the scientific, but the unscientific man who denies future possibilities. Thus though an advocate of eugenics may be applauded for his judgment if he declares that the creation of genius will for ever be impossible, yet I should not care to assert that the ultimate limitations of eugenics can thus be defined. We have yet to hear the last of Mendelism.

EUGENICS AND UNEMPLOYMENT.— Let us look now at another aspect of the promise of race-culture. When the time comes that quality rather than quantity is the ideal of those who concern themselves with the population question, it is quite evident that not a few of the social problems which we now find utterly insoluble will disappear. In this brief outline, we can only allude to one or two points. Take, for instance, the question of unemployment. We know that some by no means small proportion of the unemployed were really destined to be unemployable from the first, as for instance by reason of hereditary disease. It were better for them and for us that they had never been born. Many more of the unemployed have been made unemployable by the influence of over-crowding, to which they were subjected in their years of development. Is there, can there be, any real and permanent remedy for overcrowding, but the erection of parenthood into an act of personal and provident responsibility?

EUGENICS AND WOMAN.— Take, again, the woman

question. No one will deny that in many of its gravest forms, especially in its economic form, and the question of the employment of women, wisely or horribly, this depends (to a degree which few, I think, realize) upon the fact that there are now, for instance, 1,300,000 women in excess in this country. Is it then proposed, the reader will say, by means of race-culture to exterminate the superfluous woman? Indeed, no. But is the reader aware that Nature is not responsible for the existence of the superfluous woman? There are more boys than girls born in the ratio of about 103 or 104 to 100: and Nature means them all to live, boys and girls alike. If they did so live, we should have merely the problem of the superfluous man, which would not be an economic problem at all. But we destroy hosts of all the children that are born, and since male organisms are in general less resistant than female organisms, we destroy a disproportionate number of boys, so that the natural balance of the sexes is inverted. Unlike ancient societies we largely practice *male* infanticide. Can the reader believe that there is any permanent and final means of arresting this wastage of child-life, with its singular and far-reaching consequences,— other than the elevation of parenthood, on the principles which race-culture enjoins, even wholly apart from the question of the selection of parents? We shall not succeed in keeping all the children alive (with a trivial number of exceptions), thereby abolishing the superfluous woman by keeping alive the boy who should have grown up to be her partner, until we greatly reduce the birth-rate; as it must and will be reduced when the ideal of race-culture is realized, and no child comes into the world that is not already loved and desired in anticipation.

EUGENICS AND CRUELTY TO CHILDREN.— This ideal, also, offers us in its realization the only complete remedy for the present ghastly cruelty under which so many children suffer even in Great Britain, even in the twentieth century. Is the reader aware that the National Society for the Prevention of Cruelty to Children inquired into the ill-treatment or cruel neglect of 115,000 children in the year beginning April 1st, 1906? It has been reasonably and carefully estimated that "over half a million children are involved in the total of the wastage of child-life and the torture and neglect of child-life in a single year." Is not Mr. G. R. Sims, to whom I would offer a hearty tribute for his recent services to childhood, justified in saying, "Against the guilt of race suicide our men of science are everywhere preaching their sermons to-day. It is against the guilt of race murder that the cry of the children should ring through the land?" As regards race suicide and the men of science, I am not so sure as to the assertion. But the truth of the second sentence quoted is as indisputable as it is horrible.

Now no legislation conceivable will wholly cure this evil nor avert its consequences. At bottom it depends upon human nature, and you can cure it only by curing the defect of human nature. This, in general, is of course beyond the immediate powers of man, but evidently we should gain the same end if only we could confine the advent of children to those parents who desired them — that is to say, those in whom human nature displayed the first, if not indeed almost the only, requisite for the happiness of childhood. To this most beneficent and wholly moral end we shall come, notwithstanding the blind and pitiable guidance of most of our accredited moral teachers to-day. By no other means than the realization of the ideal defined, that every new baby shall be loved and desired in anticipation — an ideal which is perfectly practicable — can the black stain of child murder and child torture and child neglect be removed from our civilization.

RUSKIN AND RACE-CULTURE.— The name of Ruskin, perhaps, would not occur to the reader as likely to afford support to the fair hopes of the eugenist. Consider then, these words from *Time and Tide:* —

> "You leave your marriages to be settled by supply and demand, instead of wholesome law. And thus, among your youths and maidens, the improvident, incontinent, selfish, and foolish ones marry, whether you will or not; and beget families of children necessarily inheritors in a great degree of these parental dispositions; and for whom, supposing they had the best dispositions in the world, you have thus provided, by way of educators, the foolishest fathers and mothers you could find; (the only rational sentence in their letters, usually, is the invariable one, in which they declare themselves 'incapable of providing for their children's education'). On the other hand, whosoever is wise, patient, unselfish, and pure among your youth, you keep maid or bachelor; wasting their best days of natural life in painful sacrifice, forbidding them their best help and best reward, and carefully excluding their prudence and tenderness from any offices of parental duty. Is not this a beatific and beautifully sagacious system for a Celestial Empire, such as that of these British Isles?"

Apart from the point as to wholesome law rather than the education of opinion as the eugenic means, the foregoing passage must win the assent and respect of every eugenist. It indicates the promise of race-culture as it appeared to John Ruskin. The passage has been quoted in full for the benefit of the ordinary thoughtful reader but for that of the professional literary man who, in this remarkable age, so far as I can judge, reads nothing but what he writes, and thus qualifies himself for dismissing Herbert Spencer or Darwin in any casual phrase.

RACE-CULTURE AND HUMAN VARIETY.— Now let us turn to another question. Let it be asserted most emphatically that, if there is anything in the world which eugenics or race-culture does *not* promise or desire, it is the production of a uniform type of man. This delusion, for which there has never been any warrant at all, possesses many of the critics of eugenics, and they have made pretty play with it, just as they do with their other delusions. Let us note one or two facts which bear upon this most undesirable ideal.

In the first place, it is unattainable because of the existence of what we call variation. No apparatus conceivable would suffice to eliminate from every generation those who varied from the accepted type.

In the second place, this uniformity is supremely undesirable from the purely evolutionary point of view, because its attainment would mean the arrest of all progress. All organic evolution, as we know, depends upon the struggle between creatures possessing various variations and the consequent selection of those variations which constitute their possessors best adapted or fitted to the particular environment. If there is no variation there can be no evolution. To aim at the suppression of variation, therefore, on supposed eugenic grounds (which would be involved in aiming at any uniform type of mankind) would be to aim at destroying the necessary condition of all racial progress. The mere fact that all the critics of race-culture attribute to evolutionists, of all people, the desire to suppress variation, is the most adequate comment imaginable upon their critical quality.

And, of course, quite independently of the evolutionary function of variation — though this is cardinal and must never be forgotten by the politician of any school, since what we call individuality is variation on the human plane — the value of variation in ordinary life is wholly incalculable. It is not merely that, as Mr. Galton says, "There are a vast number of conflicting ideals, of alternative characters, of incompatible civilizations; but they are wanted to give fullness and interest to life. Society would be very dull if every man resembled the highly estimable Marcus Aurelius or Adam Bede." The question is not merely as to the interest of life. Much more important is the fact that it takes all sorts to make a world. What is the development of society but the result of the physiological division of labor in the social organism? And how could such division of labor be carried out if we had not various types of laborers? What would be the good of science if there were no poetry or music to live for? How would poetry and music help us if we had not men of science to protect our shores from plague? Obviously the existence of men of most various types is a necessity for any highly organized society. Even if eugenics were capable — as it is not — of producing a complete and balanced type, fit up to a point to turn out a satisfactory poem, a satisfactory symphony or a satisfactory sofa, the utmost could not be expected of such a man in any of these directions. In a word, as long as their activities are not anti-social, men cannot be of too various types. We require mystic and mathematician, poet and pathologist. Only, we want good specimens of each. "The aim of eugenics," says Mr. Galton, "is to represent each class or sect by its best specimens; that done, to leave them to work out their common civilization in their own way. . . . Special aptitudes would be assessed highly by those who possessed them, as the artistic faculties by artists, fearlessness of inquiry and veracity by scientists, religious absorption by mystics, and so on. There would be self-sacrificers, self-tormentors, and other exceptional idealists." But at least it is better to have good rather than bad specimens of any kind, whatever that kind may be. Mr. Galton thinks that all except cranks would agree as to including health, energy, ability, manliness and courteous disposition amongst qualities uniformly desirable — alike in poet and pathologist. We should desire also uniformity as to the absence of the anti-social proclivities of the born criminal. So much uniformity being granted, let us have with it the utmost conceivable variety,— more, indeed, than most of us can conceive.

This point, of course, is cardinal from the point of view of practice. No progress could be made with eugenics, it would be impossible even to form a Eugenics Education Society, if each of us were to regard the particular type he belongs to as the ideal, and were to seek merely to obtain the best specimens of that type. The doctrine that it takes all sorts to make a world — a doctrine very hard for youth to learn, yet unconsciously learnt by all who are capable of learning at all — must be regarded as cardinal truth for the eugenist. All he asks for, all he is wise in seeking, is good specimens rather than bad. Poets certainly, but not poetasters; jesters certainly, but not clever fools.

TIME AND ITS TREASURE.— Taking the modern estimates of the physicists, we are assured that the total period of past human existence is very brief compared with what may reasonably be predicted. Granted, then, practically unlimited time, what inherent limits are there to the upward development of man as a moral and intellectual being? Shall we answer this question by a study of the nature of matter? Plainly not. Shall we answer it by a study of the nature of mind? Surely not, for the study of existing mind cannot inform us as to what mind might be. One source of guidance alone we have, and this is the amazing contrast which exists between the mind of man at its highest, and mind in its humblest animal forms: or shall we say even between the highest and lowest manifestations of mind within the human species? The measureless height of the ascent thus indicated offers us no warrant for the conclusion that, as we stand on the heights of our life, our "glimpse of a height that is higher" is only an hallucination. On the contrary.

There is no warrant whatever for supposing that the forces which have brought us thus far are yet exhausted: they have their origin in the inexhaustible. Who, gazing on the earth of a hundred million years ago, could have predicted life — could have recognized, in the forces then at work and the matter in which they were displayed, the promise and potency of all terrestrial life? Who, contemplating life at a much later stage, even later mammalian, could have seen in the simian the prophecy of man? Who, examining the earliest nervous ganglia, could have foreseen the human cerebrum? The fact that we can imagine nothing higher than ourselves, that we make even our gods in our own image, offers no warrant for supposing that nothing higher will ever be. What ape could have predicted man, what reptile the bird, what amœba the bee? "There are many events in the womb of time which will be delivered" and the fairest of her sons and daughters are yet to be.

But even grant, for the sake of the argument, that the intelligence of a Newton, the musical faculty of a Bach, the moral nature of any good mother anywhere, represent the utmost limits of which the evolution of the psychical is capable. There is every reason to deny this, but let us for the moment assume it true. There still remains the thought of Wordsworth, "What one is, why may not millions be?"— a thought to which Spencer has also given utterance. What is shown possible for human nature here and there, he says, is conceivable for human nature at large. It is possible for a human being, whilst still remaining human, to be a Shakespeare or a St. Francis: these things are thus demonstrably within the possibilities of human nature. It is therefore at the least conceivable that, in the course of almost infinite time (even assuming, say, that intelligence must ever be limited, as even Newton's intelligence was limited),—some such capacities as his may be common property amongst men of the scientific type; and so with other types. We may answer Wordsworth that there is no bar thrown by Nature in the way of such a hope.

WHAT IS POSSIBLE.—This, of course, is speculation and of no immediate value. I would merely remind the reader that the doctrine of optimism, as regards the future of mankind, which the principles of race-culture assume and which they desire to justify, was definitely shared by the great pioneers to whom we owe our understanding of those principles. Notwithstanding grave nervous disorder, such as makes pessimists of most men, both Darwin and Spencer were compelled by their study of Nature to this rational optimism as regards man's future. The doctrine of organic evolution, and of the age-long ascent of man through the selection of the fittest (who have, *on the whole,* been the *best*) for parenthood, is one not of despair but of hope. Exactly half a century ago it struck horror into the minds of our predecessors. Man, then, is only an erected ape, they thought—as if any historical doctrine, however true, could shorten the dizzy distance to which man has climbed since he was simian: and man being an ape, they thought his high dreams palpably vain. But the measure of the accomplished hints at the measure of the possible, and the value of the historical facts lies not in themselves, all facts as such being as dead as are the individual atoms of the living body, but in the principles which grow out of them. It is of no importance as such that man has simian ancestors; it is of immeasurable importance that he should learn by what processes he has become human, and by what indeed, they became simian — which would have been a proud adjective for its own day. The principles of organic progress matter for us because they are the principles of race-culture, the only sure means of human progress. Our looking backwards does not turn us into pillars of salt, but teaches us that the best is yet to be, and how alone it is to be attained.

Elsewhere the optimistic argument of Wordsworth is quoted. Hear also John Ruskin: —

> "There is as yet no ascertained limit to the nobleness of person and mind which the human creature may attain, by persevering observance of the laws of God respecting its birth and training."[1]

and Herbert Spencer: —

> "What now characterizes the exceptionally high may be expected eventually to characterize all. For that which the best human nature is capable of, is within the reach of human nature at large."[2]

and Francis Galton: —

> "There is nothing either in the history of domestic animals or in that of evolution to make us doubt that a race of sane men may be formed, who shall be as much superior, mentally and morally, to the modern European, as the modern European is to the lowest of the Negro races.
>
> "It is earnestly to be hoped that inquiries will be increasingly directed into historical facts, with the view of estimating the possible effects of reasonable political action in the future, in gradually raising the present miserably low standard of the

[1] *Munera Pulveris*, par. 6.
[2] *The Data of Ethics*, par. 97.

human race to one in which the Utopias in the dreamland of philanthropists may become practical possibilities."[1]

CONCLUSION — EUGENICS AND RELIGION.— In an early chapter it was attempted to show that eugenics is not merely moral, but is of the very heart of morality. We saw that it involves taking no life — despite the unspeakable folly written about lethal chambers and the like — that, at any rate so far as this eugenist is concerned, it recognizes and bows to the supreme law of love: and claims to serve that law, and the ideal of social morality, which is the making of human worth. Eugenics may or may not be practicable, it may or may not be based upon natural truth, but it is assuredly moral: though I, for one, would proclaim eternal war between this real morality and the damnable sham which approves the unbridled transmission of the most hideous diseases, rotting body and soul, in the interests of good.

And if religion, whatever its origin and the more questionable chapters in its past, be now "morality touched with emotion," I claim that eugenics is religious, is and will ever be a religion. Elsewhere[2] I have attempted to show that religion has survived and will survive because of its survival-value — its services to the life of the societies wherein it flourishes. The religion of the future, it was sought to argue, will be that which "best serves Nature's unswerving desire — fullness of life." The Founder of the Christian religion said, "I am come that ye might have life, and

[1] *Hereditary Genius*, Prefatory Chapter to Edition of 1902, pp. x. and xxvii.

[2] "The Survival-Value of Religion," *Fortnightly Review*," April, 1906.

that ye might have it more abundantly." It is higher and more abundant life that is the eugenic ideal. Progress I define as the emergence and increasing dominance of mind. Of progress, thus conceived, man is the highest fruit hitherto. He is also its appointed agent and eugenics is his instrument.

To this end he must use all the powers which have blossomed in him from the dust. He must claim Art: and indeed in Wagner's great music-drama, at the moment when the prophetic Brünnhilde tells Sieglinde who has just lost her mate that she, the expectant mother, may look for the resurrection of the dead and the life of the world to come in the child Siegfried; and when the heroic theme is pronounced for the first time and followed by that which signifies redemption by love: then, I think, the eugenist may thrill not merely to the music, nor the humanity of the story, but to the spiritual and scientific truth which it symbolizes.

If the struggle towards individual perfection be religious, so, assuredly, is the struggle, less egoistic indeed, towards racial perfection. If the historic meaning and purport of religion are as I conceive them, and if its future evolution may thence be inferred, there can be no doubt in the prophecy that in ages to come those high aspirations and spiritual visions which astronomy has dishoused from amongst the stars, and which, at their best, were ever selfish, will find a place on this human earth of ours. If we have transferred our hopes from heaven to earth and from ourselves to our children, they are not less religious. And they that shall be of us shall build up the old waste places; for we shall raise up the foundations of many generations.

APPENDIX A

CONCERNING BOOKS TO READ

THE preceding pages are of course only tentative, preliminary and introductory. I have merely tried to make a beginning. No better purpose can be achieved than that the reader should proceed to study the subject for himself. A few pages may therefore be devoted to the names of some of the books which will be found useful. This is in no sense a complete bibliography, nor even a tithe of such a bibliography. But the reader who makes a beginning with the books here named, or even with a well-chosen half dozen of them, will hereafter need no one to tell him that the culture of the human race on scientific principles will be the supreme science of all the future, the supreme goal of all statesmen, the object and the final judge of all legislation.

Where it is thought that useful remarks can be made they will be made, but neither their presence nor absence nor their length is to be taken as any index to the writer's opinion of the relative value of the works in question.

Heredity. (The Progressive Science Series, John Murray, 1908.) By PROFESSOR J. A. THOMSON, M.A.

This is the most recent and most valuable for general purposes of all books on the subject of heredity. No layman should express opinions on heredity or eugenics until he has read it, for it is extremely improbable that they will be valuable. Professor Thomson covers the whole ground with extreme lucidity and care and impartiality. The book is readable, nay more, fascinating from end to end, and it is liberally and usefully illustrated. It is the first general treatise on heredity which leads consciously, yet as of necessity, towards eugenics as the crown and goal to the whole study, and in this respect it undoubtedly marks an epoch.

The Methods and Scope of Genetics. (Cambridge University Press, 1908.) By W. Bateson, M.A., F.R.S.

This is the inaugural lecture, destined, I have little doubt, to become historic, which was delivered by Professor Bateson on his appointment to the new Darwin Chair of Biology at Cambridge. It is purposely included here for very good reasons. The reader who begins his serious study of heredity with Professor Thomson's work, must be informed that though the author gives an interesting account of Mendelism, he is not a Mendelian, and neither his account of Mendelism nor his estimate of it is at all adequate for the present day. In truth there is the study of heredity before Mendelism and after, and though eugenics owes its modern origin to the founder of the school of biometrics, and though among his followers there are to be found many who decry and oppose the Mendelians, it is for the eugenist of single purpose to take the truth wherever it is to be found. It is now idle to deny either the general truth or the stupendous promise of Mendelism. Many vital phenomena besides heredity are studied by the statistical method, and are put down by it to heredity. The Mendelians take seeds of known origin, and plant them and note the result. They carry out experimental breeding not only amongst plants but amongst the higher animals, including mammals who, in all essentials of structure and function, are one with ourselves. It is not possible, I believe, to over-estimate the supreme importance of Mendelian inquiry for eugenics. Eugenics is founded upon heredity, and Genetics, which is Professor Bateson's name for the physiology of heredity and variation, is now working at the very heart of those natural phenomena upon which eugenics depends. This lecture of Professor Bateson's is by far the best introduction to Mendelism that exists, besides being the most recent and the most authoritative possible. With the lucidity of the born teacher (whose faculty, I have no doubt, is a Mendelian unit, not always inherited by the born observer) the author explains the essence of Mendelism. The usual expositor has not proceeded far upon his way before he is encumbering himself and the learner with the phenomena of dominance and recessiveness, which are not cardinal and are highly involved. Professor Bateson makes no allusion to them. But he gives an account of Mendelism which it is impossible to put down without finishing, and which is elementary in the highest sense of the word. In the latter pages the author preaches eugenics with a vigor and conviction not unworthy of notice as coming from the leader of a school which is utterly opposed in principle and in methods, if not in theory, to the school of biometrics founded by the founder of eugenics. I insist upon this because there is a half-instructed ignorance abroad which has heard the name of Mendel, and seeks thereby to discredit Darwin and natural selection, Mr. Galton and eugenics. Hear Professor Bateson: —

"If there are societies which refuse to apply the new knowledge, the fault will not lie with Genetics. I think it needs but little observation of the newer civilizations to foresee that *they* will apply every scrap of scientific knowledge which will help them, or seems to help them in the struggle, and I am good enough selectionist to know that in that day the fate of the recalcitrant communities is sealed."

Hereditary Genius, An Inquiry into its Laws and Consequences. (Second Edition. Macmillan, 1892. Out of print.) By FRANCIS GALTON.

This is the classical and pioneer inquiry, far beyond my praise or appraisement. The main text is not long, is easily read and is extremely interesting. The reader should acquaint himself also with Mr. Constable's recent criticism, *Poverty and Hereditary Genius.*

A Study of British Genius. (Hurst & Blackett, 1904.) By HAVELOCK ELLIS.

This is an extremely interesting book, which should be read in association with the foregoing, to which it is a criticism and supplement. The greater part of the volume is concerned with the study of genius from the point of view of heredity — in terms of nationality and race, and of individual parentage. Very great labor and scholarship have been expended to very high purpose in this work.

Inquiries into Human Faculty. (Macmillan, 1883. Out of print.) By FRANCIS GALTON.

This is the next in order of Mr. Galton's works, *Hereditary Genius* dating from 1869. It has recently been reprinted in Dent's "Everyman's Library," and can thus be purchased for one shilling.

Natural Inheritance. (Macmillan, 1889.) By FRANCIS GALTON.

Memories of my Life. (Methuen & Co., 1908.) By FRANCIS GALTON.

This is Mr. Galton's latest book, and apart from its personal fascination must be read by the serious eugenist if only on account of its last five chapters, and especially the last two, which deal with Heredity and Race Improvement. What could be more interesting and significant, for instance, than to find Mr. Galton in 1908 saying of himself in 1865, "I was too much disposed to think of marriage under some regulation, and not enough of the effects of self-interest and of social and religious sentiment." Mr. Galton comments on the wrong headedness of objectors to eugenics. I fancy, however, that the familiar misrepresentations will soon cease to be possible. The whole of this brief last chapter must be carefully read and studied. At least I must quote the following paragraph:—

"What I desire is that the importance of eugenic marriages should be reckoned at its just value, neither too high nor too low, and that eugenics should form one of the many considerations by which marriages are promoted or hindered, as they are by social position, adequate fortune, and similarity of creed. I can believe hereafter that it will be felt as derogatory to a person of exceptionally good stock to marry into an inferior one as it is for a person of high Austrian rank to marry one who has not sixteen heraldic quarterings. I also hope that social recognition of an appropriate kind will be given to healthy, capable, and large families, and that social influence will be exerted towards the encouragement of eugenic marriages."

This volume, a model for all future autobiographers, ends with the following splendid statement of the eugenic creed: —

"A true philanthropist concerns himself not only with society as a whole, but also with as many of the individuals who compose it as the range of his affections can include. If a man devotes himself solely to the good of the nation as a whole, his tastes must be impersonal and his conclusions so far heartless, deserving the ill title of 'dismal' with which Carlyle labeled statistics. If, on the other hand, he attends only to certain individuals in whom he happens to take an interest, he becomes guided by favoritism and is oblivious of the rights of others and of the futurity of the race. Charity refers to the individual; Statesmanship to the nation; Eugenics cares for both.

"It is known that a considerable part of the huge stream of British charity furthers by indirect and unsuspected ways the production of the Unfit; it is most desirable that money and other attention bestowed on harmful forms of charity should be diverted to the production and well-being of the Fit. For clearness of explanation we may divide newly married couples into three classes, with respect to the probable civic worth of their offspring. There would be a small class of 'desirables,' a large class of 'passables,' of whom nothing more will be said here, and a small class of 'undesirables.' It would clearly be advantageous to the country if social and moral support as well as timely material help were extended to the desirables, and not monopolized as it is now apt to be by the undesirables.

"I take eugenics very seriously, feeling that its principles ought to become one of the dominant motives in a civilized nation, much as if they were one of its religious tenets. I have often expressed myself in this sense, and will conclude this book by briefly reiterating my views.

"Individuals appear to me as partial detachments from an infinite ocean of Being, and this world as a stage on which Evolution takes place, principally hitherto by means of Natural Selection, which achieves the good of the whole with scant regard to that of the individual.

"Man is gifted with pity and other kindly feelings; he has also the power of preventing many kinds of suffering. I conceive it to fall well within his province to replace Natural Selection by other processes that are more merciful and not less effective.

"This is precisely the aim of eugenics. Its first object is to check the birth-rate of the Unfit, instead of allowing them to come into being, though doomed in large numbers to perish prematurely. The second object is the improvement of the race by furthering the productivity of the Fit by early marriages and healthful rearing of their children. Natural Selection rests upon excessive production and wholesale destruction; Eugenics on bringing no more individuals into the world than can be properly cared for, and those only of the best stock."

Heredity and Selection in Sociology. (A. & C. Black, 1907.) By GEORGE CHATTERTON-HILL.

This is a useful and interesting work, the nature of which is well indicated by its title. It contains many purely eugenic chapters, and cannot be ignored by the student.

The Germ-plasm, A Theory of Heredity. (The Contemporary Science Series, Walter Scott, 1893.) By AUGUST WEISMANN.

This is Weismann's great work. It should be studied by politicians and others who still interpret all social phenomena in terms of Lamarckian theory, and also by modern writers who are so much more Weismannian than Weismann.

The Evolution Theory. (Two volumes. London, 1904. Translated by J. Arthur Thomson and M. R. Thomson.) By AUGUST WEISMANN.

The Principles of Heredity. (Chapman & Hall, 1905.) By G. ARCHDALL REID.

This is a very interesting and extremely Weismannian book which contains the most recent statement of the author's remarkable inquiries into the influence of disease as a factor of human selection.

Variation in Animals and Plants. (The International Scientific Series, Kegan Paul, 1903.) By H. M. VERNON.

Variation, Heredity and Evolution. (Murray, 1906.) By R. H. LOCK.

The Origin of Species. (Murray, 1869. Last (sixth) edition. Reprinted 1901.) By CHARLES DARWIN.

The Descent of Man. (Murray, 1871. Second edition, 1874. Reprinted 1906.) By CHARLES DARWIN.

These classics now cost only half-a-crown apiece.

The beginner should read *The Descent of Man* first, I think. Some of the earlier chapters are of the utmost eugenic value, and would be found immensely interesting by modern lecturers on decadence, and the like.

Darwinism To-day. (London, George Bell; New York, Henry Holt, 1907.) By VERNON L. KELLOGG.

An interesting and scholarly recent criticism, containing much matter strictly relevant to eugenics.

The Evolution of Sex. (The Contemporary Science Series, Walter Scott. Revised edition, 1901. Originally published in 1899.) By PATRICK GEDDES and J. ARTHUR THOMSON.

A famous book, yet to be discovered by most "authorities" on the Woman Question.

A History of Matrimonial Institutions. (University of Chicago Press & Fisher Unwin, 1904.) By G. E. HOWARD.

This is a three-volume treatise, extremely comprehensive, and especially valuable as a guide to the literature of the subject. Only the professional student can be expected to read it from cover to cover, but it is valuable for purposes of reference.

The History of Human Marriage. (Macmillan.) By E. WESTERMARCK.

This rightly celebrated and epoch-making work demonstrates in especial the survival-value of monogamy, and its historical dominance as a marriage form.

The Evolution of Marriage. (The Contemporary Science Series, Walter Scott.) By PROFESSOR LETOURNEAU.

The Principles of Population. By T. R. MALTHUS. The substance of this may be conveniently read in the extracts published in the *Economic Classics* by Macmillan (1905).

The Principles of Biology. By HERBERT SPENCER. The last section "The Laws of Multiplication" *must* be read as the expression of the missing half of the truth discovered by Malthus. It is tiresome, nearly half a century after Spencer's enunciation of his law, to have to read the remarks of some modern writers who continue to assume that Malthus expressed the whole truth.

The Republic of Plato.

Apart from the lines of Theognis quoted by Darwin in *The Descent of Man,* which are some two centuries older than Plato, the fifth book of the *Republic* is the earliest discussion in literature of the idea of eugenics, and utterly wild though we may consider most of the proposals of Plato — or Socrates — to be, these early thinkers are yet more modern and more scientific and more fundamental than all their successors, even including our modern Utopia makers who have come after Darwin, in recognizing that it is the quality of the citizen which will make a Utopia possible. The following quotation will suffice to show that after more than two thousand years we can still learn from the fundamental idea of Plato's fifth chapter: —

> "It is plain, then, that after this we must make marriages as much as possible sacred; but the most advantageous should be most sacred. By all means. How then shall they be most advantageous? Tell me that, Glauco, for I see in your houses dogs of chase, and a great many excellent birds. Have you then indeed ever attended at all, in any respect, to their marriages, and the propagation of their species? How? said he. First of all, that among these, although they be excellent themselves, are there not some who are most excellent? There are. Whether then do you breed from all of them alike? or are you careful to breed chiefly from the best? From the best. But how? From the youngest or from the oldest, or from those who are most in their prime? From those in their prime. And if the breed be not of this kind, you reckon that the race of birds and dogs greatly degenerates. I reckon so, replied he. And what think you as to horses, said I, and other animals? is the case any otherwise with respect to these? That, said he, were absurd."

Plato proposed to destroy the family, and to "practice every art that no mother should know her own child." He also approved of infanticide. Nevertheless, this fifth book of the *Republic* is interesting and valuable reading, and it is especially well to note that this pioneer of Utopianism and Socialism possessed the idea which almost all living Socialists, except Professors Forel and Pearson, lack, that we must first make the Utopian, and Utopia will follow.

The Family. (G. P. Putnam's Sons, 1906.) By ELSIE CLEWS PARSONS.

This recent, scholarly and lucid book, of which any living man might well be proud, may follow the reading of the utterly unconcerned and taken-for-granted fashion in which Socrates and Plato proposed to destroy the family. Lecture VIII., on "Sexual Choice," is brief, but the references following it are extremely valuable and complete. It is evident that one of the books which will have to be written on eugenics in the near future must deal with the whole question of marriage and human selection in its historical and contemporary aspects.

"The Possible Improvement of the Human Breed under Existing Conditions of Law and Sentiment." *Nature,* 1901, p. 659; *Smithsonian Report,* Washington, 1901, p. 523. By FRANCIS GALTON.

This was the Huxley Lecture of the Anthropological Institute in 1901, and the contemporary interest in eugenics may be said to date from it.

"Eugenics, its Definition, Scope and Aims. (*Sociological Papers,* Macmillan, 1904.) By FRANCIS GALTON.

This remarkable lecture constituted a further introduction of the subject, and it is somewhat of the nature of an impertinence for the professional jester, who is not acquainted with a line of it, to dismiss eugenics with a phrase as if this lecture had never been written or were unobtainable. Mr. Galton there defined eugenics as "the science which deals with all influences that improve the inborn qualities of a race. . . ." The definition given in the *Century Dictionary* is unauthoritative, incorrect, and misses the entire point.

An extremely valuable discussion follows this lecture, and it is absolutely necessary for the student to acquaint himself with the whole of these pages (45-99).

Restrictions in Marriages: Studies in National Eugenics: Eugenics as a Factor in Religion. By FRANCIS GALTON.

These memoirs communicated to the Sociological Society in 1905, and published together with the subsequent discussions in *Sociological Papers* (1905). The three memoirs are also published separately under one cover, and I believe the few remaining copies can be obtained from the Secretary of the Eugenics Education Society.

Probability, the Foundation of Eugenics. The Herbert Spencer Lecture of 1907. By FRANCIS GALTON.

This lecture is published by the University of Oxford. It contains a very brief historical outline of the recent progress of eugenic inquiry and a simple discussion of the mathematical method of studying heredity. It must, of course, be read by every serious student.

National Life from the Standpoint of Science. (A. & C. Black, 1905.) By KARL PEARSON.

This is a reprint of a lecture delivered by Professor Pearson in 1900, together with some other valuable contributions of his to the subject. There is scarcely a better introduction to eugenics.

The Scope and Importance to the State of the Science of National Eugenics. The Robert Boyle Lecture 1907. (Dulau & Co., Second Edition, 1809.) By KARL PEARSON.

This fine lecture should be carefully read. It gives some index to the quantity and quality of the work done by Prof. Pearson and his followers since the Francis Galton Eugenics Laboratory was founded.

Population and Progress. (Chapman & Hall, 1907.) By MONTAGUE CRACKANTHORPE.

Though only published recently, part of this book goes back far. The first chapter is indeed a reprint of a eugenic article published in the *Fortnightly Review* as far back as 1872. Some of us may perhaps be inclined to forget that more than a generation ago Mr. Crackanthorpe had grasped the great truths which we are now trying to spread, and had courageously expressed them in the face of ignorance and prejudice even greater than to-day. This is unquestionably a book which every student must read but the press generally, with some notable exceptions, have fought rather shy of it. It was sent to the present writer at his request from a leading morning paper which trusts him, and he wrote a column on it, most careful in diction and moderate in opinion, which was, nevertheless, not printed. One of the leading medical papers devoted a long article to the book, written on the general principle that it is right for a medical paper to differ from any non-medical person who approaches the closed neighborhood of medical inquiry. Another leading medical paper considered Mr. Crackanthorpe's "ideal" to be "beyond present accomplishment," and feared it must have "many generations of probation before it could hope to enter the sphere of practical politics." We venture to say that *Population and Progress,* dealing, as it does, with a subject that really matters, contains more fundamental practical politics — in the true sense of that word — than has been discussed in most of our current newspapers since they were first established.

Race-Culture or Race Suicide. (Walter Scott, 1906.) By R. R. RENTOUL.

This is a second and enlarged edition of a remarkable pamphlet published by Dr. Rentoul in 1903 under the title *Proposed Sterilization of Certain Mental and Physical Degenerates. An Appeal to Asylum Managers and Others.* Dr. Rentoul's own description of this pamphlet is as follows: — "In it I called attention to the large and increasing number of the insane in the United Kingdom; to our disgraceful system of child-marriages; to the growing suicide rate; to our disgusting system of inducing certain mentally and physically diseased persons to marry; and to a slight operation which I was the first to propose as a means of checking the increase in the number of the insane, and in preventing innocent offspring from being cursed by some parental blemish."

Education. (Originally published in 1861; half-crown edition with the author's latest corrections, Williams & Norgate, 1906.) By HERBERT SPENCER.

This is the classic which marks an epoch in the personal development in every one who reads it, and which made an epoch in the history of education: the book was probably of more service to woman, owing to its liberation of girlhood, than any other of its century.

The Study of Sociology. (International Scientific Series. Originally published in 1873. Twentieth edition, 1903, Kegan Paul.) By HERBERT SPENCER.

This is, of course, *the* introduction to sociology, written for that purpose by a master, and in every respect a masterpiece. It contains many eugenic references and arguments. As far as the eugenic education of the adult is concerned, this is rightly the preliminary work.

Besides *The Evolution of Sex* and Mrs. Parson's book on *The Family,* there are many others relevant to the question of woman and eugenics, of which one or two may be noted here.

Sex and Society, Studies in the Social Psychology of Sex. (University of Chicago Press and T. Fisher Unwin, 1907.) By W. I. THOMAS.

This is a very readable and recent work, and for the general reader much the most suitable of any that I know.

Man and Woman. (Contemporary Science Series, Walter Scott. Second Edition.) By HAVELOCK ELLIS.

This is a very clear and readable book.

Youth — its Education, Regimen and Hygiene. (Sydney Appleton, 1907.) By STANLEY HALL.

This is a new and abbreviated version of Professor Stanley Hall's two well-known volumes on *Adolescence,* published in 1904. For the general reader this much smaller work is very suitable, and especial attention may be directed to Chapter XI. "The Education of Girls."

It would have been presumptuous and absurd to attempt, in the course of a merely introductory volume, to deal, by anything more than allusion to its existence, with the great question of human parenthood in relation to race. Most urgently this question, of course, concerns the negro problem in America. The student who has to trust entirely to second-hand knowledge had best be silent. Lest, however, the reader should imagine that the older doctrines of race can be accepted without reserve, he will do well to study very carefully the latter part of Dr. Archdall Reid's book, already referred to, and, with extreme caution, the following: —

Race Prejudice. (Constable, 1906.) By JEAN FINOT.

This book most of us must believe to be extreme, but it should be read: it bears on what may be called international eugenics, and the whole question of inter-racial marriage.

On matters of transmissible disease and racial poisons there is much literature. Only one or two books can be referred to here.

The Disease of Society: The Vice and Crime Problem. (Lippincott, 1904.) By G. F. LYDSTON.

This, of course, is not a pleasant book, and it is open to much criticism in many respects, but it is well worth reading, especially in association with Dr. Rentoul's work.

Malaria — A Neglected Factor in the History of Greece and Rome. (Macmillan, 1907.) By W. H. S. JONES, with an introduction by RONALD ROSS.

This is a recent historical study and may be a very substantial contribution to the study of Decadence.

Alcoholism. (Nisbet, 1906.) By W. C. SULLIVAN.

This little book of Dr. Sullivan's contains a useful and scrupulously moderate chapter on the relation of alcohol to human degeneration.

The Drink Problem. (Methuen, 1907.) By Fourteen Medical Authorities.

The Children of the Nation. (Methuen, 1906.) By SIR JOHN GORST.

Infant Mortality. (Methuen, 1906.) By GEORGE NEWMAN.

The Hygiene of Mind. (Methuen, 1906.) By T. S. CLOUSTON.

Diseases of Occupation. (Methuen, 1908.) By SIR T. OLIVER.

The Prevention of Tuberculosis. (Methuen, 1908.) By A. NEWSHOLME.

These volumes, in my New Library of Medicine, all deal in part with questions of racial poisoning and racial hygiene.

Alcoholism — A Study in Heredity. (Fisher Unwin, 1901.) By ARCHDALL REID.

Alcohol and the Human Body. (Macmillan, 1907.) By SIR VICTOR HORSLEY and MARY D. STURGE.

Hygiene of Nerves and Mind. (The Progressive Science Series, John Murray, 1907.) By AUGUST FOREL.

Inebriety — Its Causation and Control. (The second Norman Kerr Memorial Lecture, published in the

British Journal of Inebriety, January, 1908.) By R. Welsh Branthwaite.

Reports of the Inspector under the Inebriates Acts. Especially those for the years 1904, 1905, 1906.

The Cry of the Children: The Black Stain. (Jarrold, 1907.) By G. R. Sims.

The above are especially recommended to politicians. Sooner or later, as never yet, knowledge will have to be applied to the drink question as it bears upon the quality of the race. The knowledge exists, and is not difficult to acquire or understand. The references given are quite sufficient to enable any one of mediocre intelligence to frame a bill dealing with alcohol which would be worth all its predecessors put together, and would arouse far less opposition than any one of them.

Reports of the National Conference on Infantile Mortality, 1906 and 1908 (P. S. King & Co.).

In the 1906 report note especially Dr. Ballantyne's paper on the unborn infant, and in the 1908 report, Miss Alice Ravenhill's paper on the education of girls.

It must be repeated that the foregoing names are merely noted as including, perhaps, the greater number of the books with which the serious beginner would do well to make a start. That is all. It would be both unfair and unwise, however, to omit any mention of at least three wonderful little books of John Ruskin's: *Unto this Last, Munera Pulveris,* and *Time and Tide,* which add to their great qualities of soul and style some of the most forcible and wisest things that have ever been written on race-culture and its absolutely fundamental relation to morality, patriotism and true economics.

If the reader desires the name of only one book, that is certainly *The Sexual Question* (Rebman, 1908), by Professor AUGUST FOREL. This has no rival anywhere, and cannot be overpraised.

APPENDIX B

THE EUGENICS EDUCATION SOCIETY

THERE has lately been founded a society, the effective activity of which has been alluded to in preceding pages. One of the purposes of the present volume is to gain adherents for this Society and perhaps, even better still, to encourage readers in great provincial centers, for instance, to form eugenic bodies for themselves. Sir James Crichton-Browne accepted the presidency of the Society for its first year, and the cause of the helpless inebriate and the future is much indebted to him for his help in that matter. Lately, Mr. Francis Galton consented to become our Honorary President, and while we have the advice and help and direction of the august founder of eugenics, it may fairly be assumed that for responsible and authoritative statement and action, it will be well to consult the Eugenics Education Society rather than the amateur and irresponsible eugenist whom this new cause, like other new causes, will doubtless call into being.

The following is reprinted from the Society's papers: —

The Eugenics Education Society proposes, so far as its means allow:

1. To arrange for Lectures on the facts and laws of heredity, on the circumstances attending the rise and decline of ruling races and families, on the good and bad racial effects of various laws and usages, and on other kindred subjects.

2. To popularize the results of researches, such as are being pursued at the Francis Galton Eugenics Laboratory of the University of London and elsewhere.

3. To ensure that the young shall be made acquainted with the principles of Eugenics, since a knowledge of them may be expected to supply an important aid towards the formation of character.

4. To intervene whenever a proposed administrative act appears likely to impair the racial qualities of the nation, and to advocate such measures as would improve these qualities.

5. To form an appropriate Library, and to issue publications.

Offices and Library — 6, York Buildings, Adelphi, W.C.

Hours — 11 a.m. to 1 p.m., and by appointment.

For further information and for programs of lectures and meetings apply to the Hon. Secretary at above address.

The Honorary President of the Society has lately written for it the following statement which is prefaced by his revised definition of eugenics as follows: —

"Eugenics is the study of agencies under social control that may improve or impair the racial qualities of future generations either physically or mentally."

The fact that the laws of heredity apply to man equally with the lower animals and plants, and that the mental functions are subject to the same laws of heredity as the physical ones, has yet to be taken to heart by the public.

The salutary effects of natural selection in preventing the degeneracy of a race are so largely interfered with, and sometimes even inverted, by civilization, that another form of prevention is peremptorily demanded.

If we apply the general word degenerate to the insane, to the imbecile, to the habitual criminal, and to those who are naturally liable to some of the more serious diseases, it is found that a "degenerate" is no less fertile than a normal person, apparently a little more so, and that such persons frequently marry.

Each married degenerate produces on the average one child who is as degenerate as himself or herself, and others in whom the taint is latent, but liable to appear in a succeeding generation. The taint of degeneracy in our population is now alarmingly great and threatens to increase indefinitely under the present conditions.

Probably one of the first efforts in practical Eugenics will be to restrict the propagation of children by the notoriously Unfit, whose marriages are now unhindered, if not sometimes fostered by mistaken kindliness.

Efforts have also to be made in the opposite direction, namely, in creating social agencies that shall promote the propagation of the Fit, as for instance by facilitating employment to married persons of good stock, and providing their families when poor with better housing and nurture than they could otherwise obtain.

The power of public opinion being enormously great, we may rest assured that after the importance of Eugenics shall have become generally recognized, many social influences will be brought to bear, and numerous customs will establish themselves that shall further Eugenic conduct with a gentle yet almost irresistible force.

We ask for your name and your help in the most radical and hopeful of campaigns — one which appeals alike to the patriot and the moralist, the man of science and the lover of children. The Society has already done practical work in drawing effective attention to the need for rational and humane treatment of inebriety, with reference to the Eugenic ideal; but this is only one of a thousand multifarious needs. Every new member adds strength and support to our cause — the cause of the future.

The *Eugenics Review* will comprise, amongst other things:

1.— Articles by responsible writers.

2.— Editorial Notes upon such of the topics of the day as illustrate Eugenic teaching, and demand Eugenic comment.

3.— Notices of recent Books which bear upon Eugenics.

4.— Official records of the Work of the Society.

The aim of the Review will be to make known the results of all seriously conducted Eugenic investigation without bias in favor of any particular school. Its range will include —

Biology — in so far as it is concerned with Heredity and Selection.

Anthropology — in so far as it throws light on questions of race and the institution of Marriage.

Politics — in so far as it bears on Parenthood in its relation to Civic Worth.

Ethics—in so far as it promotes ideals that lead to the improvement of racial quality.

Religion—in so far as it strengthens and sanctifies the sense of Eugenic duty.

A Copy of the Review will be sent post free to all Life Members of the Society, and to all Annual Subscribers of One Guinea. For other persons, the Subscription will be 4s. 6d. a year. Single Copies may be purchased at 1s. net., or post free, 1s. 2d.

The Review will be published at the Offices of the Society, 6, York Buildings, Adelphi, London, and may be ordered of any Bookseller.

FRANCIS GALTON.

The Eugenics Education Society exists to uphold the ideal of Parenthood as the highest and most responsible of human powers; to proclaim that the racial instinct is therefore supremely sacred, and its exercise, through marriage, for the service of the future, the loftiest of all privileges. It stands "for a transfigured sentiment of parenthood which regards with solicitude not child and grandchild only, but the generations to come hereafter — fathers of the future creating and providing for the remote children." That which too many schools of thought and practice have derided or defiled it seeks to elevate and ennoble. Parenthood on the part of the diseased, the insane, the alcoholic — where these conditions promise to be transmitted — must be denounced as a crime against the future. In these directions the Society stands for active legislation, and for the formation of that public opinion which legislation, if it is to be effective, must express. Parenthood on the part of the worthy must be buttressed, guided, and extolled. The Society stands for the education of the young regarding the responsibility and holiness of the racial function of parenthood.

THE END

INDEX OF SUBJECTS

INDEX OF NAMES

Published by

Facsimile Publisher
Ashok Vihar, Delhi-110052 (India)
Website: www.facsimilepublisher.com

Distributed by

Gyan Books Pvt. Ltd.
5, Ansari Road, Daryaganj, New Delhi-110002 (India)
E-mail: books@gyanbooks.com, Website: www.gyanbooks.com

2 222000 013349